Sword of Jacinto: A Life of Sam Houston

FIRESTORM

Marshall De Bruhl

RANDOM HOUSE | NEW YORK

FIRESTORM

ALLIED

AIRPOWER and the

DESTRUCTION

of DRESDEN

Published in the United States by Random House,
an imprint of The Random House Publishing Group,
a division of Random House, Inc., New York.

RANDOM HOUSE and colophon are registered
trademarks of Random House, Inc.

All photographs, with the exception of the image of the
reconstructed Frauenkirche, are from the
collection of the Sächsische Landesbibliothek-
Staats-und Univeritätsbibliothek Dresden/Abt.
Deutsche Fotothek. Photographers are listed with
their individual works.

LIBRARY OF CONGRESS CATALOGING-IN-PUBLICATION DATA

De Bruhl, Marshall.
Firestorm: Allied airpower and the destruction of Dresden/
by Marshall De Bruhl.
p. cm.
Includes bibliographical references and index.
ISBN-10: 0-679-43534-4
ISBN-13: 978-0-679-43534-1
1. Dresden (Germany)—History—Bombardment, 1945.
I. Title.
D757.9.D7D4 2006   940.54'2132142—dc22   2006041059

Printed in the United States of America on acid-free paper

www.atrandom.com

9 8 7 6 5 4 3 2 1

FIRST EDITION

*Title-page photograph, Mathildenstrasse, by Paul Winkler,
Stadtmuseum, Dresden, 1945*

Book design by Barbara M. Bachman

FOR BARBARA

During a visit to the coast of France in the summer of 1984, I found myself standing on a platform at the top of a stairway that led down to a beach. It was a beautiful day, warm and sunny. From far below I could hear the squeals of children splashing in the mild surf, young men shouting to one another as they kicked a soccer ball around, and, occasionally, music being borne along on the slight breeze.

It was a very different scene from that of four decades earlier, when the sounds coming from the beach below were those of one of the most desperate struggles of modern times. For this was Normandy and that place was Omaha Beach.

I was on my own pilgrimage, just a few days after thousands of veterans and world leaders had come to this site for the fortieth-anniversary celebrations of the Allied invasion. I was just a boy in a small town in North Carolina when the Allies landed here to free Europe from the Nazis, but I vividly remember how my family gathered around the radio in our living room and listened to the live broadcasts from the landing sites.

My thoughts that morning in June 1984 were of the cousins and uncles who had been with the invasion force. One of them, an infantry officer, saw his promising professional baseball career ended by a German bullet in the left lung. Another, the executive officer of a paratroop unit, was killed just a few days after landing behind the beaches—coincidentally, not far from where his father was killed in World War I.

My sad but proud reflections were interrupted by the laughter of a young woman and two young men who were making their way up the long stairway from the beach. As they reached the landing where I stood, the girl suddenly exclaimed, "My God. What is this place?" The three of them fell silent.

Spread out before them in perfectly ordered rows were the 9,387 marble Christian crosses and Stars of David of the United States Military Cemetery at Colleville-sur-Mer. Most of the men buried there were about the ages of these young people when they died on the beach below, or fighting their way up the very same steep bluff, or during the bloody advance inland after D-day.

Those young people had come to spend a few hours at the beach, not to visit a battlefield or a war memorial, but they listened attentively to my brief but emotional account of the Normandy invasion, of which they knew nothing. It was as distant to them as the wars of ancient Greece. They then quietly took their leave to wander among the graves.

The ravages of the Second World War are hardly to be seen today as one travels through the cities and countryside of Europe. There are war memorials to be sure—obelisks, vast monuments to the dead, eternal flames, and in some cities the hulk of a burned-out building left untouched as a reminder to the passersby that something terrible happened here over a half century ago.

Most Americans, however, are so inured to seeing cities being torn down and rebuilt that they are like those carefree students on their holiday. They seem not to be aware, or much care, that the lovely beaches, the beautiful orchards and vineyards, and the rolling fields of France and Belgium and Germany were once soaked with the blood of hundreds of thousands of young men.

For a truer picture of the carnage of World War II, one must look to the cities, not the battle sites, which, often as not, now resemble well-tended parks. The healing power of nature is evident in the countryside. Vines, wildflowers, and grasses cover the shell holes and bomb craters. Bones of unknown war dead still work their way to the surface or are accidentally turned up by plows and spades, and hapless farmers still occasionally fall victim to the random unexploded shell or land mine long buried in the soil. But instead of ravaged farmlands and the lanes and byways ripped up by the passage of thousands of tanks and trucks and armored vehicles, the fields are much as they were before total war came to these bucolic regions.

Man-made structures can be restored and reconstituted only by other men, however, not by nature. And it was the urban environment—with its villas, houses and palaces, apartment blocks, factories, government buildings, churches and cathedrals, schools, and shops—that was the scene of the greatest devastation. This sort of destruction could never be imagined until the twentieth century and the birth and development of a new form of warfare.

This new war bypassed the armies clashing in the field. It was waged hundreds, often thousands, of miles from any battlefront. This campaign was against the civilian population, which, as war has become more brutal, has increasingly become the target and borne the brunt of military operations.

In the great cities of Germany, visitors are largely oblivious to what predated the ubiquitous glass towers, the pedestrians-only shopping areas, and the almost too wide streets and expressways. To be sure, many historic structures, indeed whole areas of cities, have been reconstructed exactly as they were. But prewar urban Germany—that congested, vibrant, thousand-year-old architectural museum—was washed away in a rain of bombs and could never be wholly reclaimed.

For some cities, such as Berlin, the rain of fire was constant, day after day, night after night. But for one city, there had been only two raids in the more than five years that Germany had been at war. Both had been relatively minor attacks, so the people of Dresden were lulled into that false security that is often a prelude to a great disaster. When their storm came, it was a firestorm, and the destruction and death were on a scale not hitherto imagined in warfare.

The Dresden raid, on 13–14 February 1945, by an Anglo-American force of over a thousand planes, has been a source of controversy, debate, and denial for six decades. It is one of the most famous incidents of the war, yet one of the least understood. It has led to rumors and conspiracy theories, to wrecked reputations, and to charges of war crimes. And it is another reason for the question that has been asked millions of times after the battlefields have been cleared, the wounded gathered up, the dead buried, and the monuments raised. It is a simple question: Why?

The Dresden story is one with particular relevance to our own era. The moral issues presented by war and, especially, aerial bombardment are timeless. The efficacy of bombing continues to be an article of faith among not only leaders of armies but leaders of nations—even though noncombatants, people far from the lines of combat, are most often the victims. In Germany, hundreds of thousands of civilians—mostly women, children, and old men—died as the cities were blasted away.

Since the advent of airpower in World War I, the bombardment of civilians has been decried but never stopped. Indeed, as historian Michael Sherry has put it, "Limited or ambitious men, both in and out of the military, often sanctioned a kind of casual brutality." For almost a century, military planners and political leaders have been beguiled by this particular form of warfare—believing that it holds the promise of a quick and speedy end to hostilities.

The lessons of Guernica, London, Rotterdam, Coventry, Hamburg, Berlin, Tokyo, Hiroshima, Nanking, Nagasaki, and Shanghai are consistently ignored. More recently, the massive bombardments during the Vietnam War and the reprisal bombing in Cambodia, the destruction of Afghanistan, the bombing of Iraq in the two gulf wars, and the devastation of the cities and villages of the former Yugoslavia remind us that airpower still reigns supreme among the planners.

However, there have been raids so controversial as to raise serious doubts about the usefulness and certainly the morality of the bombing of cities. Since 1945, the debate has centered for the most part on the atomic bombing of two Japanese cities—Hiroshima and Nagasaki. The horror of those two events has overshadowed the destruction of dozens of other cities by more conventional means. Nagasaki and Hiroshima served for the last half of the twentieth century as the greatest symbols of the horrors of nuclear warfare, and the result has been rather a tolerance of bombing as long as it is not nuclear. However, the great air raid and firestorm that consumed Dresden, Germany, was as awesome and dreadful as any raid of the war. Both the physical destruction and the casualties were truly horrific.

• • •

I first became interested in the Dresden raid in the summer of 1965, when I made a trip to Coventry to see the new St. Michael's Cathedral, designed by Sir Basil Spence. The medieval church was destroyed in the famous raid by the German Luftwaffe in November 1940. Early on, it had been decided to leave the ruins and tower of the old church as a memorial and build a new, modern St. Michael's immediately adjacent.

During my tour through the church much was made of the comparison between the bombing of Coventry and the raid on Dresden four years later. And in spite of the fact that we were then in the midst of the Cold War and Dresden lay in one of the most extreme of the Soviet satellites, a certain understanding had developed between the two cities. The new cathedral, in fact, featured a cross made from melted and twisted metal from the ruins of Dresden.

The next summer I went to Dresden. Even after two decades, signs of the war were still evident everywhere. What had once been one of the busiest thoroughfares in the world—the Pragerstrasse, which ran from the central train station to the city center—was still a vast open field, through which one walked to the rebuilt Zwinger, that rococo exuberance that houses one of the world's greatest art collections. The museum had been faithfully restored and reopened as both a symbol of civic pride and propaganda for the Communist regime.

Ruins can inform, and it was not too difficult to reconstruct, in the mind's eye at least, the grandeur that was Dresden. And, of course, to mourn its loss. The blackened ruins of the royal palace, the opera house, the theater, the Albertinum museum, the great cathedral, or Hofkirche, along with dozens of other ruined buildings lay behind chain link and board fences, where they awaited a promised restoration—which, in some cases, would not be done for decades. Indeed, the restoration still continues, most recently with the reconstruction of the symbol of Dresden, the Frauenkirche. The ruins of the Church of Our Lady—a vast pile of rubble in the Neumarkt—served for fifty years as a war memorial and the center of the annual commemoration of the bombing.

The questions that have since 1945 swirled around the great raid that destroyed what was arguably the most beautiful city in Germany and for many the most beautiful in Europe have never been satisfactorily answered.

I can only hope, as all chroniclers of history must hope, that my work contributes to a better understanding of those times when no weapon was considered inappropriate and all targets—whether persons or places—were considered appropriate.

CONTENTS

"Ash Wednesday and St. Valentine's Day, an inharmonious combination," confided Prime Minister Winston Churchill's private secretary to his diary on 14 February 1945. A thirty-year-old former diplomat—he had been transferred from the Foreign Office to Downing Street in 1939—John Colville wrote those words from the relative comfort of London. He had not been included in the British delegation to the Yalta Conference, which had ended, for better or worse, three days before.

Churchill himself was now en route home from the Crimea, and on this "inharmonious" day he was in Athens. As his motorcade made its way through the streets of that ancient city, he gloried in the adulation of hundreds of thousands of Greeks, who hailed him not only as their liberator from the hated Germans but also as a bulwark against a Communist takeover of the country.

It was one of Churchill's greatest public triumphs, and there had been many. "Were you there, Charles?" he said to his physician, Lord Moran, after the group reached the British embassy. "I have never seen a greater or more demonstrative crowd."

Twelve hundred miles away, in the streets of another city, the sounds were not those of a cheering throng but the insistent klaxons of fire engines and ambulances, the crash of collapsing buildings, and the screams of the wounded and the dying. The sun had risen on this combined Ash Wednesday and St. Valentine's Day in Dresden, Germany, to reveal a city laid waste.

Baroque bell towers stood silently over smoking and burned-out shells of eighteenth-century churches that just hours before had seemed to owe more to the art of the confectioner than to that of the architect. The Altmarkt and the Neumarkt, the ancient city squares, were now surrounded by roofless, gutted buildings and littered with the burned, twisted, melted-down hulks of cars, trucks, and streetcars.

The Brühl Terrace—the so-called balcony of Europe, that great esplanade overlooking the river Elbe—had been turned into jagged bits of masonry and broken statuary. The adjoining avenues and boulevards were obliterated. Only charred stumps marked the location of century-old plane and linden trees. The narrow streets of the Altstadt, the Old City, had simply disappeared. Palaces, museums, and galleries were now unidentifiable heaps of smoking rubble.

In the great public park called the Grosser Garten, high-explosive bombs had plowed up the ground and created hundreds of deep craters. The ancient trees were leveled or splintered. And everywhere in the park lay thousands more of the dead and dying—refugees from the east who had sheltered there in their flight to the west, as well as native Dresdeners who had fled to this oasis to escape the bombs and the flames. For two centuries people had found refuge here amidst nature. This time, they had met their end.

The monuments and statues in every square and park in the city had been replaced by mounds of corpses. Thousands and thousands of the dead were carried out of the ruined buildings, to any available open space. There the survivors attempted the impossible task of identification. But when entire families, entire neighborhoods have died, who remains to identify the dead?

Two waves of bombers from British Bomber Command had attacked the unsuspecting and undefended city—the first at just past ten o'clock on the eve of St. Valentine's Day and the second a little after one o'clock the following morning. The initial raid created the firestorm, and the second, as designed, helped spread the conflagration that destroyed everything in its path.

At midday, as Churchill was being hailed in Athens, a third wave of planes, from the U.S. Eighth Air Force, appeared over the stricken capital of Saxony. The American raid, which lasted just ten minutes, has been called the most cruel element of the triple blow against Dresden. Such a series of closely spaced and coordinated raids against a major German city—code-named Operation Thunderclap—had first been promulgated by air planners in the summer of 1944. And the results of the raids of 13–14 February against Dresden were precisely as envisioned by the planners of Thunderclap.

The two nighttime British raids had been spaced so as to cause maximum damage and chaos and create the unusual but longed-for phenomenon of a firestorm. Now the bombs from the American B-17s fell on emergency workers and rescuers as they struggled to put out the fires and extricate victims from the rubble.

When this third wave departed, the great city that was known as "the Florence on the Elbe" was already only a memory. In less than fourteen hours the work of centuries had been undone.

FIRESTORM

CHAPTER ONE

"THE BOMBER WILL ALWAYS GET THROUGH"

Aerial
Bombardment:
Theory and
History

War, despicable and despised, has nevertheless been one of mankind's most widespread and popular activities. "Human history is in essence a history of ideas," said H. G. Wells, a noble idea in itself. However, human history is more realistically described as a history of warfare. The chronicles and annals, century after century, millennium after millennium, are dominated by war.

Mercifully, there have been periods of peace; but, for the most part, they have been brief. The era beginning with the end of the Napoleonic Wars in 1815 to the outbreak of World War I in 1914 was relatively calm. To be sure, there were smaller wars aplenty—the Mexican War, the Franco-Prussian War, the Sino-Japanese War, the Boer War, and the Spanish-American War—and one large one, indeed: the American Civil War.

However, for a full century there was no great multinational conflagration such as the Seven Years' War or the Napoleonic Wars. Then came a period of hitherto unimaginable ferocity. The three decades from 1914 to 1945 might well be regarded as a modern Thirty Years'

War, interrupted by a turbulent recess before the principals returned to the battlefield and even greater bloodletting.

· · ·

The frightful and bloody battles of World War I remained fresh in the minds of both victor and vanquished throughout the 1920s and 1930s. Time did nothing to erase the memories. The contests for small patches of ground in France and Flanders and the Eastern Front had resulted in millions of dead and maimed. Families around the world grieved for their dead sons, brothers, and fathers and recoiled at the idea of another such conflict. It was inconceivable to most civilized people that the world would ever again witness such carnage.

Battle deaths among the Central Powers (Germany, Austria-Hungary, Bulgaria, and the Ottoman Empire) were 3,500,000. Among the Allies, who lost 5,100,000 soldiers, the French nation was scarred like no other. Most of the Western Front was on French soil, and over 1,380,000 Frenchmen died on the battlefield or from war wounds, almost 3.5 percent of the entire population of the country. Twenty-five percent of all Frenchmen between the ages of eighteen and thirty died in World War I.

The other Allies suffered great casualties as well. Britain, with 743,000 deaths, and the commonwealth, with another 192,000, were particularly stunned by the losses, as was Italy, with 615,000 dead.

United States battle-related deaths were nowhere near those of most of the other belligerents. Just 48,000 Americans died in battle in World War I. Disease caused the greatest number of deaths; more than 62,000 Americans were carried off by the great influenza epidemic of 1918.

While America has honored its war dead—indeed, the Tomb of the Unknown Soldier and the Vietnam Veterans Memorial in Washington are major tourist attractions—its wars have generally faded from memory. The simpler monuments in the cities, towns, and villages of America have become a familiar part of the background of everyday life and eventually are barely noticed as people go about their daily tasks. Memorial Day is now more than likely a day devoted to pleasure than to remembering the dead or decorating their graves. As each generation of veterans dies out, their contributions slip into history.

This has been so from the American Revolution to the First Gulf War. Each war and the reasons for fighting it become hazy with time. For decades after the Civil War, veterans' reunions, stirring speeches, and grand parades kept the memories and the sacrifices fresh in both the North and the South. Today, few people notice the bronze or granite Union or Confederate soldier who keeps watch over countless village greens and courthouse squares.

In Europe, which has suffered the devastations of centuries of warfare, memory has not been so quick to fade. War memorials and burial grounds have not been allowed to disappear into the background. This is especially true in France and Belgium, the scene of so much carnage. One cannot ignore the perfectly maintained burial grounds that dot the landscape and that reflect the nationalities of the dead interred there. There are the somber Germanic memorials, the rather more nationalistic American tributes, the sad formalism of the French, and the tranquillity of the English cemeteries. In the latter, the flower of an entire generation lies at peace in gardens much like those in Kent or Surrey or the Cotswolds.

The Great War stayed fresh in the memory of the survivors, and in the interwar years thousands of people from both sides made pilgrimages to decorate the graves of the dead in France and Belgium. The senseless battles, the mindless charges and assaults, and the mountains of dead hovered over every postwar conference, every planning session, every strategic discussion. Diplomacy, however misguided, had as its end the avoidance of any repetition of the Great War.

The memories of World War I did not serve just to underscore the need for a permanent peace. In the defeated countries, memory also fostered revanchist emotions, a desire for revenge. "The world must be made safe for democracy," the American president had said in his message asking Congress to declare war on Germany in 1917. No sooner had the war ended than Wilson's words began to echo with a hollow sound. Absolutism rose instead: Communism in Russia, Nazism in Germany, Fascism in Italy, and a virulent militarism and expansionism in Japan.

Another war seemed inevitable to many, and when it came it would prove to be the most devastating conflict in the history of mankind. And there was one great difference between World War II and any preceding war. Because of a new method of warfare, with its more powerful weapons, great numbers of the dead would be noncombatants, far from the front lines.

Among less traditional military planners of the major powers, this new weapon was of particular interest in that it was potentially capable of such power and destruction that it might ensure permanent peace. The airplane might well prove to be the weapon that would put an end to warfare itself.

· · ·

In 1914, when World War I began, powered flight was still in its infancy. The Wright brothers' first flight had been just a little more than a decade before, in December 1903. The infant was a robust one, however, and grew so quickly that there seemed to be some new breakthrough almost daily.

In 1908, the Wrights shipped one of their aircraft to France, where Wilbur flew a series of demonstrations of the plane at the racetrack at Le Mans. In the delirious crowd was Louis Blériot, a French aviation visionary who would make history himself in less than a year. On 25 July 1909, Blériot flew the English Channel from Calais to Dover. The flight was short, only thirty minutes, but it was a powerful portent.

Governments immediately began buying aircraft for their militaries. By the beginning of World War I, the French air force comprised 1,000 planes. The British had an equal number, and the Germans 1,200.

But the birthplace of aviation lagged far behind the European countries' exploitation of aircraft for their militaries. The isolation from Europe and its gathering problems was a strong argument against increased spending for any arms, least of all aircraft, and the American isolationist politicians were aided and abetted by the military traditionalists. Many of the ranking generals were veterans of the Indian wars of the 1880s and were blind to the importance of the airplane; and the admirals, naturally, were wedded to the doctrine of invincible sea power and its most visible component, the battleship. Consequently, when war came, the U.S. Army Air Service had less than 250 aircraft, few of them combat-worthy.

Even in those nations with a relatively advanced air force, airplanes initially were used almost exclusively for reconnaissance over enemy lines. In short order, however, other, more aggressive uses recommended themselves. The first recorded aerial bombardment occurred as early as 1911. In the Italo-Turkish War, Italian pilots dropped small bombs on Turkish troops in Tripoli. The next year, in the First Balkan War, two Bulgarian airmen leaned out of their cockpit and dropped thirty bombs, weighing just a few pounds each, on Edirne, Turkey.

These two minor engagements, with just a handful of bombs and only minor damage, did little to advance the cause of aerial bombardment, and little more was thought about it by most military planners.

There were a few isolated bombing incidents at the beginning of the war—all but two on the Continent—but they were little more than calling cards. Then, on 19 January 1915, the first fatalities occurred. A German dirigible raid, the first of fifty-two in World War I, killed four people in England. In the next three years, another 556 people were killed from bombs dropped from German zeppelins. The first raid on London was on 31 May 1915.

The zeppelin raids were by no means a strategic threat to England, and the casualties were minuscule, at least compared to what was occurring across the Channel. It was not lost on the populace and the politicians, however, that 90 percent of the casualties were civilians.

Two years after the commencement of the dirigible raids, the Germans increased the pressure on English civilians. Gotha bombers began dropping 1,000-pound bomb loads on the British Isles. The first raid, on 25 May 1917, killed 95 people, 80 percent of them civilians. On 13 June the bombers attacked London. Not surprisingly, the attacks on the congested British capital caused a far greater number of deaths and injuries than other German air raids, and as would be the case in World War II, the attacks caused a great public outcry.

There were other parallels with the great conflict that was to come. British defensive measures forced the Germans to give up daylight bombing by August 1917, and the following May they ended their aerial bombardment of England. While they were active in the skies over England, the German raids totaled just 27. There were 836 deaths, however, and 72 percent of them were civilians.

The British also were active in aerial bombardment in World War I, and they had the honor of staging the very first long-range air raid. Three two-seater Avro 504s bombed the zeppelin sheds at Friedrichshafen on 21 November 1914. The raid accomplished little—one of the planes was shot down and the pilot almost murdered by an enraged mob—but it proved that long-distance aerial bombardment was not just theoretical. It was practicable.

Total civilian and military deaths in the three years of dirigible and bomber attacks on Great Britain were, according to historian John Terraine, "less than those sometimes suffered by a single division of the citizen army on the Western Front in *one day.*"

The effect of the German bombing cannot be measured in lives lost or property destroyed. Neither of those measures was of much consequence. The aerial bombings ushered in a whole new way of looking at war. By May 1918 it was clear that morale bombing would henceforth be a powerful force in military planning. Aerial theorists soon appeared to codify and give philosophical weight to the arguments of the men in the field.

· · ·

The first great proponent of airpower, the preeminent theorist, was Giulio Douhet, an Italian general and aviator. Douhet was no stranger to controversy. In World War I, he was court-martialed—and imprisoned—for exposing the weakness of Italy's air force. Vindicated when the Italians were defeated at Caporetto, he subsequently became head of the Italian army aviation service. In 1921, Douhet published *Il dominio dell'aria* (The Command of the Air), which soon became the bible of airpower apostles, priests, and converts. Early in his work, in a few well-chosen words, Douhet laid out the essential elements of his thesis.

"As long as man remained tied to the surface of the earth, his activities had to be adapted to the conditions imposed by that surface," said Douhet. "Since war had to be fought on the surface of the earth, it could be waged only in movements and clashes of forces along lines drawn on its surface." Far removed from these lines of combat, civilian populations had good reason to feel distant from the battlefield. "The majority went on working in safety and comparative peace to furnish the minority with the sinews of war," he said.

This state of affairs arose from the fact that *it was impossible* to invade the enemy's territory without first breaking through his defensive lines.

But that situation is a thing of the past; for now *it is possible* to go far behind the fortified lines of defense without first breaking through them. It is airpower which makes this possible.

The airplane has complete freedom of action and direction; it can fly to and from any point of the compass in the shortest time—in a straight line—by any route deemed expedient. Nothing man can do on the surface of the earth can interfere with a plane in flight, moving freely in the third dimension. All the influences which have conditioned and characterized warfare from the beginning are powerless to affect aerial action.

By virtue of this new weapon, the repercussions of war are no longer limited by the farthest artillery range of surface guns, but can be directly felt for hundreds and hundreds of miles over all the lands and seas of nations at war. No longer can areas exist in which life can be lived in safety and tranquility, nor can the battlefield any longer be limited to actual combatants. On the contrary, the battlefield will be limited only by the boundaries of the nations at war, and all of their citizens will become combatants, since all of them will be exposed to the aerial offensives of the enemy. There will be no distinction any longer between soldiers and civilians.

In yet another bold break with tradition, Douhet also called for separate, autonomous air forces. These independent air arms might coordinate their activities with the army and the navy, which might, indeed, have their own planes; but they would in no sense be subordinate.

Soon, the English military historian and theorist B. H. Liddell Hart provided powerful support for the Douhet doctrine. Great destruction could be visited on urban areas and the civilian population if the bombs and the means of delivering them were developed. There would be no front lines, with great armies throwing themselves against each other. Instead, said Liddell Hart, fleets of bombers would "jump over the army which shields the enemy government, industry, and the people and so strike direct and immediately at the seat of the opposing will and policy."

However, the theorists surmised, these new weapons would never actually be used. They were to be deterrents to war. Indeed, the very threat of such terror would lead to the quick end of any war—if, indeed, diplomacy between potential adversaries had allowed the situation to deteriorate to that point. But if war did come, said Liddell Hart, and cities such as London were bombed, "Would not the general will to resist vanish . . . ?"

Another airway theoretician, J. F. C. Fuller, was more quantitative, assigning an acceptable number of dead that might be necessary to achieve a greater goal. "If a future war can be won at the cost of two or three thousand of the enemy's men, women and children killed . . . then surely an aerial attack is a more humane method than the existing traditional one."

The men who flew in the fledgling air forces of World War I quickly embraced the new theories. Douhet was hailed as one of the great military thinkers, for he had given airmen a philosophical underpinning— as, in the nineteenth century, Alfred Thayer Mahan had done for the admirals and Carl von Clausewitz for the generals. It is not such a large step from theory to dogma; early on, minds were set in a strategy that would govern thinking about aerial warfare.

A new era in warfare thus began. The unthinkable would prevent the unimaginable. In the event, warfare did not change, of course. The weapons being extolled by Douhet and Liddell Hart not only did not prevent another world war but would themselves cause even more destruction and death—particularly among the noncombatants. Even greater armies contested the field, and those bombers that were supposed to have deterred the war or to bring it to an early end instead flew over them night after night, day after day, year after year, taking the war, as predicted, to the ground combatants' homes, far from the battlefield.

. . .

Few branches of the military forged such close bonds as the flying corps. The other services had distinguished themselves in World War I and served just as heroically, but the pilots were different. They were an elite group, few in number, better paid, and isolated by their mastery of a still unusual, even unique skill. In addition, they benefited from their messianic zeal. For them, airpower had become a new religion.

The bonds formed by these pioneers would be lasting and help them build a devastating war-making machine in the decades ahead. Much has been said in condemnation of so-called old-boy networks, but such networks went far in defeating Axis tyranny.

However, upstarts too can soon become the old guard, with an entrenched doctrine and calcified thinking. When the admirals and generals insisted that the airplane was just another weapon, not a revolutionary method of waging war, the airpower enthusiasts were quick to circle the wagons. And just as quickly they began to overstate the effectiveness of their new weapon and create inter- and intraservice rivalries that would last for decades.

General Jan Christian Smuts and Major General Hugh Trenchard were among the chief proselytizers in the United Kingdom. As Smuts wrote to Prime Minister Lloyd George on 17 August 1917:

Air power can be used as an independent means of war operations. . . . Nobody that witnessed the attack on London on 7th July, 1917, could have any doubt on that point. Unlike artillery an air fleet can conduct extensive operations far from and independently of both Army and Navy. As far as can at present be foreseen there is absolutely no limit to the scale of its future independent war use. And the day may not be far off when aerial operations with their devastation of enemy lands and destruction of industrial and populous centres on a vast scale may become the principal operations of war, to which older forms of military operations may become secondary and subordinate.

On 1 April 1918, these two visionaries saw their dream realized. The Royal Air Force, the RAF, was founded, with Trenchard himself as chief of the air staff.

The views of Trenchard, Smuts, and the other early apostles of airpower and their glowing predictions of the future of airpower continued to rankle the old-line admirals and generals in both England and America who saw the airplane as little more than a toy and pilots as a brash group of show-offs. In 1919, the American secretary of war, Newton D. Baker, reflected this mind-set. Of aviation, he said, "the art itself is so new and so fascinating, and the men in it have so taken on the character of supermen, that is difficult to reason coldly."

· · ·

Oddly, it was an advocate of disarmament who gave the pro-bomber proponents their most potent axiom. On 10 November 1931, Prime Minister Stanley Baldwin said in the House of Commons, "I think it is well also for the man in the street to realize that there is no power on earth that can prevent him from being bombed. Whatever people may tell him, the bomber will always get through. The only defence is offence, which means you have to kill more women and children more quickly than the enemy if you want to save yourselves."

Baldwin was, of course, denouncing aerial bombardment and what he perceived, correctly, as its inevitable escalation. But in one of those not unusual twists that result in a speaker's words being used in a way he never intended, the prime minister's statement was taken up by the proponents of the invincible, self-defending heavy bomber. "The bomber," they cried, "will always get through."

The opposing group was equally mistaken in their expropriation of the prime minister's remarks, although they at least were in philosophical agreement. The fear of aerial bombardment led many in his and later governments, as well as the public, to attempt to placate Hitler and then to acquiesce in his designs on neighboring states.

. . .

Wise military leaders learn from their mistakes and are quick to embrace new weaponry and technology. They always seek to devise more effective methods for fighting the next round of engagements. Not for them the adage that military men always seem prepared to fight the last war. Prescience is not without its price, however.

The military landscape is littered with the wrecked careers of revolutionaries who ran afoul of the system when they tried to institute new and untried tactics or weapons of warfare. Billy Mitchell, that brilliant but impolitic apostle of airpower, is perhaps the twentieth century's most resonant example.

General Mitchell, who had learned firsthand the effect of airpower as head of the American air service in France in 1917–18, was the most visible and voluble of the alleged air supermen, and he carried on a ceaseless and often intemperate campaign for airpower and an air service. In this he was supported by other zealots, several of whom, in the next two decades, would carry Mitchell's plans to fruition. They included Henry (Hap) Arnold, Carl Spaatz, and Ira C. Eaker, among others.

Mitchell's ideas were anathema to the traditionalists in the army and the navy, who were quick to protect their territories, but it was the latter service that was his particular target, and eventually the navy rose to his challenge that airplanes could sink capital ships.

A demonstration was set up off the Virginia Capes in July 1921. As Mitchell predicted, air service planes sank a captured German destroyer, a cruiser, and, to everyone's consternation, the battleship *Ostfriesland.*

To further drive home his point and to prove that the first engagement was not just a fluke, Mitchell repeated the lesson in September. Army planes bombed and sank the decommissioned battleship *Alabama.*

Even so there were still doubters, and in September 1923, Mitchell sought to convert them as well. He arranged for the destruction of two more old battleships—the *Virginia* and the *New Jersey.*

But the bombs that sank obsolete warships were not the only ones dropped by Billy Mitchell. In a series of articles for the *Saturday Evening Post*, he went all out in his advocacy of airpower and his criticism of those who could not see that it was the future of warfare. He accused the military's top brass of muzzling their subordinates and preventing them from telling the truth.

Mitchell had crossed the line between advocacy and insubordination. He was demoted to colonel and transferred to a remote base in Texas. He had, of course, become the darling of the press, and before his departure he pulled off another coup—or stunt. He took arguably the most popular and widely read American of his time, Will Rogers, for a much reported first airplane ride.

But Mitchell was not just a publicity hound. He was genuinely concerned with aviation and was determined to overcome the American reluctance to build an air force. Even from his exile in the outback he would not be silenced, particularly when he was given two spectacular disasters as a springboard.

On a misconceived public relations mission to Hawaii, a navy flying boat, the PN-9 No. 1, ran out of fuel and ditched at sea. The crew was rescued after ten days adrift in their plane, but the navy was accused of dereliction. Worse was the destruction of the dirigible *Shenandoah*, which went down while the search for the missing flying boat was still going on. The aircraft had been ordered to fly into a severe thunderstorm to maintain its schedule of public appearances in the Midwest.

Mitchell's response was immediate and scathing. He charged that the loss of the *Shenandoah* was "the result of incompetency, criminal negligence, and the almost treasonable negligence of our national defense by the War and Navy departments."

Ironically, the flying boat and the dirigible had both been dispatched in order to gain publicity for navy air and as an effort to counter Mitchell's charges that the air arm was being ignored.

The Coolidge administration and the military could not ignore such a broadside from a military officer, and their response was swift. Mitchell was court-martialed.

Both Carl Spaatz and Hap Arnold testified for the defense, which the country knew was a defense of airpower as well. Though Mitchell's point was made, his career was over. He was given a five-year suspension, but he chose to resign from the army and continue his crusade as a civilian.

Forty years later, Spaatz made it clear that his testimony at the trial had to do with advocating airpower. Mitchell's insubordination was, indeed, actionable by a military court. Spaatz said that he and Arnold and Mitchell's other friends "had no quarrel with the administration of military justice as it applied to him. . . . He brought it upon himself and I think he did it deliberately."

Mitchell is mostly remembered for his advocacy of aerial bombardment, and bombers were, to be sure, the mainstay of his envisioned air force. But he also believed in fighter planes. Indeed, he felt that 60 percent of any air force should be pursuit planes—small defensive fighters that would be employed to destroy an enemy's air force.

Claire Chennault was another advocate of fighter planes. His public stance also angered his superiors, but he left the army quietly in 1937 for medical reasons. The next day, however, he traveled to China, where he organized and trained the Chinese air force.

Work on fighter planes had been effectively halted, and the United States aircraft industry did not develop a first-rate fighter, either for escort or pursuit, until 1940—for the British Royal Air Force.

Some good did come from the Mitchell scandal. Both the public and Congress benefited from the discussion, and at least one important step was taken in regard to airpower. The Morrow Board, an investigative body appointed by Calvin Coolidge, recommended the creation of the Army Air Corps, and Congress passed the Air Corps Act of 1926. For airpower advocates it was only half a loaf—there would be no separate and autonomous air force—but it was clearly better than none.

The chief objection to building up this new force was in no small degree a moral one in the eyes of many congressmen and the public. Building more planes and a greater air force directly contravened the recently negotiated naval treaties. What use was it, detractors argued, to limit the tonnage of capital ships and go all out in building planes and an air force?

Military opponents of the Army Air Corps were, of course, willing to embrace any argument to limit its growth, and thus the new aviation branch of the army remained a stepchild—underfunded, understaffed, and shunted aside by the traditional services.

According to the findings of the Morrow Board, "The next war may well start in the air, but in all probability it will wind up, as the last one did, in the mud." Events justified this statement, at least in Europe. Adolf Hitler began with air attacks, but the war ended with ground troops fighting street by street in Berlin. In the Pacific it was otherwise. The Japanese began their expansion with air attacks—the raid on Pearl Harbor, while certainly the most well known, was just one of many—and the war was brought to a rapid conclusion by the Americans with the most famous air raids in history, Hiroshima and Nagasaki.

· · ·

The Morrow Board notwithstanding, aviation could not be ignored. The thought of flight has always engaged the imagination of mankind, and in 1927 Charles Lindbergh's solo flight across the Atlantic galvanized the world. While the civilian population was celebrating Lindbergh's singular accomplishment and was set to dreaming of a new age of travel and communication, the more prescient of the military establishment saw his flight as further proof of a theorem.

To be sure, other pilots had flown long distances before Lindbergh— as early as 1919 a U.S. Navy crew had flown a seaplane across the Atlantic—but his nonstop, solo feat brought hitherto unimagined interest in the possibility of flights across oceans and continents.

And clearly long-distance planes could be used for something far more sinister than aerial stunts. They were obvious vehicles for the delivery of weapons of destruction. Bombers were the ideal machines for terrorizing the civilian population and destroying the manufacturing centers of an enemy nation. Theory could indeed be joined with practice. Wars could be fought and won without the use of invading armies.

Tradition dies hard, and nowhere does it take as long or succumb as slowly as in the military. In Germany, also, the old-line generals and admirals were just as suspicious of and patronizing toward this new form of warfare as their French, British, and American counterparts. But if airpower was indeed to prove to be the weapon of the future, they were just as determined to control its growth and its deployment, and until Hitler came to power they did just that.

Dictators do not suffer the constraints of a congress or a parliament, and they can also overrule objections from the general staff. Hitler saw the terroristic advantages of bombing or the threat of bombing, and the buildup of the German air force, the Luftwaffe, was given high priority in his plans to rearm Germany. By 1937–38, almost 40 percent of the German defense budget was allocated to the Luftwaffe.

Joseph Goebbels, the propaganda minister, began to trumpet the legend of the invincible Luftwaffe, and his half-truths and outright lies went unquestioned by foreign air ministries and visiting dignitaries who were beguiled by the Nazi regime and who swallowed whole the propaganda.

None of the visitors to Nazi Germany was as credulous or as influential as that quintessential American hero Charles Lindbergh, who on his return to America after visiting Nazi Germany naively extolled the myth of German airpower. In 1939, the Lone Eagle made two radio addresses and wrote an article for *Reader's Digest*, in which he cautioned his fellow Americans against involvement in any European war and reminded them of the special obligation that Anglo-Saxons owed to one another.

Little wonder that Roosevelt responded with hostility to such rhetoric, which gave the isolationists a powerful weapon. "I am absolutely convinced that Lindbergh is a Nazi," he said to his secretary of the treasury, Henry Morgenthau.

Lindbergh was wrong in other ways as well. His projections of the Luftwaffe's strength and aircraft production were incredibly wide of the mark. However, unlike his political pronouncements, they had a salutary effect. They spurred the administration to action.

The myths of the German war machine and German technological superiority were strong, and remain so still. They are not easily dispelled.

Perhaps it would be wise to heed historian A. J. P. Taylor: "The decisive difference between the British and the Germans is the British . . . knew what they were doing and the Germans did not."

However, in the 1930s the threat of the German air force was very real to the more immediately endangered Czechs, Poles, French, and British, who would have to bear the first onslaught of any German moves east or west. Most Americans were content to go about their business, protected by the great moat of the Atlantic Ocean.

The isolationist sentiments that prevented America from joining the League of Nations had grown stronger. If Americans needed proof that the United States should stick to the affairs of the Western Hemisphere, what better examples were there than the rise of Hitler, Mussolini, and the Japanese warlords?

American involvement in World War I had come to be seen by millions of Americans as a futile exercise. Indeed, the American public had begun to question the aims and the results of World War I as soon as it ended. Now the general feeling seemed to be "We bailed them out, and here they are—at it again."

In just fifteen years the war clouds that had been dispersed in 1918 began to gather again, but the new storm threatened to be much more violent. However, none of the American armed services was preparing itself for a modern war. Tactics were still based on those of World War I. The navy paid little attention to the U-boat threat, the army was deficient in knowledge and training in the new mechanized warfare, and the air corps, in spite of its gains in acceptability, still was mired in the strategy of another era. This was to be expected; after all, their equipment was of an earlier era.

· · ·

Events, however, soon began to dictate strategy. By the fall of 1938 only the most obtuse could not, or would not, admit to the evil designs of the National Socialists in Germany and the inevitability of a new, or resumed, world war. Franklin Roosevelt certainly was under no illusions about the nature of Hitler's government. On 14 November 1938, in response to the Nazi pogrom against the Jews known as Kristallnacht, or the Night of Broken Glass, he recalled the American ambassador from Berlin. There was no break in diplomatic relations, however, and much to the dismay of his admirers and future chroniclers, there the matter rested.

As historian and Roosevelt biographer Kenneth S. Davis stated, "He was determined to conserve every bit of his depleted political capital for expenditure on matters he deemed of supreme importance, and the Jewish refugee crisis was not one of these. . . . National defense on the other hand was paramount."

That same day, Roosevelt assembled a group of close advisers at the White House to discuss his plans for expanding the American air force. Among them was the new chief of the U.S. Army Air Corps, Hap Arnold, who was now a major general. The president immediately made known his concern about the woeful state of the air corps. The total number of operational planes was about 1,600, and fewer than 90 were being built each month. Roosevelt wanted an air force of 20,000 planes and a production capacity of 2,000 planes a month.

The American president, like the German Führer, believed in the power of numbers. He seemed not to have concerned himself with the equally important training and operations of an expanded air corps. When he was challenged on this he bristled that he "had sought $500,000,000 worth of airplanes, and he was being offered everything except airplanes."

Roosevelt did listen to the objections, especially those of General George Marshall, who, as usual, was able to rise above the army's natural but parochial opposition to the huge new expenditure for a competing military arm and support the plan—if it included training and operations. Otherwise, America, too, would have only a "shop-window" air force. The president acquiesced, but he made it clear that any such additions to the program would have to come from the original appropriation.

The American public had bought the argument that warplanes represented real power to a potential enemy. Had not Hitler proved that at Munich? Even fervid isolationists might endorse the buildup of an air force—as a deterrent. And if deterrence failed and war did come, then the planes could be used as offensive weapons. But the battle would be far from America's shores.

As Michael Sherry has said, the new aerial policy put forth by Roosevelt "squared with the dominant prejudices and priorities of Americans: alarm over fascist aggression, aversion to military expeditions abroad, desire to preserve American isolation, and faith in aviation as a benign technology."

Even though a public opinion poll in 1938 showed that 90 percent of Americans thought there should be a larger air force—in almost the same numbers the public felt that there should be a larger army and navy, as well—Roosevelt knew that he could not hope to have a force anywhere near the scale he envisioned. His plans were just too ambitious for the new Congress and the country. The president scaled back his request to a total of 10,000 planes and a monthly production of fewer than 1,000.

Hap Arnold moved immediately to bring in his old friend to help him implement the new presidential directive. Carl Spaatz was transferred to Washington in late November 1938, on temporary assignment from nearby Langley Field, in Virginia. Early in the new year the job became a permanent one. He was now chief of planning of the office of the chief of the air corps.

Spaatz soon learned the vast distance between the president's wishes, no matter how urgent and well-founded, and the Congress, which had to grant the wishes. Even in times of international crisis, the adage still applies: "The president proposes, but Congress disposes." And Congress was still not in an internationalist mood.

The final air corps plan was nowhere near what the president had in mind, but at least it was a start. Congress appropriated $180 million with a ceiling of 5,500 planes.

Even this modest number of aircraft was not practicable. Foreign governments were desperately seeking to build up their own air forces, which they could do only with the aid of the American aircraft industry. The Americans clearly could not supply both the army air corps and the Allies.

To Arnold's chagrin, Roosevelt came down on the side of those most directly threatened by a rearmed and aggressive Germany. The American military had to give its place in line to England and France. And, perhaps even more galling, a hundred scarce fighter planes were earmarked for Claire Chennault's Chinese operations, the famous Flying Tigers.

Many have argued that Roosevelt's plan all along was not to build up the American air forces—which would account for his disregard for support and training facilities—but to manufacture airplanes for the Allies.

In spite of the clear threat posed by a rearmed and aggressive Germany, the war in Europe still did not engage the attention of the American military, which continued to deal primarily with hemisphere defense. Indeed, at a 1940 conference that discussed the various options that the U.S. military might face in the foreseeable future, an offensive war in Europe was ranked fifth.

There was, however, real fear that Germany and Italy might establish bases in South America, not a far-fetched idea at all since both countries already had commercial air service to Latin America. The tiny American bomber fleet had the range to reach South America, but no fighter plane had anywhere near that range, which made little difference to the planners. Fighters were still considered as interceptors only, not escorts. Self-defending bombers were still an article of faith among air planners.

In a 31 October 1939 memo to Ira Eaker, H. S. Hansell said that "long range bombers must rely on their own defensive power to get them out of trouble." Hansell's view was not particular to him. At the time he was assistant executive officer for public relations for Hap Arnold.

This particular orthodoxy of the airpower enthusiasts—that bomber formations, with their multiple guns covering every part of the sky, were therefore invincible—went down in flames over the North Sea in just a few weeks, but it took years for the lesson to be fully absorbed.

The question as to why American or British fighters could shoot down German bombers over Great Britain but German fighters would presumably be ineffective over the Reich, or at least enough so that Allied bombers would get through, was never seriously raised. But startling proof came that the theory was false came on 14 December 1939.

Five of twelve Wellington bombers were shot down by Luftwaffe fighters off Wilhemshaven, the great German naval base. Bomber Command maintained that it was flak that did the damage, and therefore in a follow-up raid on 18 December the twenty-four Wellingtons dispatched were ordered to maintain an altitude of 10,000 feet. Two of the planes turned back, but out of the twenty-two effectives, twelve were shot down by German fighters. And worse, all of the action was miles out to sea. No plane had reached Germany itself.

Theorists and supporters of the self-defending bomber formation immediately searched for reasons for the disaster that would not call into question the underlying strategy. The major cause of the catastrophe, stated a report, was poor leadership. The pilots had not maintained the tight formation necessary for mutual defense.

Two other contributing factors, both technological, were admitted to and would be addressed. The fuel tanks were not self-sealing, and the gun turrets on the Wellington had a field of fire of only eighty degrees. New fuel tanks were ordered and waist guns installed. But the strategy of the self-defending bomber fleet remained unquestioned—until 12 April 1940.

On that day, disaster struck again. Nine out of eighty-three aircraft were shot down in a daylight raid on Stavanger, Norway. However, only sixty had been attacked by the German fighters, which elevated the loss rate considerably—from an unacceptable 11 percent to a catastrophic 15 percent.

Planners began to entertain the possibility that perhaps the bomber would not always get through—at least not in daylight. There now occurred what RAF historians Martin Middlebrook and Chris Everitt have called "undoubtedly the most important turning-point in Bomber Command's war." Henceforth, the Wellingtons and Hampdens and their four-engine successors would fly only at night.

· · ·

In America, meanwhile, the master politician Franklin Roosevelt kept his eye on the voters. Given public opinion and political opposition, Roosevelt could never have placed the country on a war footing. He could, however, maneuver to place the country in a position to aid its allies, particularly Britain.

Roosevelt met with Winston Churchill on 9–12 August 1941 at the Atlantic Conference in Newfoundland. They were attended by high-ranking officers from all of the services and the heads of the civilian planning agencies. As Wesley Frank Craven and James Lea Cate observed, it was "obvious to any literate citizen that those officers had not boarded the *Prince of Wales* [Churchill's flagship] to discuss the Four Freedoms."

The two leaders did release a manifesto called the Atlantic Charter, which called for the renunciation of territorial expansion or territorial changes not sanctioned by the people affected. In the postwar world, people would be guaranteed self-determination, equal access to trade and raw materials, international economic cooperation, improved labor standards and social security, freedom from fear, freedom from want, freedom of the seas. Further, aggressor nations would be disarmed.

The charter would later serve as the basis for the United Nations, but, as Craven and Cate rightly said, Roosevelt and Churchill had more immediate concerns on their minds in Newfoundland. Their main purpose was to move neutral America closer to war with Germany, which Roosevelt correctly perceived to be an immediate threat to the United States.

Indeed, a month earlier Roosevelt had requested the secretary of war to provide him with "the overall production requirements required to defeat our potential enemies." The air corps estimates were assigned to the new Air War Plans Division. In early August, Lieutenant Colonel Harold George, Major Kenneth Walker, Major H. S. Hansell Jr., and Major Laurence Kuter produced the famous document AWPD-1, which set forth the initial air force policy for the bombing of Nazi Germany— four months before the United States was at war with the Third Reich.

The priority targets for a bombing campaign as set out in AWPD-1, after the destruction of the German Luftwaffe, were (1) the electric power grid, (2) the transportation system, and (3) the oil supply and production facilities. The fourth item on the list was, most tellingly, the civilian population.

Just after Pearl Harbor a new directive was issued, AWPD-4, which stated clearly that "a powerful air force, waging a sustained air offensive against carefully selected targets, may destroy the sources of military power." Not only were the authors saying that airpower alone could bring about the end of the war; AWPD-4 was also seen by the other services as a call for a larger slice of the appropriation pie by the air commanders and, of course, a separate and equal United States Air Force.

A year later, in December 1942, Hap Arnold ordered a review of the bombing plan by a group of civilian analysts and intelligence personnel. In the new directive, AWPD-42, the pro-air rhetoric was toned down a bit. Further, in a classic example of the ongoing conflict between civilian and military planners that can bedevil any defense establishment, the Committee of Operations Analysts (COA) determined that the operations recommended by the drafters of AWPD-1 were in some cases not feasible.

In their revised list of priorities, after the destruction of the German air force, the electric power system, the power grid, was now third in order of priority. As the war progressed, target priorities were changed several times—oil, for example, went to the top of the list—but the electric power system of the Third Reich was never reassigned primacy.

Hansell, in 1972, said this decision was "one of the tragic mistakes of the war." And there is more than a little justification for his opinion. In a modern industrial society, which Germany certainly was in 1941, everything comes to a halt when the power goes off. This was made startlingly clear in the United States, beginning in the mid-1960s, when a series of blackouts brought great sections of the country to a complete halt. In each of those cases, the causes were fairly simple—defective switches combined with human error. No structural damage had occurred in the system. The total destruction of power plants, transmission lines, and substations would have caused a long-term or complete breakdown in the Third Reich.

• • •

Capital ships and tanks, to use Craven and Cate's felicitous phrase, "carried with them the reassuring weight of military tradition." Strategic bombers were new and exotic and unproved weapons. Hap Arnold and Carl Spaatz had to show that they could win a war.

They were fully aware of the setbacks at British Bomber Command and the now-proscribed daylight operations. But the strategy was not at fault, they reasoned. The primary strategy was sound. The necessary element for its successful prosecution was the proper weapon, which the British did not possess. A four-engine, heavily armed daylight bomber would prove the point, and such a plane was becoming operational in the United States. The B-17, the legendary Flying Fortress, properly deployed and manned, would be able to look after itself in any situation.

Since offensive war was anathema and Americans recoiled at the thought of bombing civilians, the military couched its plans, as it always does, in palatable, defensive terms. Thus until bombers became a retaliatory force and began to visit death and destruction on the cities of Europe, they continued to be touted as deterrents to aggression. The purpose of bombers was to prevent war, not make war. The public accepted this line of reasoning, even though events in Europe should have made it clear to them that the opposite was true.

The American president had responded to the invasion of Poland two years earlier by imploring the European belligerents to renounce the bombing of cities and the civilian populace. Roosevelt's call for restraint was heeded, more or less, for a few months.

Purely military installations and naval vessels remained the primary targets until 14 May 1940, when the Dutch port city of Rotterdam was devastated by the Luftwaffe. It was now clear that civilians would not be spared in any all-out bombardment by either side.

Americans, meanwhile, in spite of Roosevelt's sympathies, were still in no mood to involve themselves in a new European war. Their fears were embodied in such organizations as the ultraisolationist America First Committee.

The committee's chief spokesman was Charles Lindbergh, who in a radio address in late May 1940, while the British and French were facing annihilation at Dunkirk, dismissed the president's plan for thousands of warplanes as "hysterical chatter."

But the public sensed that perhaps the airplane might be the weapon that would keep the country safely removed from involving itself in Europe's headlong rush into disaster. Polls showed that while support for a larger air force had fallen, it was still at 73 percent. Americans clearly felt that if war should come, the airplane was the best way of keeping it a very long arm's length from the United States.

CHAPTER TWO

THE ARCHITECTS
OF DESTRUCTION

The Bomber
Barons and
Total Air War

Most of the men who ran the air war in World War II began their careers as airmen in the same patches of sky over the battlefields of the Western Front in World War I—the first air war. They were part of that small cadre of brash young men who, in their primitive biplanes and triplanes, helped usher in the age of aerial warfare. While still in their early twenties all of them became heroes, veterans of the dogfights and seat-of-the-pants flying that characterized combat above the trenches of the Western Front.

They were young and often reckless, but they knew instinctively that their aircraft were not the "toys" derided by more conventional military men, and they would live to see the Spads, Sopwiths, and Fokkers of their youth evolve into the Mustangs, Hurricanes, Messerschmitts, Flying Fortresses, Junkerses, Halifaxes—and even jet planes and rockets—that would redefine military strategy. In a little over two decades, the small bombs they casually tossed from their open cockpits, like so many firecrackers, would give way to the incendiaries, the massive blockbusters, and even the atomic bomb itself.

But the development of airpower by no means proceeded in anything resembling an orderly progression. The road to a coherent and practicable air policy was filled with twists, turns, cutoffs, and detours. The rights-of-way were littered with discredited strategies, failed weapons, and not a few damaged reputations and wrecked careers.

However, by the late 1930s, the theorists and philosophers of airpower had carried the day. There was a U.S. Army Air Corps, a Royal Air Force, and a Luftwaffe. Of the three, Germany and Great Britain had made their air arms autonomous, separate institutions—Britain at the end of World War I and Germany after the accession of Adolf Hitler. Interservice rivalries and politics forestalled such a move in the United States, where the air force, which had been created as a branch of the army, would remain so until after World War II.

But theories had to be put into practice. It was now the turn of the men of action, pragmatic men who could take the directives of a prime minister or a president or a führer and get the planes built and the men trained to fly them.

However, just as the stubborn orthodoxy of the army and navy had been overcome, the airmen also espoused and defended policies and strategies long after they had been proved wrong. The almost blind adherence to the doctrine of the self-defending bomber was as misguided as had been the insistence on the invulnerability of the battleship.

Technology was promoted extravagantly only to be summarily cast aside for newer, even more ambitious schemes. Aircraft manufacturers and arms makers had a more than patriotic interest in promoting their own hardware. The profits to be made were enormous. And, of course, the generals and admirals, even as they prepared for and fought a war, kept a wary eye on the rival services.

· · ·

Billy Mitchell's contemporaries, both in the United States and abroad, fared somewhat better than he had done with their crusades to promote airpower. They too had learned from the grand rehearsal of World War I, and they were equally zealous; but they knew how to proselytize without being impaled on their own swords. Indeed, they would be rewarded with the highest honors and military rank.

Hugh Trenchard, an early and lifelong advocate of the power of bombardment from aircraft, had said in 1923, "It is on the bomber that we must rely for defence. It is on the destruction of enemy industries and, above all, on the lowering of morale . . . caused by bombing that ultimate victory rests."

Trenchard never lost his enthusiasm for airpower or his zeal for aerial bombardment, and even after the "father of the RAF" retired from the military and was raised to the peerage, he continued his proselytizing. The enemy, he always maintained, could be defeated by taking the war directly to its homeland, and he never retreated from his early pronouncement that "the moral effect of bombing stands to the material in a proportion of 20 to 1."

In 1942, on the eve of the battle of El Alamein, Lord Trenchard said to Churchill's physician, Lord Moran, "We must avoid the stupendous drain on manpower of an attempt to win victory by land warfare. You must get this into the Prime Minister's head. If he puts his faith in bombers, it will save millions of lives." As we will see, this view was echoed by almost every air commander until the end of World War II.

The first commander in chief of Bomber Command, Sir Edgar Ludlow-Hewitt, was one of the few who disagreed. He argued that long-range bombing was going to have to be conducted at night and with fighter escorts. If England engaged in a sustained campaign against Germany, he warned, the bomber fleets would be completely wiped out in just a few weeks. But his heresies did not stop there.

Ludlow-Hewitt also began to insist that a major component of any buildup had to be operational training units. Otherwise the RAF, and by extension Bomber Command, would be just a so-called shop-window air force. So much for twenty years of RAF orthodoxy. Ludlow-Hewitt paid for his outspokenness. He was relieved as head of Bomber Command in April 1940.

Bomber Command then went through a rough patch for almost two years, until it found its proper strategic role in the prosecution of the war. Some of the problems were administrative, some were due to a lack of proper bombing platforms—the available planes simply could not do the job required—but most were due to a lack of judgment as to how the bombing should be carried out.

Air Marshal Sir Charles Portal, a fervent disciple of Hugh Trenchard's, was appointed to succeed Ludlow-Hewitt, but in just six months he moved up to the post of chief of the air staff.

From this powerful position—he attended every major planning session and was part of the British delegation at conferences in Casablanca, Washington, Tehran, and Yalta—Portal played a crucial role in developing the doctrine of the massive bombing of German cities.

His November 1942 plan called for completely destroying, through the use of heavy bombers, not only Germany's industrial capacity but also 6 million German dwellings. Not only would the proposed joint Anglo-American campaign "dehouse" 25 million people, it was estimated that there would be 900,000 civilians killed and another 1 million seriously injured. The plan was approved by the Chiefs of Staff on 31 December 1942.

Portal then flew with Churchill in the prime minister's plane to the Casablanca Conference, which began on 14 January 1943. There it was officially decided that through round-the-clock bombing Germany's military, industrial, and economic systems were to be systematically destroyed. In addition, although it was not publicly stated, attacks would also be directed so as to destroy the will of the people to resist. In other words, morale bombing was to be official policy.

· · ·

When Air Marshal Portal left Bomber Command, he was succeeded by Air Marshal Sir Richard E. C. Peirse. As a young naval aviator in World War I, Peirse had distinguished himself, and after he transferred to the RAF his rise was rapid. He was commander of the British forces in Palestine, and by 1936 he was an air vice marshal and then director of operations and intelligence at the Air Ministry. When he came to Bomber Command in October 1940, he was vice chief of the air staff, and with his impeccable background and knowledge it seemed that any problems with the command would soon be set right.

It was not to be. During Peirse's tenure at High Wycombe, Bomber Command began to suffer disastrous and unsustainable losses of planes in raids over the Continent. Worse, the revelation that the British bombing had been nowhere near as accurate as reported caused an uproar. Thus, in December 1941 it was clear that drastic measures had to be taken. Peirse was relieved.

His replacement would become more famous—some would say more infamous—than any of the men, both civilian and military, who were responsible for the bombing campaigns of World War II. Indeed, he has come to symbolize the power or weakness, failure or success, effectiveness or folly of aerial bombardment of civilian populations.

Unlike his less colorful associates, the new head of Bomber Command was known by a variety of nicknames. He was affectionately called "Bert" or "Bud" by his friends, the "Chief Bomber" by Winston Churchill, and "Butch" by his "bomber boys."

"Butcher" was the term favored by his detractors, who included Joseph Goebbels, an expert in such things. He said of Harris, "You have only to look into his eyes to know what to expect from such a man. He has the icy-cold eyes of a born murderer."

However, it is as "Bomber Harris," the name bestowed by an admiring public, that he is best known. But whatever the sobriquet, Air Marshal Sir Arthur Travers Harris would, over time, stand as the prototypical airman of World War II.

■ ■ ■

Harris was born on 13 April 1892, while his parents were on home leave from India, where his father was a civil servant. The family soon returned to the subcontinent, where the boy lived until he was five, when he was sent back to England for schooling.

Harris therefore saw almost nothing of his parents in his formative years. In that way, his childhood was strikingly similar to that of another controversial British military hero and a colleague of his in the British army, Bernard Law Montgomery, as well as Winston Churchill's.

And Harris responded in much the same way as did those two worthies. He became independent, strong-willed, and supremely self-confident and self-sufficient. Perhaps because of the enforced solitude of his youth, Harris was also attuned to the loneliness of a soldier's life and sympathetic to the needs of his men, qualities that would later endear him to his subordinates.

At age eighteen—he said he was fed up with the snobbery of England—Harris fled to Rhodesia, where he took up farming. That British colony was not beyond the reach of world events, and in August 1914, with the outbreak of war, Harris joined the army. He fought in the successful campaign against the Germans in southwest Africa, and with the German surrender there in July 1915, his war was ostensibly over. The real war, in Europe, was only beginning, however, and by that autumn Harris was back in England, where he was accepted for pilot's training with the Royal Flying Corps at Brooklands.

Aside from riding as a passenger in a Maurice Farman Longhorn and a BE2c, Harris's pilot training comprised less than half an hour of dual instruction. He then took a plane up by himself. Thus between 7 October 1915, when he arrived back in London, and 6 November, Harris went from the infantry to pilot's training to being an officer in the Royal Flying Corps.

Harris was then assigned to the Central Flying School at Upavon, which was only marginally more rigid than the one at Brooklands. As Harris said, "I completed the long course. . . . The Long Course, ye Gods! . . . I suppose it must have been about ten hours."

His first active-duty station was at Northolt, in Middlesex. When his new commander asked the young pilot if he could fly in the dark, Harris replied, "I can't fly in the daylight, so maybe I can fly in the dark."

The remark was not atypical. Harris was famous for the barbed comment, but he was also a man of dry wit and droll humor. He liked to drive fast and was once stopped for speeding near an air base. "You might have killed someone, sir," said the policeman in an attempt to chastise the air marshal. "I kill thousands of people every night," replied the head of Bomber Command.

Harris's squadron was put on antizeppelin duty, charged with intercepting and destroying the airships that Germany was using to bomb London at night. Harris literally had to teach himself night flying. It was dangerous work and many men were killed, but the experience taught him that thorough training was the essential element for an air force. Of equal importance, here was the beginning of his theories about the use of planes at night to bomb enemy cities. Later, when he was head of Bomber Command, these two ideas would reach full fruition.

Harris recalled his later combat duty in France—flying the Morane Parasol, the Morane Bullet, the Sopwith 1½ Strutter, and finally the legendary Sopwith Camel—in his usual style, which was a combination of the testy, the arrogant, and the self-deprecating.

He seemed to have come out of the war more bemused than enlightened. "We just flew about," he said. "There didn't seem to be any plan."

Harris, his offhanded comments aside, gained valuable ideas from his derring-do over Flanders' fields. The military planners and the public would in time learn the value of the airplane as a strategic and tactical weapon. Harris never doubted the airplane's future. It was to be his crusade to turn this potent new weapon, this "toy," into the primary means of attacking the enemy. He was given the opportunity to do so when he was asked to stay on in what was now the Royal Air Force.

Hugh Trenchard, the first chief of the new RAF and chief of the air staff from 1919 to 1929, managed to hold off the skeptics who had not let up in their efforts to undermine the RAF and keep them at bay. He thus kept the RAF alive, but it was barely breathing.

Harris, in *Bomber Offensive*, his postwar memoir, wrote scathingly of the campaigns against the air services by the old guard during the interwar period. "Thereafter for nearly twenty years," he said, "I watched the army and navy, both singly and in concert, engineer one deliberate attempt after another to destroy the Royal Air Force. Time after time they were within a hairbreadth of success; time after time Trenchard, and Trenchard alone, saved us. If they had succeeded they would have abolished our air power as they succeeded in abolishing our tank power, while retaining the Camberley drag hunt."

Regarding the vaunted battleship, Harris said that their "bones now lie where air power so easily consigned them, littering the floors of the ocean or obstructing the harbours of the world."

As an acolyte of Trenchard's, Harris had paid close attention to his new ideas, and Smuts's manifesto would become his credo when he became head of Bomber Command. Harris early on saw the power of bombs as a deterrent when he was stationed in India in 1921. One twenty-pound bomb dropped onto the grounds of the palace of the emir of Afghanistan, who had launched an insurgency against Great Britain, had been enough to convince that worthy to negotiate.

After his tour in India, Harris was sent to Iraq, where the RAF was charged with subduing another restive, even rebellious populace. Between 1922 and 1924, the RAF heavy bombers destroyed villages and killed or injured thousands of the rebels before calm was restored.

But the lessons of India and Iraq, while instructive, were improper for the wars of the 1930s and 1940s. The intimidation of petty tribal chieftains, illiterate villagers and nomads, or eastern potentates, who had never seen an airplane, was a far easier task than cowing the populace of a major industrial power ruled by a fanatic.

After his service in India and the Middle East, Harris returned to England and began his unremarkable but steady rise through the officer ranks of the Royal Air Force, eventually joining the Air Ministry, where he became deputy director of operations and intelligence, and then, within a year, head of the Planning Department.

Harris and others in the military in England were successful in their efforts to counteract those who scoffed at the idea that German bombers might be able to so immobilize Britain that it would be isolated. Further, their argument that in the event of such a disaster only a bomber force could continue to wage offensive war against Hitler began to be taken seriously. But, as in America, the pacifists and the isolationists wielded enormous power and used it either to block or to much reduce military spending.

Nowhere was this shortsightedness more evident than in the decision not to fund an RAF entry in the Schneider Trophy high-speed flying contest in 1931. The Labour undersecretary of state for air saw no reason for the government to fund a "sporting event."

Lady Lucy Houston immediately agreed to donate £100,000, a plane was built, and the RAF won the race. But the trophy symbolized something far more important. The research and development that produced

the winning plane and its engine were crucial to the design and manufacture of the Rolls-Royce engines used in the famous Spitfire fighter
and the Lancaster bomber. Later, Harris credited this eccentric widow of
Sir Robert Patterson Houston, along with Fighter Command, of winning the Battle of Britain.

When Adolf Hitler came to power in 1933 and began to rearm Germany, the RAF had only 850 first-line aircraft. By 1935, the Führer
could brag to a British delegation headed by Foreign Secretary Sir John
Simon that the Luftwaffe already had that many planes and would soon
have 2,000.

Hitler's boast, which was intended to intimidate any potential enemies, spurred advocates of British rearmament to action—in particular,
Winston Churchill, who in dozens of speeches and articles called for a
much enlarged Royal Air Force to counteract what he saw as the coming
German threat. Although Churchill was mocked by the opposition and
ignored by many in his own party, he did have some success with his
campaign.

When faced with the incontrovertible fact of German rearmament,
the British government approved plans to produce 816 new bombers by
1937. This number was increased to 990 in February 1936. In addition,
production of new fighter planes was to begin.

Harris was troubled by the air staff's plan, which included light
bombers, medium bombers, and fighter-bombers—any one of which,
he said, would be obsolete by its delivery date. He called instead for a
plane with a range of one thousand miles and a top speed of 250 miles
per hour—in other words, a heavy bomber.

He was able to influence strategic planning as one of three authors of
a 1936 report entitled "Appreciation of the Situation in the Event of
War Against Germany in 1939." Few military documents have proved to
be so prophetic. Harris and his coauthors, Forbes Adams and Tom
Phillips, predicted exactly the German war aims and strategies and the
only possible defense for Great Britain.

A quick advance by Germany into France and the Low Countries
would give the Germans the air bases from which to make concentrated
attacks on the United Kingdom, which was clearly vulnerable to such as-

saults. Germany would then, they warned, do everything to guarantee a quick end so that Britain would not have time to mobilize for war.

In other words, the only course for the next two to three years was to prepare the country for defense against the coming German air raids. Harris was sure that the RAF could hold off the Germans with the fighter force that was in the works, and England could thus hold out until the offensive bomber force was in place. But the medium bombers could not be ready until 1940 at the earliest, and the heavies not until 1942.

The three authors also offered the opinion that any war with Germany would ultimately be decided on land. Harris would, of course, totally abandon this theory. He came to believe strongly that bombers alone could end the war.

Because even the thought of bombing cities and towns was still anathema, the three RAF officers were careful not to dwell on the fact that a bomber offensive would kill and maim thousands of enemy civilians. They had, however, made it clear that perhaps as many as 150,000 Englishmen would be killed or injured by German bombardment.

Now came the job of mobilizing industry to build a war machine. The RAF comprised just 1,000 first-line aircraft in 1936. Great Britain ranked fifth among the world's air powers. Harris wanted to have at least 2,000 first-line planes by 1939 with a reserve force of 200 percent.

British intelligence that the Luftwaffe would produce 2,500 first-line planes by that date and its reserve would be 100 percent was right on the mark. Production for the Luftwaffe in 1939 was 2,518 planes. However, in 1940 German production rose to 10,247.

· · ·

In 1937 it appeared to the advocates of aerial bombardment that they had won their campaign for increased aircraft production and procurement, and Harris happily accepted his promotion to air commodore and the command of a bomber group. But the triumph over the admirals and generals and the pacifist politicians was short-lived.

In an almost exact replication of what was happening in Germany and the United States, the decision was made to concentrate on medium bombers instead of the more expensive heavies. Almost as serious were the cuts in the reserve forces.

However, much good also came out of this reordering of priorities, which concentrated on defensive aircraft. The Hurricane and Spitfire fighter planes, which won the Battle of Britain, are the most resonant examples.

The British realized early on that their aircraft industry could not meet even reduced goals in any reasonable time, and the RAF had to turn to the United States. Harris was part of a British mission that arrived in Washington in April 1938 to negotiate with the Americans for planes and equipment.

He was singularly impressed with American efficiency and enthusiasm, particularly the executives and engineers at the Lockheed Aircraft Corporation. The British ordered "batches of Hudsons and Harvards." As Harris wrote after the war, "The Hudsons beyond doubt pulled us out of the soup when we used them for anti-submarine patrols . . . and the Harvards broke the back of our problem in finding training aircraft."

But his praise extended only to the civilian sector. As for the U.S. Army Air Corps, "I am at a loss to understand where the myth of American air power and efficiency arose," he reported back to England.

Harris acidly observed that the Americans "have one or two 'stunt' units which can, and occasionally do, put up 'stunt' performances." In short, said Harris, the Americans had only "an elaborate and expensive piece of window dressing, which comes perilously near to being little more than a jest when judged by the standards of any first class air power. . . . Their major obsession," said Harris, "is that all their geese are swans, and that everybody else's are, at the best, ducks."

It is clear, using Harris's standards, that no country, in 1938, was a first-class air power. Certainly Great Britain was not, and in the not too distant future, events would prove how ineffective Germany's "shop-window" Luftwaffe actually was.

Harris did praise the American advances in navigation and recommended that Britain should order navigation and communications equipment from the United States. However, the item that the British were most anxious to learn about was off-limits. Harris ran into a stone wall when it came to the Norden bombsight. No information was available.

Given his scornful dismissal of the American air force, it is surprising that he became friends with the commander, Hap Arnold, and his deputy, Ira Eaker.

Harris's reputation for speaking his mind made it unlikely that the American commanders did not hear of his remarks, but they refrained from responding to the testy Briton, who was doubtless venting some of his rage against the shortsighted bureaucrats at home. It cannot have been pleasant for this proud and touchy man to have gone hat in hand to the Americans.

By 1939, the situation began to change. Hap Arnold and Carl Spaatz, who were charged with a quantum expansion of the U.S. Army Air Corps, now ran head-on into balancing their needs with the needs of the RAF. Spaatz was flatly opposed to sending planes abroad when the American air force, if one could even call it that, was so deficient. No doubt Harris became aware of Spaatz's opposition, which may have colored his somewhat negative view of the American airman when they had to work together so closely later in the war.

Just before Harris's mission to Washington in 1938, the forty-five-year-old bachelor officer had become engaged to twenty-year-old Therese Hearne. When he returned from the United States, they were married and soon afterward Harris began a second tour in the Middle East as air officer commanding Palestine and Transjordan.

The British attempt to adjudicate the troubles between the Jewish settlers and the Arabs often led to armed clashes, assassinations, and open revolt. Harris applied the techniques developed ten years earlier in India and Afghanistan, and once again airpower proved to be a useful tool of intimidation.

He returned to England in midsummer 1939, just after his promotion to air vice marshal, and when the war began he became head of 5 Group, one of the five bomber groups that made up Bomber Command, with headquarters at Grantham, an ancient and historic town on the Witham, in Lincolnshire.

The winter dragged on, and Hitler still did not press his presumed advantage after the invasion of Poland by moving west. This period, the so-called Phony War, which lasted from October 1939 until April 1940, was a time of waiting and watching, and for Harris it was a particularly dispiriting period.

"I have in the course of my lifetime rarely been so depressed," he said. His surroundings did little to lift his gloom. Grantham had once been the haunt of King John and Richard III, but Harris's troubles were of more recent vintage. He felt he was in a backwater and saddled with equipment that in his opinion was useless.

Harris, in his pursuit of his military ideals, spared no one throughout his career in his relentless advocacy of better training, planes, and weaponry. When he saw the prototype of the twin engine Avro Manchester in September 1940, he said that the only use for the plane as presently configured was for "throwing away crews."

He was particularly derisive concerning the small escape hatches on the Avro Manchester. Someone at the Air Ministry should realize that if a man has to jump out of an airplane he should be able to take his parachute, Harris sarcastically observed.

Despite Harris's criticisms, some two hundred Avro Manchesters were built and delivered to the RAF; but, as he predicted, they were a failure and were withdrawn from service in less than two years. The plane did serve a useful purpose, however. It would be the basis for the aircraft that became the backbone of the bomber fleet, the Lancaster.

In the same memo addressing the shortcomings of the Manchester, Harris's credo regarding aerial bombardment was simple. Heavy bombers should be used only for nighttime operations. Daylight bombing had been proved to be a "busted flush." As he put it, this was a "childishly obvious fact."

Arthur Harris's first concern was always the welfare and safety of his crews, which endeared him to the rank and file of the RAF. He was particularly distressed by what he saw as foolhardy actions by pilots to save a plane or avoid civilian casualties on the ground if a plane crashed. Trained pilots and crew, he said, were far more important than either a plane or any unfortunate civilian who happened to be in the way.

Planes and crew, as vital as they were, existed for only one reason, to rain destruction on the enemy, and Harris early on pressed for the development of more powerful bombs. The Germans had by the winter of 1940 demonstrated the destruction that could be caused by large high-explosive bombs, and intelligence indicated that the Nazis were developing a 4,000-pound version.

Harris was quick to trade on the German advances and to adopt the Luftwaffe's bombing policies. It mattered not at all to him where ideas came from. Effectiveness was the only criterion. In a memorandum he laid out the two principal bombing methods as he saw it.

The first was so-called precision bombing, wherein factories, communications centers, and other industrial sites were hit directly, or nearly so, by heavy fragmentation bombs.

The other method was the Luftwaffe's. Light-case bombs with huge amounts of explosives were dropped with little regard for accuracy. Damage was more widespread; it interrupted all essential services and so damaged buildings that production would be halted. The effect could be increased exponentially if the high explosives were accompanied by incendiaries. This plan would evolve into the system that would become standard bombing procedure. Incendiaries were used to set the fires and the high explosives—2,000-pound, 4,000-pound, and even larger bombs—would crash through, destroying roads, water mains, and the electrical supply.

Thus, in late 1940, Bomber Command, as Harris had always argued it would, became the only British means of engaging the Germans directly on the Continent.

In June 1941, Harris returned to the United States as head of a delegation charged with expediting the purchase and delivery of American war matériel. Harris had not tempered his view of America—the only thing worse than going there, he said, was staying at the Air Ministry—but only someone of his rank and experience could deal with the American officers on equal terms, so he accepted the assignment.

Harris particularly disliked Washington, though he managed to hide his disdain. And he was wise enough to realize that there were many in the Roosevelt administration who were sincerely trying to help his be-leaguered country.

He reached out to them, and to one in particular: a man who was sin-gled out and praised unstintingly by both Harris and Churchill—Harry Hopkins. The mild-mannered midwesterner was a strong intervention-ist, and he now became Harris's personal conduit to his boss, the presi-dent, who already was bending every effort, and not a few laws, to overcome the ingrained opposition to foreign involvement by powerful leaders in the Congress and the majority of his countrymen.

Harris toured the country, visiting aircraft factories and training fields and forging firm alliances with other military men with whom he would work closely in the coming months and years. He also came to ad-mire George Marshall—whom Churchill called "the noblest Roman of them all"—and he developed strong relationships with Robert Lovett and Averell Harriman, two other influential figures in the Roosevelt ad-ministration and strong anglophiles.

On 22 June 1941, just days after Harris arrived in Washington, Ger-many invaded the Soviet Union. The opening of this second front, in the east, with the diversion of much of the Third Reich's war-making po-tential, relieved a great deal of the immediate pressure on Great Britain; but Harris and his countrymen's most fervent prayers had yet to be an-swered.

They had not long to wait. On 8 December, the day after the attack on Pearl Harbor, Roosevelt went before the Congress and asked for a de-claration of war against Japan. And on 11 December, in what historian Martin Gilbert has called "perhaps the greatest error, and certainly the single most decisive act, of the Second World War," Hitler declared war on the United States.

America was now firmly and officially allied with Britain in the war, but, paradoxically, Harris's job did not become easier. The equipment he had obtained with such difficulty was now needed by Britain's new ally.

There was also the question of which theater of operations the United States would consider the more important. In order to ensure that it would be Europe, Churchill left England the day after Hitler's declaration of war, bound for Washington and his second meeting with Roosevelt in ten months. In the delegation was Air Chief Marshal Sir Charles Portal, chief of the air staff.

After the first meeting of Roosevelt and Churchill with the Combined Chiefs of Staff, Portal pulled Harris aside and informed him that he was going to recommend to the prime minister his appointment as head of Bomber Command. The next day Harris was told that Churchill, who was impressed by the close relationship that Harris had developed with Roosevelt and Hopkins, had agreed.

Harris may have ingratiated himself with the president and his trusted adviser or, more likely, they with him, but their goodwill seems not to have tempered his view of things American. Roosevelt's boast to Harris that the average American could quickly learn to fly a plane— "because you see our boys are all used to mechanical things—they can drive a car long before they are legally allowed to"—was swallowed at the time by the air marshal.

In his postwar memoirs, however, he let fly. "Well," he said, "the answer to that sort of statement is that any moron can drive a motor car and it is generally the moron who takes most delight in doing so."

On 10 February 1942, Harris sailed from Boston for home, aboard HMS *Alcantara*, a passenger liner that had been converted into an armed merchant cruiser. While he was at sea, the famous area-bombing directive was sent to Bomber Command. Along with the decision to fly only at night because of the enormous losses, it had become clear that precision bombing, with the equipment then at hand, was also not possible. The only appreciable damage that could be meted out to the enemy was to bomb the cities. After all, as Harris had observed more than once, that is where the industry was. And while the area-bombing directive was drafted while he was in the United States, its contents could hardly have come as a surprise. In any event, he embraced it wholeheartedly.

Harris also maintained, somewhat disingenuously, that while morale bombing of Germany was high on others' lists of priorities, it was never a major priority of Bomber Command. As he said, "The idea that the main object of bombing German industrial cities was to break the enemy's morale proved to be wholly unsound." His argument had to do not with morality, however, but with practicality.

How could it have been effective, he argued, when in the brutal police state that was Nazi Germany there was never a possibility that the people could successfully rebel against the regime? As Harris said, the Gestapo was firmly in control and the leaders of the Reich made a clear distinction between the morale of the people and their conduct. The people suffered terribly from the raids, but they still reported for work. He might also have added that millions of workers in the Reich and the occupied territories were slave laborers.

Harris, ever the advocate of airpower, did not rule out morale bombing. "I do not, of course, suggest that bombing is not a useful weapon against morale," he wrote, citing the successes of the Luftwaffe in 1939 and 1940 in Poland and Holland. But, he added, the German "attempts to break the morale of Britain by bombing altogether failed."

Here one encounters again the oft-stated, contradictory arguments for morale bombing of civilians. On the one hand, it might work if one's own planes are doing the bombing. On the other hand, it is not effective if the enemy is dropping the bombs.

A letter written by a survivor of the Dresden raids and firestorm is instructive on this point. "The damage surpasses all one could imagine. . . . But we must not give up. Somehow we have to get through it all as it seems to be our duty."

On 23 February 1942, Harris assumed his new post, commander in chief, Bomber Command. He quickly settled in at the headquarters five miles from High Wycombe, in Buckinghamshire, and at once began to develop and refine the bombing practices that in the next three years would blast Germany's cities into heaps of rubble. Also buried in the dust of the cities of the Reich was the fine distinction between morale and area bombing.

• • •

The Billy Mitchell episode had served to put the issue of American airpower front and center, where it belonged, but it did nothing to tamp down interservice rivalries. The American military was not completely blind to the potential of airpower, but the American generals and admirals saw the airplane only in terms of tactical support for ground troops and naval vessels. And they certainly did not want any air arm to be on a par with the U.S. Army and the U.S. Navy—not in congressional appropriations, not in strength, and certainly not in influence.

There were minor but encouraging advances, however. The National Defense Act of 1920 established the U.S. Army Air Service, within the U.S. Army and equal to the infantry and the cavalry—at least in theory. The reality was otherwise. The act required that 90 percent of the officers in the air service be rated fliers. In addition, anyone transferring into the air service had to pass the stringent physical requirements. For senior military officers, this was, by and large, not possible. They were too old. The air service was therefore staffed with junior men in the military hierarchy.

In July 1923, the future head of the U.S. Army Air Forces, thirty-seven-year-old Henry Harley (Hap) Arnold, and the future head of the Eighth Air Force, thirty-two-year-old Carl Spaatz, held only the rank of major. Clearly, this lack of seniority hampered any serious buildup of the air service, whose officers did not have the clout in the army to advance their views—much less impose their will.

As sometimes happens, this detriment turned out to be an asset. These relatively young men were obliged to perform the tasks of men much older and much more senior in the regular army. And, of course, among themselves they were not bound by the archaic rules and attitudes of the traditional services.

Hap Arnold was a true aviation pioneer. Anxious to get out of the infantry, he'd applied in 1909 for a transfer to the Aeronautical Division of the Signal Corps. His application was approved in 1911, when the War Department contracted with the Wright Brothers to buy three airplanes. The transaction included pilot training at the Wright Brothers Flying School outside Dayton, Ohio, for Arnold and a fellow officer, Thomas DeWitt Milling.

Although Arnold worked closely with both Wright brothers at the school and factory, he never flew with either of them. The Wrights concentrated on the mechanics of aircraft with the students. An assistant took them up in the planes.

After total air time of about six and a half hours, Hap Arnold found himself a licensed pilot, one of the first in the United States. He and Milling were the only two pilots in the United States Army.

Arnold's early flying career was distinguished by his winning the Mackay Trophy for an outstanding military flight, but it was also marred by one crash and one near crash, which he admitted so unnerved him that he voluntarily removed himself from active flying duty in 1912. His subsequent marriage reinforced his decision to stay on the ground. But after unrewarding tours back in the infantry, he once again felt the pull of aviation, and in November 1916, at age thirty, he returned to the air.

When America entered the war in 1917, Arnold, in the belief that any future promotions would depend on frontline experience, applied several times for postings to Europe. His superiors felt he was needed in Washington, so his requests were denied until November 1918. He finally made it to the war, but just barely. He arrived in France on 4 November, just a week before the Armistice. Thus, to his everlasting regret, his illustrious career lacked one important element: actual aerial combat.

But the War Department experience would prove just as valuable in more important ways in the years to come. During his time in Washington he had seen firsthand the problems that would bedevil the buildup of a proper air force—research and development, aircraft manufacturing, the training of pilots, and the building of the infrastructure necessary for a proper air arm. It would take years to solve the problems—if indeed they were ever solved to Arnold's satisfaction—but this hands-on experience in Washington laid the foundation.

Arnold's World War I tour in Washington also involved the development of an experimental aircraft that in retrospect was more prescient than its designers imagined. The Liberty Eagle, or "Bug," as the plane was called, was an unmanned biplane loaded with explosives. It employed a rudimentary form of the system used to launch and guide the V-1, or Buzz Bomb, the weapon developed by the Germans and used with deadly effect against the cities of England in 1944–45.

The Bug never flew successfully, and the project was abandoned and forgotten by the military. It was thus consigned to the same shelf as two other revolutionary ideas that were conceived early on by the Americans but never developed until years later: midair refueling and wing tanks.

The interwar years were difficult for a career officer in any branch of the military. Wartime promotions were revoked, and Arnold briefly found himself reduced in rank from colonel to captain before it was settled that he would have the permanent rank of major—a bitter pill for a thirty-four-year-old. He also (at least he so believed) suffered from his defense of Billy Mitchell. Beginning in 1926, he was "exiled," as he put it, to a string of air fields in the Midwest for five years.

Meanwhile, other airmen found themselves in a similar situation, existing on the fringes of the American military establishment. Among them were James Doolittle, Carl Spaatz, and Ira Eaker, with whom Arnold forged strong ties and who in two decades would help him transform the United States into the greatest air power in the world.

In 1931, Arnold's career began to look up, with his promotion to lieutenant colonel and his appointment as commanding officer of March Field, in California. And in 1934, he was awarded a Distinguished Flying Cross and another Mackay Trophy for his command of a group of ten Martin B-10 bombers on a round-trip flight from Washington, D.C., to Fairbanks, Alaska.

The following year, Arnold was promoted to brigadier general, temporary, and in January 1936, he was posted back to Washington as assistant chief of the U.S. Army Air Corps.

Arnold's military credentials were certainly impeccable, but he had also cultivated powerful friends in the Roosevelt administration, in particular the president's closest confidant (some would say alter ego), the redoubtable Harry Hopkins. Through Hopkins he gained the respect and confidence of the president himself, and on 21 September 1938, Arnold was given the top Army Air Corps job, chief of the air force, and a second general's star. Henceforth the president relied on Arnold for advice on all matters concerning airpower, and Arnold's was a major voice at the Big Power conferences.

In June 1941, the U.S. Army Air Forces was created and Arnold's title became chief of the army air forces, part of the promotion being so that there would be an American equivalent of the British air marshals at the upcoming Atlantic Conference in Newfoundland being arranged secretly by Hopkins.

Arnold also attended the conferences, at Quebec, Cairo, and Potsdam; but it was at Casablanca in January 1943 that he did perhaps his most important and, some would say, controversial work. There he helped craft the bombing directive for the massive Allied air campaign against the Third Reich.

Arnold, to his chagrin, realized soon after arriving in Casablanca that the British air staff had convinced Churchill that only night bombing could succeed. After all, daylight raids had been a disaster for the RAF and had been abandoned. This was no small matter, since the Americans had been trained only for daylight operations.

The American commander wisely left it to his more experienced and knowledgeable subordinates—in particular Eaker, who at the time was head of the Eighth Air Force in England—to make the case for daylight raids. Thus the policy of round-the-clock bombing of the Third Reich—the Americans by day and the British by night—was born.

There was no argument about the ultimate purpose of the combined bomber offensive, which was to bring about "the progressive destruction and dislocation of the German military, industrial and economic system." But there was a secret directive as well: "the undermining of the morale of the German people to a point where their capacity for armed resistance is fatally weakened."

During the war and after, the Americans insisted that their unchanging and official policy throughout was always the precision bombing of military targets, and that civilians were never purposely targeted. It is clear, however, from the Casablanca directive that terror bombing of civilians was an official, albeit unannounced, policy of both the RAF and the Eighth Air Force. And Hap Arnold, as the ranking American airman present, doubtless played a major role in formulating the policy that by war's end had caused the death of an estimated 600,000 German civilians.

■ ■ ■

If Arthur Harris is indeed the archetype of the World War II airman, the man responsible for the rebirth, expansion, and subsequent policies of the German air force was an archetype of a very different sort. Harris and the other bomber barons are now known chiefly by students of the period, but as so often happens with history's true scoundrels, Hermann Göring's fame is widespread and enduring.

But Göring's place in history comes from his politics, not his military prowess. He was part of Adolf Hitler's innermost circle and was one of the most notorious criminals of the Nazi era.

Göring's position in the Third Reich, in that it was both military and political, was much higher than that of any of his opposite numbers among the Allies, but his direct control of the Luftwaffe put him in a rather similar operational position. And he is, of course, irrevocably tied to his conquerors, although, unlike them, he left no aviation legacy.

The virulently anti-Semitic Göring was the namesake and godson of Hermann von Eppenstein, an Austrian-born Jew who had converted to Catholicism. Eppenstein was not only the godfather of Hermann and his siblings, he was also the lover of Göring's mother for fifteen years.

Eppenstein had been ennobled, and in keeping with his position he maintained two castles—Schloss Veldenstein, at Neuhaus an der Pegnitz, near Nuremberg, and Schloss Mauterndorf, at Salzburg, where the Göring family lived after the father retired from the diplomatic service. It was among the medieval towers and battlements of the castles that young Hermann discovered his love for the Germany of myth and legend. He also developed a taste for opulence and grandeur.

Young Hermann had an illustrious career in the German air force, downing twenty-two enemy planes, for which he received Germany's highest military decoration, the Pour le Mérite. When Manfred von Richthofen, the legendary Red Baron, was killed, Göring became commander of his squadron.

Like millions of his countrymen, Göring left the military a bitter and resentful man. In Munich, where he had gone to study at the university, he met the man who would harness his nation's resentments and ride them to power.

Adolf Hitler and his fledgling National Socialist Party, the Nazis, promised to right the wrongs visited on Germany. What did the methods matter if the Führer could reverse the decline of Germany, abrogate the hated Versailles Treaty, and restore the Fatherland to its rightful place in the world? Hitler's rage and anger were focused on two groups in particular. The chief authors of German defeat and humiliation, he said, were the Bolsheviks and the Jews.

Adolf Hitler's message was easily assimilated by the twenty-nine-year-old war veteran, and he was welcomed into the Nazi Party in October 1922. Two months later, Hermann Göring, godson and protégé of an Austrian Jew, was head of the SA, the Sturmabteilung, or Storm Troopers, Hitler's elite guard.

The bond between the two men was further strengthened when Göring was wounded in the Beer Hall Putsch in 1923. He fled Germany to avoid imprisonment and spent the next four years in exile. He returned to Germany in 1927 and renewed his relationship with Hitler. When the Nazis won twelve seats in the Reichstag in the 1928 elections Göring took one of them, alongside Joseph Goebbels.

By 1932, the Nazis were strong enough that they were able to force the election of Göring as president of the Reichstag. By the time of Hitler's triumph—the accession to the chancellorship in 1933—Hermann Göring's future was assured.

The old loyalist was given three cabinet posts. He was made minister without portfolio, which meant, to use his own word, he was the Führer's "paladin." As minister of the interior for Prussia, which included the capital, he had control of the police of the most powerful state in Germany.

He soon made known his intentions, bragging that he alone would be in charge in Prussia. Thus was born an organization whose name would become synonymous with torture, murder, and suppression of all dissent—the *Geheime Staatspolizei*, or Gestapo.

In the dog-eat-dog world of Nazi politics, Göring's power always depended on the will or whim of the Führer, who encouraged infighting among his subordinates. It was, after all, a basic Nazi belief that the most worthy man would triumph and come out on top. And if he did so, was he not, according to the doctrine of the survival of the fittest, ipso facto the best man for the job, whatever that job may be? Thus, in a series of intrigues, Göring lost control of the Gestapo to Heinrich Himmler, and also lost the interior ministry for Prussia.

However, there remained the seemingly innocuous third cabinet post, air traffic minister. That one would prove to be the most important, at least as concerns the military, of Göring's government assignments. He at once began to combine the civilian air clubs and aviation organizations into the German Air Club and German Air Sport Union.

Goebbels immediately began to beat his propaganda drums. He warned the German people in the most strident terms of the nation's vulnerability to air attack and the need to build up a defense. A National Flying Day was held at Berlin's Tempelhof Airport on 15 June 1933, and a week later the Goebbels-controlled press fired the first shot in the air war: "Red Plague over Berlin: Foreign Planes of an Unknown Type Escaped Unrecognized; Defenseless Germany."

The 1926 Pact of Paris allowed Germany air police protection, and Göring moved immediately to take advantage of this clause and exploit the scare invented by the propaganda minister. He successfully negotiated with Sir John Siddeley, the British aircraft manufacturer, to provide aircraft to Germany.

Former wartime comrades of Göring's—in particular, Karl Bodenschatz, Erhard Milch, Bruno Loerzer, and Ernst Udet—were only too anxious to join him in building the German air force, but the emphasis was placed on training younger men for a modern air force. One of the first to be enlisted was twenty-one-year-old Adolf Galland, the future head of the Luftwaffe fighter command.

The putative Lufthansa trainee, along with several other young men, was sent for secret training as a fighter pilot with the Italian air force. Within the year, as Hitler became bolder, Galland and other of the Italian-trained pilots were transferred to the military and commissioned as officers.

In fairness—if such a word can be used in such a context as Hitler's Germany—no man could have fulfilled all the duties that were assigned to Hermann Göring. Not only was he to oversee the buildup of the German air force, but he was also in charge of overseeing the economic plans of the Reich and then of the conquered territories. It would be as if in America one person were placed in charge of the Federal Bureau of Investigation, the Treasury and Commerce departments, the Office of Management and Budget, and the air force. Failure was inevitable.

Before the collapse, however, there were years of stunning successes, or so it seemed to the outside world. In the early years of the Reich, Göring was by no means a hands-on manager of the Luftwaffe. He attended few staff meetings and was seldom seen in his office at the Air Ministry. His chief role was ensuring that funds were available for the vast buildup envisioned by a capable group of subordinates—Walther Wever, Helmut Wilberg, and Robert Knauss.

These three men were fervid believers in the philosophy of Giulio Douhet and advocated early on the building of a large bomber fleet to deter any aggression from Germany's enemies and to take the war to the enemy homeland if necessary. Their philosophy was embodied in "Luftwaffe Regulation 16: The Conduct of the Aerial War."

Although the regulation stressed that the purpose of an air war was to destroy the enemy's military forces—"The will of the nation finds its greatest embodiment in its armed forces"—there was no doubt in its supporting arguments that any segment supporting the military was a fit target for attack: factories, rail lines, administrative centers, power plants, and so on. In other words, the civilian population would not be spared in the event of a war.

In June 1936, the hitherto relatively smoothly functioning bureaucracy of the Luftwaffe received a blow from which it never recovered. Lieutenant General Walter Wever, the chief of staff, was killed in an air crash in Dresden.

Forthwith, Göring began to take a more active role in Luftwaffe planning and policies, and he appointed his old friend Ernst Udet chief of aircraft production. Udet, who was little more than a glorified test pilot, had no knowledge of aeronautics or airplane design.

By this time, although the resurgence of the German military machine was a reality, much of the power attributed to it was a bluff. However, when visitors from abroad were shown the new planes and the factories and introduced to the dashing young Teutonic pilots, they spread the word of the powerful armada that Germany was building and could launch against any potential enemies.

General Joseph Vuillemin, a French air commander, was led to believe—and did believe—that the test-model Heinkel bomber that roared overhead during his visit to a Luftwaffe airfield was in full production. Heinkel was said to be producing seventy He 111s a month.

In addition, it was said that the Messerschmitt Me 109 fighter was also being turned out in vast numbers, and the French delegation was treated to an awesome display of firepower from a jacked-up Me 110—again, only a prototype passed off as being in full production.

But the Luftwaffe was, in reality, as historian Michael Sherry has pointed out, a "shop-window" air force. It was "designed to intimidate or to demonstrate resolve," but it had very little to back it up. In no area was it as it was presented. Not only were the planes for show but command structure was weak, as were logistics, training, and reserves.

In Poland, in September 1939, the weaknesses were quickly made manifest to the knowing, but they were concealed by the rapidity of the assault and conquest of the country. Newsreel pictures of the Stuka dive-bomber attacking men on horseback reinforced the image of a technologically superior nation. The reality was otherwise. The Luftwaffe lost 285 planes and 734 men in the four-week campaign.

Hitler himself was taken in by the propaganda extolling the invincible Luftwaffe, and the Führer was lavish with honors and high position for the man he saw as its progenitor. It would take him years to realize that his trust in Göring was misplaced, but by then the war was lost.

Göring's great failing was that he did not use his influence and proximity to educate Hitler on the importance of strategic airpower and to institute a rational plan for research, development, and production of aircraft. In this he was, of course, like most yes-men. Whatever the Führer said was correct.

Otto Dietrich, Hitler's chief of press relations from 1933 until 1935, offered interesting insights into Hitler's attitude toward airpower. According to Dietrich, the Führer had no feeling for airplanes. In fact, he did not like to fly himself, although he had used an aircraft to telling effect while campaigning for office.

The Führer, however, never hesitated to interfere in design or production, and thus designers and builders were allowed to develop whatever struck their and the Führer's fancy at the moment rather than concentrating on proven aircraft.

Göring has often been painted as something of a buffoon, a beer hall glad-hander, an incompetent who succeeded to his positions of power through his doglike devotion to Adolf Hitler. And, indeed, there is truth to these assessments. There is also the fact it was his devotion and loyalty and proximity to the Führer that were integral to the founding and early growth of the Luftwaffe.

For all his failings, Göring turned out to have been a realist about German power in 1939 and the consequent ability of the Reich to wage war. The vaunted air force was something of a sham, and he knew it. But he said nothing, and it would be a year before the truth became obvious.

German medium bombers might be able to carry a thousand pounds of bombs to England, but they would have to do so without anywhere near effective fighter escorts. Therefore, it was essential to knock out the British fighter squadrons if the bombers were to get through. Thus when Göring laid down the priorities and the strategy for the Luftwaffe in January 1940, he made it clear that the aircraft industry and the RAF establishments were far and away the most important targets.

But there was the added danger that such precision required. The Luftwaffe would have to operate in daylight or when there was a full moon. Otherwise, said Göring, many of the raids on aircraft factories would have to be undertaken by single aircraft or small groups of planes to ensure surprise.

Although he would have to revise his thinking in the light of the harsh realities, in January 1940 Hermann Göring characterized night raids as merely "nuisance raids," which would be carried out only to keep the British on edge. As for the bombing of cities, he said, "An endeavor will be made to avoid for the time being considerable casualties among the civilian population."

On 7 September 1940, when it seemed that success in the Battle of Britain was within reach, Göring reversed this policy. It was the greatest strategic blunder of the many that the head of the Luftwaffe made. The bombers were redirected to the cities of Britain, particularly London, and when the Blitz ended in November, Germany had lost hundreds of planes and men and Hitler and Göring's grand plan to conquer Britain was finished. But neither man was ever able to reconcile the fact that it was their strategy that was at fault and not the men charged with carrying it out.

Indeed, when apprised that RAF fighters were appearing in ever-increasing numbers to shoot down his bombers, Göring exulted, "That's just what we want! If they come at us in droves, we can shoot them down in droves."

"In the face of such arguments no fruitful discussion was possible," wrote German historian Cajus Bekker. "The Luftwaffe's supreme commander had lost touch, to a disturbing degree, with operational problems. He dwelt in a world of illusions."

CHAPTER THREE

WEAPONS FOR THE
NEW AGE OF WARFARE

The Race for
Aerial Superiority

America, Germany, and Britain produced a remarkable array of aircraft as they prepared for and fought World War II. In the race to win defense contracts and reap the immense sums allocated for building up air forces, competition was fierce and was not limited to the industrial sector. Politics, both civilian and military, played a role as well.

As in America, where there were ruthless interservice rivalries and each branch had its own sometimes peculiar demands for aircraft, so was it in Great Britain. The Germans had a somewhat different problem, in that the byzantine workings of Hitler's inner circle and the underlings who aspired to be part of it often led to procurement decisions that had little to do with offensive or defensive needs.

Whether in democratic or totalitarian societies, technological breakthroughs ran up against an almost willful blindness by military leaders and politicians, who, in pursuit of their own agendas, could be oblivious to what was needed by the men who had to fly or defend against the fighters and bombers in combat.

In Great Britain the first bombers put into service, the twin-engine Wellingtons, Hampdens, Whitleys, Manchesters, and Blenheims—which bore the brunt of the aerial offensive from 1939 until 1942—

were all deficient, often in many important ways. But each had its partisans, and crucial time was lost before it was clear that twin-engine aircraft, even in great numbers, would never be equal to the task set for Bomber Command: the obliteration of Germany.

The first of the four-engine heavy bombers to see action with the RAF was the Short Stirling. The initial order was delivered to the RAF in August 1940. The Handley Page Halifax followed in November of the same year. The Avro Lancaster lagged somewhat behind these first two heavy bombers. Production did not begin until early in 1942. But massive production of the heavy bombers would not really get under way until even later, when much of it was farmed out to countries in the commonwealth.

Indeed, when Arthur Harris assumed command in late February 1942, the total operational night-bomber strength of Bomber Command was only 469 aircraft, of which just 53 were the new four-engine bombers. There were an additional 78 day bombers, all of them twin-engined.

American aircraft manufacturers were just as anxious to gain as large a piece of the armaments pie as their British and German counterparts, and they too trotted out various designs and prototypes that they promoted as the bombing platform that would guarantee U.S. superiority. By the time the American aircraft industry finally geared up, the country was on a war footing. There was little time to try many different aircraft and then pick the one that worked best, but a plethora of manufacturers, contractors, and subcontractors turned out dozens of mockups and prototypes of bombers, fighters, and transports.

When the dust settled, however, just three twin-engine medium bombers, two four-engine heavy bombers, and three fighters carried the brunt of the American campaign in Europe. The largest bomber of all, the B-29 Superfortress, was not deployed until mid-1944 and only in the Far East.

The Douglas Boston medium bomber was first produced for the French air force, but with the fall of France in 1940 the planes were diverted to Britain, where they were instrumental in whatever early successes Bomber Command had.

The Martin B-26 Marauder was a versatile tactical bomber that was used with great success by America and the Allies. It became fully operational in the summer of 1941, and some 5,000 saw action during the war.

The best-known of the American twin-engine bombers was the North American B-25 Mitchell, which first flew in January 1939 and was in full production by February 1941. This plane, of which some 10,000 were built, gave the Allies a much-needed psychological lift on 18 April 1942 when General James H. Doolittle led a group of sixteen B-25s from the aircraft carrier *Hornet* in the western Pacific and successfully raided Tokyo. The raid was little more than a calling card, but it served notice that the Japanese home islands were in striking distance of a determined enemy.

Arguably the best-known American heavy bomber of World War II was the Boeing B-17, the legendary Flying Fortress. Its predecessors were the 1931 twin-engine Boeing B-9, the first single-wing, all-metal bomber, and the 1933 Martin B-10.

It was clear soon after its introduction that the B-9 was more useful as a model for the nascent airline industry than for the air corps, and by 1934 Boeing was already at work on a successor. In July 1935, the XB-17, as it was called, was introduced at the Boeing plant in Seattle. The prototype flew on 28 July, and the following month the plane flew nonstop to Dayton, Ohio. A new era in aerial bombardment had clearly begun. The air corps ordered sixty-five of the new bombers. The euphoria was brief. In October, the XB-17 crashed on takeoff.

The cause was pilot error, but the accident served as ammunition for jittery congressmen who were not unlike their counterparts in Britain and Germany. Could you not, they asked, have many more twin-engine bombers for the same amount of money? The B-17 program was kept alive, but barely; the order was reduced to just thirteen planes.

The first operational B-17 was delivered to 2nd Wing, GHQ Air Force, in January 1937. The remaining twelve planes on order from Boeing trickled in over the next two and a half years, until the thirteen-plane order had been fulfilled. The 2nd Wing thus had the only operational squadron of four-engine heavy bombers—which was the American bomber force—in September 1939, when Hitler invaded Poland and World War II began.

The B-17 was the plane that the theorists had long called for. It so bristled with armaments that it surely justified its name, Flying Fortress. No attacking fighter force would be a match or be a danger. This bomber would always get through.

This unshakable faith in the plane's invincibility created a dangerous situation in the air force that would take years to rectify. The development of new fighter planes ceased to have any priority. They weren't needed by a self-defending bomber fleet, said the advocates of bombardment.

This universal blindness to the need for development of a powerful single-engine interceptor or escort is well illustrated by an October 1934 visit to a BMW plant in Germany by the vice president of Wright Aeronautics. The BMW director sent along the American's remarks to Ernst Udet, head of aircraft production for the Luftwaffe, who forwarded them to Erhard Milch, secretary of state for air.

"According to the American habit [he] spoke quite frankly and we thereby received very valuable information," said the BMW director. The single-seat fighter "had played out its part." Only a twin-engine plane could ever hope to catch one of the new bombers, of which, he said, the best was the new Curtiss A-18, a twin-engine bomber with 850-horsepower engines.

Because the Allies had delayed the full-scale peacetime development of a long-range, heavy bomber force, the planes perforce had to be put into service before many of the operational problems were even recognized, much less corrected. Sometimes fatal design flaws thus came to light under the grueling and dangerous conditions of actual combat.

The first sale of heavy bombers to Great Britain comprised twenty of the new B-17Cs, and Bomber Command crews came to America to train in the planes at McChord Field, near Tacoma, Washington, in January 1941. This group of RAF Flying Fortresses began to be ferried across the Atlantic in April.

Additional training was necessary in Britain, but by summer all seemed ready for the new American bomber's combat debut. On 8 July 1941, three B-17s were dispatched to raid Wilhemshaven in daylight. Two of the planes successfully bombed the docks, and all three planes returned to their home base. It was a reasonably auspicious beginning but by no means a true test.

Harris's withering assessment of the Americans and their equipment would prove to be on target. American Anglophobia and British smugness aside, the criticisms seemed justified. The subsequent performance of the U.S. plane was disappointing.

In fifty-one sorties, eight of the aircraft were lost either in combat or to accidents, and only 2,240 pounds of bombs could definitely be said to have fallen on the assigned targets. No enemy fighters were shot down. Harris ordered a halt in their use in operations on the Continent.

Was this record the fault of the plane or the way in which it was deployed by the RAF? There were design problems to be sure, but the problems were exacerbated by Bomber Command policy. The B-17 was slow and was designed to operate in daylight, and the British were wedded to high-altitude nighttime operations. Since many of the planes were delivered with no heating system, the B-17s' guns froze, their windshields frosted over, and their engines did not operate efficiently. Worse, since the engines had no flare dampers, the exhaust flames could be seen for thirty miles, which made the planes an easy target for enemy interceptors and antiaircraft batteries.

And the RAF never used more than four of the aircraft at a time, thus ensuring that there could be no proper bomb pattern. As far as the British pilots were concerned, Hermann Göring's taunt that the B-17 was a "flying coffin" was all too accurate. The British B-17 operational difficulties might very well have been the result of not using the plane properly, but when the Americans arrived in force, they too had serious problems with the plane.

On one U.S. raid, when the thirty-eight B-17s were en route back to their home base in England they were suddenly attacked by German fighters. But only two of the Fortresses could return fire because the windows had frosted up. Fortunately for the helpless crews, the enemy interceptors were at the limit of their range and had to turn back.

Most of the problems with the Flying Fortress were ironed out over time, and slowly the fleet was built up so that by the end of November 1944 there were over 1,300 operational B-17s with the Eighth Air Force.

The problems with another American plane, the B-24 Liberator, were more substantial and were the results of basic design flaws. This plane was designed to carry four tons of bombs—one ton more than the B-17—and was supposed to fly at greater speeds and higher altitudes.

However, the plane's armament proved so deficient in combat that it immediately had to be increased. The added weight increased fuel consumption and lowered both the speed and the operational altitude. To compensate, the bomb load was reduced by a ton and half—from 8,000 pounds to 5,000 pounds. And, of course, the range of the plane was also substantially reduced.

The B-24 had other problems as well, which gave it a reputation as a hard plane to fly and a poor bombing platform. The normal upward angle of the nose of the plane in flight was made even more pronounced once the speed was reduced. This change in the plane's attitude further reduced the visibility for the pilot, the navigator, and the bombardier, who sat in the nose turret. It took a crew of great skill to man the plane and overcome General Doolittle's complaint that 75 percent of mission failures were caused by poor navigation. Doolittle's low estimate of the plane's operational abilities could not be raised by increasing the crew's navigational skills, however.

As late as 25 January 1945, he wrote to Lieutenant General Barney M. Giles, chief of the air staff, "It is my studied opinion that no minor modifications will make the B-24 a satisfactory airplane for this theater." This, after the plane had been in service for five years and undergone countless modifications. Giles replied on 10 February that the staff was about at "the end of their rope" as far as the B-24 was concerned. Arnold really blew his stack when he learned during an inspection trip that some five hundred modifications were then being done on the plane.

However, one Liberator did prove to be particularly airworthy. The pilot and crew managed to bring the critically damaged plane back to England, but it was clear that they were not going to be able to land it safely. They headed the aircraft out to sea, set the autopilot, and then bailed out. But the plane turned around at the coast and for ten minutes flew around the airfield at Woodbridge until the tail fell off and the plane "landed" on the runway.

And the sad honor of being the last American bomber on a combat mission to be shot down over Germany in World War II fell to a B-24. On 21 April 1945, the *Black Cat* fell victim to antiaircraft fire at Regensburg.

Official assessments of the B-24 were not much shared by the pilots who flew the plane, it seems, although their copilots were not so enthusiastic. Seventy-nine percent of the pilots who were surveyed felt that the B-24 was the best plane for the job. Only 58 percent of copilots agreed. Figures for the B-17 were much higher: 92 percent and 88 percent, respectively.

· · ·

The bombing campaign against Germany would never have achieved the success it did without the development of a long-range fighter that could escort the bombers all the way into the Reich and back. Otherwise, as Bomber Harris said repeatedly, daylight bombing was a "busted flush."

Chief among these planes was the North American P-51 Mustang, the greatest fighter plane of World War II. Like virtually all new planes, the Mustang had a rocky beginning. (The de Havilland Mosquito was the single exception; it was a success from the start.) Originally built to British specifications, the P-51 made its first test flight in November 1940, an amazing one hundred days from the first design, and the initial British order began arriving in Great Britain just a year later, in November 1941.

It was immediately obvious to the British that the new plane, with its American-built Allison engines, was underpowered and was not effective at higher altitudes. It was thus used only as a low-altitude reconnaissance fighter. There was also another drawback. In a masterpiece of British understatement, one analyst said, "The only criticism of the P-51 is the shedding of wings."

The structural problems were soon solved, but not until the British installed a Rolls-Royce Merlin engine and changed the propeller to a four-bladed airscrew did the Mustang begin to come into its own. Eventually, with more modifications, the P-51 could fly at 437 miles per hour and climb to 20,000 feet in seven minutes; it had a range of 2,300 miles.

The British improvements in the plane were immediately undertaken by North American Aviation during manufacture of new planes in the States, most notably the installation of a Packard-built Merlin engine, instead of the General Motors Allison. By the end of World War II, over 15,000 P-51 Mustangs had been built.

Two other major American fighters played an important role in the air campaign in northern Europe: the P-47 Thunderbolt, from Republic Aviation, and the Lockheed P-38 Lightning. Along with the P-51, these fighters also had the capability of flying deep into Germany, and after their introduction the air war took a dramatic turn.

Republic began work on the Thunderbolt a month before the first design for the Mustang. Unlike the short gestation of that plane, the prototype of the P-47 took somewhat longer. There were many design problems, and the plane did not fly until 6 May 1941. The first production model did not come off the assembly line until March 1942, but by 1944 more than 10,000 of the fighters had seen service.

It was the largest of the American single-engine fighters—empty, the Thunderbolt weighed more than five tons—but its great size was for many its primary asset. Many pilots who otherwise would have died in less rugged planes managed to bring a shot-up Thunderbolt back to England.

Small numbers of the planes began to arrive in Great Britain in November 1942, and twenty-three P-47s flew their first Eighth Air Force operation, a high-altitude sweep over Holland, on 8 April 1943.

The most glamorous of the three American fighters, both to the men who flew them and to little boys who built and collected model airplanes in the 1940s, was the Lockheed P-38 Lightning. It had two engines, twin tails, and a cockpit suspended in the middle; no aircraft of World War II was so instantly recognizable.

Work began on the P-38 as early as 1936, when twin-engine aircraft were still considered the best alternative, but the first versions of the plane were dogged by design flaws and accidents. A prototype flew in January 1939, and all seemed well until, after a record-breaking coast-to-coast dash, the plane crashed on a golf course on Long Island. The pilot survived the crash, but it set back production by a good two years.

However, many modifications and versions later, production began. In 1943 the P-38 was the first fighter to be ferried across the Atlantic to England, where it became one of the big three fighters with the Eighth Air Force. Later models of the P-38 had an operating range of 2,300 miles and could stay aloft for ten hours. They could also carry two 2,000-pound bombs. This was remarkable in a fighter, since it was not so much less than the bomb load of a B-17.

But the plane's high rate of engine failure—many pilots blamed the low-grade British aircraft fuel, the British weather, or both—put it at a decided disadvantage next to the more reliable Mustangs and Thunderbolts, which also could penetrate deep into Germany. But in spite of the problems with the plane, over 10,000 of them were built.

Its speed and maneuverability made the P-38 a superb plane for photo reconnaissance and for Pathfinder duty, but its career in Europe was a brief one. It is last mentioned in the *Mighty Eighth War Diary* on 15 October 1944. Two P-38s were in charge of control and operation of two explosive-laden, unmanned B-17s on a mission to Heligoland. Sixteen P-51s provided the escort cover.

By late 1944, the P-47 was also all but phased out for support on deep penetration raids. For example, all of the escort fighters that were dispatched to support the American raid on Dresden on 14 February 1945 were P-51s.

· · ·

Harris and his American counterparts notwithstanding, a twin-engine bomber was not a completely retrograde idea in the 1930s. Nor was the idea of using the same material that the Wright Brothers had used in their first plane as far-fetched as it first seemed. Indeed, one of the most successful warplanes ever built had two engines and was made almost entirely of wood. The legendary Mosquito—the "Mossie," the "Wooden Wonder," or "Freeman's Folly"—was first proposed in 1938, and a prototype appeared in 1939. Fifty were ordered, but the minister for aircraft production, Lord Beaverbrook, canceled the order. Only the perseverance of the plane's advocates—in particular Air Chief Marshal Sir Wilfred Freeman; hence the less kind label attached to the plane—kept the program alive. With the flight of the first Mosquito in November 1940, its backers' faith was borne out. Its great potential was immediately apparent. In November 1941 the plane became operational.

With its light wooden frame, two powerful Rolls-Royce Merlin engines, and no defensive armor to add to its weight, the Mosquito depended on speed and maneuverability for defense. With a crew of two, pilot and navigator-bombardier, the plane cruised at over 300 miles per hour and could reach maximum speeds of over 400 miles per hour with a 2,000-pound bomb load. It operated at a ceiling of 36,000 feet and had a range of 1,500 miles. It was not only the fastest piston-engine bomber in World War II, it was one of the fastest and most effective combat aircraft of any kind.

The Wooden Wonder went through various metamorphoses, including the installation of armaments on many models, which enabled it to be used in a multitude of ways by the RAF: bomb marker, night fighter, pure bomber, ground attacker, and photo reconnaissance plane. The bomb capacity eventually hit 4,000 pounds on some versions, but even then the plane had no trouble reaching Berlin and even beyond.

The Mosquito flew so many missions over the German capital that it is difficult, if not impossible, to document them all. Goebbels railed against it in entry after entry of his diaries. "In the evening we again had the regulation Mosquito raids on Berlin," he wrote. "The population of the capital is gradually becoming habituated to the necessity of spending one or two hours every evening in the air-raid shelters."

In addition to its spectacular record as a pure combat aircraft—pilots of Mossies shot down 600 German aircraft and as many V-1 flying bombs—the Mosquito was, of course, the mainstay of the Pathfinders and the bombing-marker groups.

• • •

As with the Eighth Air Force B-17 Flying Fortress and the B-24 Liberator, two British heavy bombers were the workhorses of Bomber Command: the Avro Lancaster and the Handley Page Halifax.

Harris's condemnation of the 1939 Manchester twin-engine bomber did not halt production of the aircraft, but when it entered service its failings were quickly apparent. The Rolls-Royce Vulture engines could not power it enough to climb rapidly, and the maximum ceiling was much less than expected.

The virtues of the basic design were recognized, however, and if the plane could be reconfigured to accept four Rolls-Royce Merlin engines, it might just be able to do the job. This was done, and by early 1942 the new bomber, rechristened the Lancaster, began to come off the production lines. With a crew of seven and a standard bomb load of 18,000 pounds, the Lancaster had a top speed of 275 miles per hour and a range of 3,000 miles.

By 1 March 1942, only four of the aircraft were on active duty, but their numbers would increase rapidly. By war's end Lancasters would account for 60 percent of the bombs dropped on Europe by Bomber Command—everything from the small incendiaries to the 22,000-pound Earthquake.

The Handley Page Halifax also grew out of an aborted two-engine medium bomber, which was also to be equipped with the inadequate Rolls-Royce Vulture engines. The decision to replace the Vultures with Merlins was taken more quickly, however, and the prototype Halifax flew in October 1939. The first planes went to service with Bomber Command in March 1941.

The Halifax and the Lancaster were roughly equal in number of crew, speed, and basic flight range, but the Halifax's range was less than the Lancaster when carrying a full bomb load of 14,500 pounds.

. . .

Göring's plans for the expansion of the Luftwaffe were predicated on a war beginning no earlier than the mid-1940s, by which time, he felt, Germany would be invincible. Until that time expansion should come about through annexation, as in Austria, or through the threat of war, as in Czechoslovakia.

But even in his pursuit of offensive weapons for the German air force, the Führer was equally blind to the possibilities. In 1934 development had begun of a four-engine aircraft purported to be for the civil airline, Lufthansa. This so-called airliner flew nonstop to New York in

1937, earning much publicity for the Reich and causing apprehension in London and Washington. The plane eventually metamorphosed into a heavy bomber, the Focke-Wulf Fw 200 Condor.

Two other four-engine bombers were also in development by the Nazis. Junkers was at work on the Ju 89, which was nicknamed the Ural Bomber since its chief function was to strike deep into the Soviet Union when the time came. Dornier was also developing a heavy bomber, the Do 19.

In 1937 the decision was made to abandon research on these promising four-engine aircraft and concentrate on producing two-engine planes, which could be manufactured more quickly and, of course, more cheaply.

Although a four-engine bomber was officially proscribed, aircraft designer Willy Messerschmitt was never one to take no for an answer. He had continued to work on such a plane, and a prototype was flown in December 1942. The Me 264, christened by the optimists the Amerika Bomber and the New York Bomber, was designed to carry a bomb load to North America and return. The reality was somewhat different. It was soon clear that the bomber could do no such thing. Late in the war, it was even suggested that perhaps Me 264s could raid the East Coast cities of the United States and then ditch in the Atlantic, where the crews could be rescued by U-boats.

The lag time between prototype and production of aircraft was just too great, and thus it is unlikely that the Me 264 could have ever seen active service, particularly so in the light of the demands on the airplane industry at that stage of the war. Then too, as Armaments Minister Albert Speer said in his memoirs, explosives were in too short supply to make the heavy bombs for such a plane. Only three Me 264s were ever built.

The decision by Hitler and Göring to concentrate on twin-engine bombers was not completely to the detriment of Junkers. Although it had to scrap its four-engine plane, the firm built more than 15,000 twin-engine Ju 88 bombers in various models and configurations, some of which, in versatility and usefulness, resembled the British twin-engine Mosquito. The Ju 88 was used as a bomber, a reconnaissance aircraft, and as a night fighter. In the latter role it was particularly deadly against the British bomber fleets

Heinkel and Dornier were also the beneficiaries of the twin-engine bomber diktat. The Heinkel He 111, which first flew in 1936, was the chief Luftwaffe bomber during the Battle of Britain, and by war's end over 7,000 of the various models of this plane had been built.

The Dornier Do 217 series of twin-engine bombers also served somewhat successfully in many capacities—bomber, night fighter, and reconnaissance—and was a major component of the Luftwaffe during the Blitz. But like the other German twin-engine medium bombers, with their limited ceiling, short range, and slow speed, it too came to grief in the skies over Great Britain in 1940. The Heinkels, Dorniers, and Junkerses and their fighter escorts, which were operating at the outer limits of their range, were no match for the British fighters.

Göring's protégé Udet was only too happy to comply with the twin-engine bomber directive. Udet had pulled off something of a coup when just a few months after Hitler became chancellor in 1933 he had gone to the United States and arranged to buy two Curtiss XP-17 Hawk aircraft and spirited them out of the country aboard a German merchant ship.

In December 1933, Udet put on a spectacular display of the diving capabilities of the Hawk, which was instrumental in the development of the Ju 87—the famous *Sturzkampfflugzeug*, an unwieldy German term for dive-bomber that would become familiar to the world in its abbreviated form, *Stuka*.

Udet became blinded by the publicity surrounding the early but misleading successes of his brainchild and was so besotted with the Stuka concept that he was oblivious to the aircraft's shortcomings. For example, no version of the plane, and there were many, was ever to fly faster than 250 miles per hour.

He therefore saw no reason why all new planes could not be redesigned as dive-bombers, even the four-engine Heinkel He 177. Although it had the potential of being the German equivalent of any of the Allied heavy bombers, the He 177 was never put into active production and was eventually scrapped.

Udet's obstinacy proved nearly fatal for the development of aircraft in Germany, which went to war with a plane that was already obsolete. Indeed, it had already been decided to halt production of the Ju 87 by the time Germany invaded Poland in 1939. However, Göring knew that Germany was not armed for a long war, so every type of plane that had had any success was kept in service. Therefore, not only was the Ju 87 retained but its production was increased.

General Herhudt von Rohden, in a report after the war, stated what the planners were up against. "We [Germany] were prepared for a short war and could not keep pace with the production of the Allies; consequently, there was on hand a too large number of obsolete aircraft, which were suitable only for the Russian front."

Although Göring initially supported a heavy bomber for the Luftwaffe, he quickly divined that Hitler opposed it, and as always, he deferred to the Führer. As he said, Hitler was interested not in the size of the Luftwaffe bombers but in how many there were.

Just as in America and Great Britain in the mid-1930s, the materials necessary for manufacturing four-engine bombers were diverted to turn out many more twin-engine planes. But the Allies were quick to see the advantage of a heavy bomber and reversed course.

Still, Göring never completely abandoned the idea of a heavy bomber, and somewhat quixotically thought that one might be in full production by the mid-1940s. But the decision made in 1937 meant that years of necessary research and development were lost.

Meanwhile, a version of the Condor was developed for the Japanese, and a modified version of the plane was the one used in the campaign against the Allied convoys in the North Atlantic. But this bomber, the Fw 200C Condor, was an unstable aircraft, given to breaking up in the air or during the stress of landing, and only 278 were ever built.

The decision to halt research and development of a four-engine bomber came back to haunt Erhard Milch. In a surprisingly frank speech in 1943, the field marshal and secretary of state for air was openly critical of his fellow Nazis and obliquely praised the British effort.

Milch, of course, had kept his mouth shut when it would have mattered. General von Rohden was especially critical of Milch and all those other colleagues who, he said, "tried to assume as little responsibility as possible in order to be able to prove that they were not responsible personally." In the general's opinion, "The unmaneuverable and unwieldy four-engine bomber was the decisive weapon of World War II."

Erhard Milch's belated outspokenness about the shortsightedness of the leadership cost him. He became increasingly isolated within the Nazi hierarchy, and by 1944 he had been forced to give up his posts in the government. Milch may have been marginalized but he was still a true believer in National Socialism. He was found guilty of war crimes at Nuremberg and served seven years in prison.

Udet came to an earlier and equally ignominious end, although it was hidden from the public. Göring's decision in 1940 to halt further research and development of new aircraft and to build only planes with a proven record in order to try to end the war quickly led Udet to brag, "The war is over! To hell with all our aircraft projects—they'll no longer be needed!"

The Battle of Britain exposed the fallacy. Udet realized that the Luftwaffe was not going to save Germany and that his own decisions had contributed to the coming calamity. He began to be slowly stripped of his duties by Göring and pushed aside. Seeing enemies on every side, on 17 November 1941 he wrote a note on his office wall, saying that he had been sacrificed by Göring to the Jews in the Air Ministry, and committed suicide.

Udet's suicide note presumably referred to Milch, who in spite of his rabid Nazism was himself half Jewish, and Lieutenant General Helmut Wilberg, who was also legally a Jew since his mother was Jewish. These two high-ranking generals were among the hundreds of thousands of so-called *Mischlinge*, literally "half-breeds," according to the Nazi racial laws.

But through influence, favoritism, or the whim of the Führer, a successful applicant received a paper certifying that he was of German blood and could henceforth be so described in all official documents. Hitler took a keen interest in the issue and personally decided on all of the applications. Thousands of these *Mischlinge*, ranging from privates and seamen to generals and admirals, were granted the *Deutschblütigkeitserklärung,* an official "declaration of German blood."

The sycophancy and infighting that prevented the development of a heavy bomber were replicated in the procurement processes for a single-seat, single-engine fighter that could challenge the best of the British and American planes.

Here, again, that poisonous mixture of politics, intrigue, and Darwinian struggle that characterized Hitler's court came into play. Loyalty to the Führer and the Nazi Party permeated every aspect of German life and nowhere more so than in the military, where a major component of personnel evaluations was the adherence to National Socialist ideals.

In the early days of World War II, the Messerschmitt Me 109 had a great success, but when it went up against the British in the Battle of Britain its flaws became apparent. The plane's limited range, just a little over 400 miles, meant that it could stay over England for just a few minutes before having to head back to bases in France. Many Me 109s had to ditch in the Channel.

Subsequent versions of the plane went through many alterations, but its range never exceeded 600 miles, and in no way was it ever the equivalent of the British or American single-engine fighters that escorted the Allied bomber fleets over the Continent.

Although the Messerschmitt remained the fighter of choice—more than 30,000 of the various models were built—another fighter, the Focke-Wulfe Fw 190, had its partisans because of its greater speed. But even this plane had a limited range and under the best conditions could stay aloft only three hours from takeoff to landing.

In spite of their shortcomings, the German fighters were able to inflict massive damage on their bomber fleets until the long-range Allied support fighters began their deep penetration of the Reich in early 1944. It is still a matter of great speculation as to how the air war would have evolved if the Germans had early on pushed ahead with the development of a revolutionary aircraft, in a field in which they had a commanding, if not insurmountable, lead at the end of the war.

Willy Messerschmitt had been working on a successor to the famous Me 109 and Me 110 for years, but the aircraft visionary had quite a different sort of fighter in mind to supersede those redoubtable aircraft.

An experimental jet plane flew as early as 1939, and if Hitler and

Göring had been more farsighted and Milch and Udet not so hesitant, jet fighters could have been flying in great numbers by 1942. The 540-mile-per-hour Me 262s would have eliminated the much slower Allied fighter escorts, and once the P-51s were out of the way the Allied bombers would have been easy prey for the more conventional Me 109s and Fw 190s.

Messerschmitt was considered something of a serial liar by people who had to deal with him. No matter what he was asked, he always painted a rosy picture. Planes were on schedule. The planes could carry impossible bomb loads. Everything was in order.

Messerschmitt may have had personality flaws, but he did know something about airplanes. The Me 262, the world's first operational jet, made its maiden flight on 18 April 1941. The first turbojet engines were problematical, but many of the obstacles were overcome by July 1942, when it looked as if the Luftwaffe would have a plane that was superior to any fighter in the world and could defend the homeland against any bomber attacks. There the matter rested.

Hitler was still obsessed with the idea of light bombers, and further development of the new fighter was scaled back. It was no longer a priority item. However, when the Me 262 was shown to him at a Potemkin-like display of aircraft at Insterburg on 26 November 1943—the planes were still prototypes and nowhere near production—the Führer seemed to soften his views somewhat. But there was a catch. Hitler wanted the Me 262 to be redesigned as a high-speed bomber even though both he and Göring were made well aware that no bombsight was suitable for the plane and that the maximum bomb load would be just two 250-kilogram bombs. There was still no rush to fully develop the plane.

Messerschmitt may have been a liar, an optimist, and a dissembler, but he was correct in saying that turning the Me 262 into a dive-bomber would make it just another airplane—one that would be ineffective in opposing the now daily onslaught of Allied fighters and bombers.

It was not until there was real fear that the Allies were themselves developing jet aircraft that Hitler began to come around, or so it seemed. In January 1944, a London newspaper reported considerable advances by the British in jet-propulsion technology. Hitler, who was kept apprised of reports in the foreign press and often reacted to them, reinstated full production of the advanced plane—but, he decreed, as a bomber.

The Allies had learned of the German advances in the new technology in March 1944. Intercepted messages to Tokyo from the Japanese military attaché in Berlin revealed that the Germans would have an operational jet-propelled aircraft in 1944 or early 1945.

Two months later, in May 1944, in a stormy session at Berchtesgaden, Hitler discovered that the Me 262 had not been redesigned as a high-speed bomber and was still classified as a fighter. He pressed for his original orders to be carried out, and Göring complied.

The Luftwaffe thus had two versions of the plane, a single-seat fighter and a two-seat fighter-bomber. Several of the bomber version of the aircraft were available in August 1944, but they had little success in stopping the breakout from the Normandy beachhead. The single-seat fighters met with more success against the bomber fleets. But once again it was too little too late, although the possibilities of the Luftwaffe's new defensive weapon caused great apprehension among the Allied commanders.

Sources differ on how many jet aircraft Germany actually produced. The figure of 1,294 given by Cajus Bekker in *The Luftwaffe War Diaries* seems a reasonable number. Most of these were built in March and April of 1945. However, not more than 300 jets ever saw combat, and never more than three or four at a time were sent against the thousands of bombers and fighters that now ranged at will over the Third Reich.

And, of course, there was another problem, as serious as the tardy development and introduction of the Me 262: the severe shortage of trained pilots, without whom there could be no widespread deployment.

The German jets may have been few in number, but their actions served as a telling reminder of what might have been if Messerschmitt had been heeded two years before. In October 1944, according to Bekker, a jet *Gruppe* shot down twenty-two Allied planes. It is easily imagined what the carnage would have been if the planes could have been flown in force instead of in the pitifully small numbers that were deployed, especially once the Me 262 was equipped in early 1945 with a new form of rocket that could be fitted beneath the wings. On 10 April 1945, Luft-waffe jet aircraft shot down ten American bombers over the Berlin area.

Much has been written about oil shortages and lack of fuel for air-planes in the waning days of the Third Reich. This did not present a great problem for the jet plane, which ran on low-grade fuels such as kerosene. However, the planes used such vast quantities that they could stay aloft for only a short time. The Me 262 used forty liters of jet fuel per minute to taxi to its takeoff position. To conserve fuel and allow the plane to extend its flight time, the Me 262 was often towed to its takeoff position by oxen.

The problem of unsupportable fuel consumption was also shared by another Messerschmitt aircraft, the single-seat, rocket-propelled Me 163. Its great speed and rate of climb enabled the pilot to reach operational altitudes in just two minutes, but it could stay airborne for a maximum of only ten minutes, which could be lengthened by the risky expedient of cutting the engine and gliding. This aircraft was, as a consequence, never a serious threat to the Allies.

• • •

Late in 1944 a delusory chapter in jet aircraft development in Germany began to unfold, around the Volksjäger, or "People's Fighter." The He 162 was designed to be built by semiskilled workers, using as few strate-gic materials as possible, which meant that the chief structural material in the plane was wood.

In the twelve-year Reich, probably no other decision was taken with such little regard to reality as the Volksjäger. The director of the project, a rabid Nazi, fervently believed that the new plane could be flown by even teenage boys and could take off and land on any meadow or high-way.

In the furtherance of this scheme, Hitler Youth were given a quick course in piloting gliders and then immediately set to learning to fly a jet plane. Predictably, the results were disastrous. The plane never saw action and only 116 of them were ever completed, even though thou-sands were in some stage of production when the war ended.

The Volksjäger was not the only fantastic scheme concocted as the Third Reich crumbled. Several flying bombs were reequipped to carry a pilot who was to bail out after directing the bomb into an Allied bomber. Several volunteers were killed while testing the idea, and the plan was shelved.

Another bizarre plan was hatched by a fanatical woman aviator Hanna Reitsch. She suggested replicating in Germany the Japanese kamikazes, and in the desperate last month of the war pure suicide missions, under the code name Werewolf, were carried out. Some 130 pilots died crashing their planes into bridges and enemy bombers. In a tortured parody of a Wagnerian immolation, they went to their own fiery deaths accompanied by marches and the national anthem, all broadcast over the radio.

· · ·

All war planes had but one overriding purpose, which was destruction. They were designed to shoot down enemy aircraft; reduce enemy cities to rubble; destroy factories, refineries, and communications systems; and kill and demoralize the civilian population.

The Allied offensive was spectacularly successful in attaining all the goals except the last. Just as the German bombing of Britain, had, if anything, stiffened British will to resist, so did the bombing campaign have the same effect on the German civilian population.

Although Goebbels himself fretted that the German people might succumb to the terror of aerial bombardment, German civilians showed no slackening of morale when the bombing campaign against them was escalated to staggering proportions. In spite of the psychological toll and the sleeplessness, the inhabitants of Berlin went about their business— that is, those who were still in the capital. Many thousands of Berliners, like the citizens of all other sizable German cities, had long since been evacuated. But those who remained cheered the propaganda chief when he toured bombed-out cities. Large crowds, predominantly female, hailed him wherever he went.

The Germans were thus like their British counterparts, who did not succumb in the face of terror from the skies—be it the bombers of the Blitz and the Baedeker raids or the V-1s and V-2s. British civilians cheered the prime minister and the royal family whenever they toured the bombed cities.

As Molly Painter-Downs reported in her "Letter from London" in the *New Yorker* magazine, "London has accepted its sirens with the usual exciting British display of complete impassiveness. . . . People have queued up for the public shelters as quietly as if waiting to see a motion picture." Indeed, the chief question seemed to be where the best place to seek shelter was, with Harrods being a clear favorite of shoppers because it provided comfortable chairs and first-aid workers. One of the chief complaints was that there was no smoking allowed in the air-raid shelters.

The situation was much the same in Berlin and the other cities of the Reich. People went about their daily business whatever the thinking of the military commanders of both sides, who continued to believe that carrying the war to the civilian populace was the way to victory.

And just as commanders believe their armies are invincible, so did they believe in the invincibility of their people. The obvious paradox seemed never to be addressed: Why would one nationality succumb to terror bombing and not another?

At the Casablanca Conference in January 1943, the bombing strategy of the Allies was codified, and Trenchard and his disciples remained persuaded until the end that if the bombing of Germany was intensive and massive enough, it would have the desired effect. The Germans had failed in 1940 and 1941 only because they had not carried their campaign to the necessary extreme.

Carl Spaatz was one of those who fully endorsed Trenchard's view that airpower could win the war, and on 8 May 1943, just before Churchill and Roosevelt met again in Washington at the Trident Conference, Spaatz wrote to Lyle G. Wilson, "We have ample evidence to clearly indicate they [B-17s] can blast their way through any defenses and destroy the will to fight in any nation which may oppose us."

And on 24 May 1943 he wrote to Arnold, "In our day to day operations at the present time, we feel any area can be completely neutralized, even blown into oblivion, by high altitude attacks, without incurring any serious losses on our part."

Spaatz went even further in November 1943. He told Harry Hopkins, who stopped over with Roosevelt in North Africa, where Spaatz was overseeing operations in the Mediterranean, that Operation Overlord, the planned invasion of Europe, was not going to be necessary. Beginning in April or May 1944, raids from both England and Italy would bring Germany to its knees in three months. If Spaatz was correct, the war would end in August or September 1944, and no Allied troops would be needed in northern Europe except as an occupying army.

Round-the-clock bombing had already begun, in February 1943, but it was a modest effort compared to the vast air fleets that would be launched against the Third Reich by the Allies later in the war. Nevertheless the effect for the first year and a half was not anywhere near what the air planners had hoped, and there were disturbing portents.

At the Octagon Conference in Quebec in September 1944, the Combined Intelligence Committee reported that the German people still strongly supported the war effort and this was unlikely to change unless there was a "military debacle." As for a surrender by Hitler and his government, the intelligence experts said flatly that neither the present government nor any Nazi successor was likely to surrender.

The commanders in the field held the key to the end of the Reich, said the intelligence experts. Once they saw the hopelessness of their situation they would begin to surrender, albeit in piecemeal fashion.

• • •

At the end of 1944, the United States had 2,970 heavy bombers with the Eighth Air Force in the United Kingdom and another 1,512 with the Fifteenth in the Mediterranean area. Of these, 2,980 were operational, and each aircraft had two crews and thus could be used every day.

Spaatz, the commander designate of the United States Strategic Air Forces in Europe, would formally assume his new post on 1 January 1944. He would soon learn that conditions over northern Europe and the Reich, in particular, were much different from the relatively undefended sunny skies of the Mediterranean. The lessons of the previous three months were there for anyone who cared to learn and profit from them. But orthodoxy was still the order of the day.

On 17 August 1943, it became clear that bombers in daylight raids, no matter how strongly self-defended, were extremely vulnerable to the German fighter squadrons. Two Eighth Air Force missions that day, in the morning to Regensburg and in the afternoon to Schweinfurt, were among the costliest of the war.

Of the 376 B-17s dispatched on the two raids, 345 were effective, that is, reached the targeted cities. The bombers were escorted, but only in the first stage of the mission, by 240 P-47s. In August 1943, the P-47 Thunderbolt, even with an extra 108-gallon gas tank underneath the belly, had a maximum escort range of only about 375 miles. The "little friends" thus had to turn back near the German-Belgian border. After that the bombers were on their own.

As soon as their escorts peeled off and headed back to England, the B-17s immediately came under attack by swarms of waiting German fighters. There was also intense antiaircraft fire from the ground. Before the day ended there was a trail of wrecked American Flying Fortresses extending from the Low Countries, across Germany, and south to the Mediterranean. The terminus for the Regensburg raid was North Africa, where the Allies had several air bases.

Sixty planes were lost and 168 damaged. No air force could sustain such losses, but the catastrophe that was the Schweinfurt-Regensburg raid was not immediately evident—certainly not to the true believers. The next day General Harold L. George sent a euphoric "Secret: Eyes Only" message to Arnold.

Today I saw air power used in manner which if continued will without slightest doubt accomplish collapse of Nazi economic structure by Christmas. With this statement Harris agrees. Today's operation must have struck shattering blow at the very foundation of Nazi morale for Nazi air force as well as those in high command. Saw it demonstrated that American bombardment aviation can penetrate in daylight to very vitals of Germany against most powerful air defenses in the world, fighting its way against concentrated enemy pursuit for two hours and then perform superb precision bombing. That this is kind of lesson Nazi command can understand. They cannot help but realize the hopelessness of their resistance.

While losses were heavy the history of war cannot show where equal expenditure of efforts were so productive in depriving an enemy of those things he needs to continue the fight. Preliminary reports indicate that Messerschmitt plant at Regensburg completely destroyed. Damage at Schweinfurt uncertain due to heavy smoke over area which precluded definite photo reconnaissance but destruction appears to be extensive. . . .

My reason for sending this message is because I realize some folks without knowledge of the facts might think the price paid for such air operations is too great. If they understand these facts then this day's operations will go down in history as a glorious achievement of American air power. . . .

With double the bomber force the losses today would have been no greater but percentage would have been so reduced that continuous operations would be assured. Vital objective now is unquestionably the destruction of Nazi fighter force. With this accomplished the rest of the job is in the bag.

General George, who had helped draft AWPD-1, was clearly still in the grip of air force orthodoxy, but his almost giddy message to Hap Arnold could not and did not disguise the catastrophe. The Schweinfurt-Regensburg losses could not be ignored by even the most zealous advocates of the self-defending bomber fleet. The Eighth shifted its attention to close-by targets in western Europe, well within fighter-escort range of bases in England. American bombers did not return to Germany until 6 September. Again, the raid—Stuttgart and various targets of opportunity—was a disaster. Of the 338 planes, only 262 were counted effective. Of these, 45 were lost and another 116 damaged. Casualties—killed, wounded, or missing in action—totaled 362.

During the rest of the month the only large raids in Germany were attacks on the port cities of Emden and Bremen. But these targets were relatively near, and the bombers had fighter escort out and back. During this time, small numbers of B-17s flew night missions with the RAF, with little success. Otherwise the Eighth restricted its activity to France and the Low Countries.

Finally, on 10 October 1943, the Eighth returned in force to Germany. Out of 313 bombers dispatched to Münster, only 236 were effective. Again, the losses were horrendous—30 planes down and 102 damaged. One bomber group, the 100th, lost 12 out of 14 bombers.

There was worse to come. Just four days later, on 14 October, a bomber force of 320 B-17s and 29 B-24s returned to Schweinfurt. The B-24s were part of a force of 60 planes, but the others were unable to rendezvous because of bad weather. Even those that had successfully formed up failed to join the bomber stream because of the weather. Instead, they flew a diversionary mission to Emden. They were fortunate.

The carnage of this second Schweinfurt raid caused a major reassessment. Another 60 bombers were lost out of the 229 effectives, a staggering 26 percent. The casualties totaled 639, most of them killed.

The Schweinfurt raids were a perfect example of orthodoxy triumphing over common sense. The primary targets were the factories manufacturing ball bearings, without which, it was reasoned, the Germans would not be able to produce aircraft, rolling stock, or almost anything else that moved. This line of reasoning, a variation on the theme "For want of a nail . . . ," can be traced back to at least one prewar incident related by H. S. Hansell.

"We discovered one day," said Hansell, "that we were taking delivery on new airplanes, flying them to their points of reception, removing the propellers back to the factories and ferrying out additional airplanes. The delivery of controllable pitch propellers had fallen down. Inquiries showed that the propeller manufacturer was not behind schedule. Actually, it was a relatively simple, but highly specialized spring that was lacking, and we found that all the springs made for all the controllable pitch propellers of that variety in the U.S. came from one plant and that that plant in Pittsburgh had suffered from a flood."

As historian Steven A. Parker observed, "This observation led

Hansell and the other planners to conclude that the loss of one specialized item, such as the spring, could have a tremendous effect on industrial output in time of war and could ground airplanes just as effectively
as if enemy forces had shot them up or if enemy bombs had destroyed
the factories."

George was right that Arthur Harris agreed that Germany could be
destroyed by Christmas 1943 through massive bombing. Harris made
such projections himself. But he disagreed vehemently with the Americans as to whether daylight raids were the proper method.

As for the Schweinfurt raids, his view was that such raids were futile—the Germans had plenty of ball bearings in reserve until they
could repair the plants or disperse them elsewhere—and the Americans
seemed to agree, judging by their subsequent actions. There were no
more deep penetrations into German airspace by American bombers
until early 1944.

Although the myth of the self-defending bomber force had exploded
over the skies of Germany along with dozens of American bombers,
myths die hard. Spaatz himself did not begin to cast aside orthodoxy
until he assumed, or reassumed, command in Great Britain, where he
soon realized that fighter escorts were the key to success.

Unlike Ira Eaker, the unfortunate interim commander who had run
the air war from Great Britain while Spaatz was in the Mediterranean,
Spaatz was able to call on vast numbers of the new long-range fighters.
Within a month of his taking command of the Eighth Air Force, hundreds of bombers and their fighter escorts began to reappear over Germany almost daily. The command of the air would never again be in
doubt.

CHAPTER FOUR

THE FATAL
ESCALATION

Air War Against
Civilians

In turbulent times a few outsized figures arise and often become the personification of the national will. Sometimes these individuals are not just responding to the turbulence but are the authors of it—Adolf Hitler is a resonant example.

Other twentieth-century figures who for good or ill became the embodiment of their nations were Franklin Roosevelt in the United States, Joseph Stalin in the Soviet Union, Mao Tse-tung in China, Mahatma Gandhi in India, and Charles de Gaulle in France. Great social or political movements were set in motion by these men and became inseparable from them—the New Deal, Stalinism, Maoism, nonviolence in the pursuit of independence, and Gaullism.

The argument is endless over whether the times make the man or the other way around, but Winston Churchill's life and career does provide much fodder for those who share his view that men make the times—no matter that most of his actions were reactions to events set in motion by a counterpart across the Channel in Germany.

Indeed, Adolf Hitler is a compelling argument that men do make the times. The founder of the Nazi Party, Hitler was a charismatic figure who became the very embodiment of his nation. He was the face, voice, and driving force of the Third Reich. Without the Führer, that dismal period in German history could not have come about.

Churchill was able, through oratory and an almost mystical belief in his mission, to rally the British people in the darkest period of his country's long history. Not so incidentally, he was busily fashioning his own myth as well.

After the fall of France in June 1940, England was alone and dangerously vulnerable to Adolf Hitler's threatened cross-Channel invasion. The Führer's Operation Sea Lion called for creating a corridor between two massive minefields backed up by U-boats and protected by airpower. Hundreds of thousands of German soldiers would then traverse this corridor in barges and ships to invade the British Isles.

Churchill, much after the fact, in his memoirs, maintained that no such scheme could ever have succeeded. Germany, he said, never had the resources, particularly the ships and crews, for such an operation. More important, according to the prime minister, who never missed an opportunity to stress the singularity of the English people, the Germans never understood what he called "the sea affair."

Said Churchill, "For centuries, it has been in our blood, and its traditions stir not only our sailors but the whole race. It was this above all things which enabled us to regard the menace of invasion with a steady gaze."

Churchill's postwar retrospective somewhat downplayed the greatest danger to England since the Spanish Armada in 1588. In 1940, an invasion seemed real enough, particularly to the Royal Navy and the RAF, which bore first responsibility for turning back or destroying a Nazi onslaught. Churchill himself fretted a great deal about it to his aides and the War Cabinet. His secretary John Colville recorded in his diary on 21 September: "The PM seems rather more apprehensive than I had realized about the possibility of invasion in the immediate future and he keeps ringing up the Admiralty and asking about the weather in the Channel."

The next day, 22 September, General Frederick Pile, head of the Antiaircraft Command, was at Chequers, the prime minister's country residence, for lunch. Churchill told the general that he had a "hot tip" that the invasion was to be at three o'clock that afternoon. "However, I stayed to tea," said the general, "and no invasion took place."

The "hot tip" had come from the Americans, who had intercepted a message relaying the information that the Japanese were to invade French Indo-China on 22 September at 1500 hours. Somewhere between the translation of the original message and its retransmission from Roosevelt to Churchill, England had been substituted for the French colony in Southeast Asia.

On 15 October, Churchill's comments to the War Cabinet showed how anxious he had been all along about the invasion threat: "Should October pass without invasion, which cannot yet be assumed, we should begin the reinforcement of the Middle East."

Publicly, however, the prime minister was sanguine. He never faltered, whether delivering a radio address, responding to questions in Parliament, or meeting with a head of state. And no one dwelt much on the successful cross-Channel invasions in English history—the early Saxons, the Vikings, the Roman legions, and, of course, the Normans under William the Conqueror in 1066.

A more recent invasion had been unopposed, that of William of Orange and his army in 1688. Churchill's great ancestor John Churchill was commander of the defending forces and was thus at least supposed to be nominally loyal to his king and patron, James II. Instead he went over to the side of the usurper William. He was rewarded with the earldom of Marlborough.

But Britain was now to be tested as never before. It was clear to the admirals and generals that an invasion could be successful only if the RAF failed to beat back an attempt by the Luftwaffe to destroy the British air force and thereby establish German air superiority over England and the Channel. Hitler and his generals knew that Sea Lion depended completely on invincible air cover. Thus began the greatest air battle in history, the Battle of Britain.

• • •

The Luftwaffe offensive divided into three discrete but overlapping phases. In mid-July 1940, massive bombing of naval convoys in the

Channel and the southern port cities began. A month later the Luftwaffe began to concentrate on the destruction of British airfields, supply depots, and aircraft factories. The last, desperate phase, the indiscriminate bombing of British cities, particularly London, was initiated in early September.

At the beginning of hostilities, Franklin Roosevelt had asked all sides to desist from bombing undefended towns and cities and the civilian populace. The moratorium was observed for several reasons, not all of them moral. Great Britain was particularly happy to comply since Bomber Command did not want to send its relatively few bombers against the German fighter defenses.

Everyone, of course, knew that the restriction on the bombing of cities could not hold forever. Air raids on civilians by all the belligerents were inevitable. In that event, said Göring, much of the German fighter fleet would eventually have to be used to protect the homeland. To that end, the Reichsmarschall disclosed plans to construct coastal defenses as far as Biarritz, near the Spanish border. This formidable defensive perimeter would require vast numbers of fighter planes and men.

Bomber Command introduced a small cloud in Göring's rosy picture on the first day of the war. Britain declared war at 1100 hours on 3 September 1939, and by early afternoon a Blenheim reconnaissance bomber appeared over the German coast. This was more bluff than substance, of course. Britain was in no position as yet to do much more. Nevertheless, it was a portent of the future.

Göring estimated that it would take three days for his Luftwaffe to destroy the RAF fighter defenses. After that, the German bombers would be able to roam at will over the British Isles. His enthusiasm for the air campaign was based on some truths. The Luftwaffe pilots were better trained, and many of them had become seasoned in the Spanish Civil War, the invasion of Poland, and the campaigns in the Low Countries and France.

However, Göring made a mistake that no military commander ever should but many often do. He underestimated the strength and determination of his opponent. The British had, contrary to the accepted view, rough parity in numbers of first-line fighter planes. Only about 700

Me 109s were available for the Battle of Britain, and the Germans had no long-range single-engine fighter. Worse, replacement planes only trickled to the front. In the four months of the campaign, just 775 Me 109s were produced. The British produced twice as many fighters in the same period so they could fill the gaps in the first line.

More important, the British pilots, in their Supermarine Spitfires and Hawker Hurricanes, proved more than a match for the Germans and their Messerschmitts. As one Luftwaffe fighter pilot said, "The Spitfires showed themselves wonderfully manoeuvrable. Their aerobatics display—looping and rolling, opening fire in a climbing roll—filled us with amazement."

Then, too, the British had the advantage of operating close to their own bases. They could land, refuel, and rejoin the battle in a very short time. London was at the outer limit of the range of the Me 109, and the German fighter pilots, no matter how the battle was going, had no choice but to head back to France when their fuel ran low.

Another surprise for Reichsmarschall Göring was the discovery that the British were far ahead in the development of an early-warning system called RDF, radio direction finding, which would become better known as radar. The device was so classified that not even the Americans were told of it.

The Germans had a form of radar, but they were by no means as far along in deployment as the British, who by late 1938 had in place along the Channel coast facing Europe a chain of early-warning stations. The Germans had exactly two radar installations in the summer of 1940—one in the Ruhr and a portable one on the French coast to track enemy convoys.

There was also another top secret enterprise of inestimable importance in the Battle of Britain and, indeed, for the entire Allied war effort. At Bletchley Park, the headquarters of the British intelligence codebreaking operation called Ultra, cryptographers had succeeded in cracking the German Enigma code. Even with the key to the German ciphers, it was still no quick and easy job to decrypt messages; it was with some pride that veterans of the effort told of delivering decoded messages to headquarters in times as brief as two and a half hours after they were intercepted.

This was still a considerable delay, considering the proximity of the Luftwaffe airfields in France, but it was possible to anticipate and act on any plans involving missions only a few hours in the future. These developments—early warning and decryption—were important elements in the RAF triumph in the Battle of Britain, but Churchill, as was his wont, credited a less quantifiable element for the success of his countrymen. The British pilots, said Churchill, "had supreme confidence in themselves as individuals and that determination which the British race displays in fullest measure when in supreme adversity."

Another factor that bedeviled both the Allies and the Germans—one that is frequently mentioned but never emphasized enough—was the weather. The weather in northern Europe—English weather, in particular—was and is extremely variable and difficult to forecast with any degree of accuracy. Aircraft formations were easily dispersed in the dense cloud cover or fog that swept in without warning, targets were hard to find, and the bomber groups were often fatally separated from their fighter escorts.

An unresolved source of contention concerning the weather was the understandable reluctance of the U.S. and Royal navies to provide hourly weather reports from the convoy escorts in the Atlantic. Such information would have been of immeasurable help to the forecasters, but it would have also given away the position of the ships to the roaming U-boat wolf packs.

Whatever the reasons for the final British victory—men, machines, meteorology, or mistakes by the enemy—it was very nearly a British defeat. The Germans came perilously close to realizing their goal of destroying British airpower. The RAF fighter pilots might have had the edge over their Luftwaffe counterparts, but attrition took its toll. Although reserves were dangerously thin, the planes could be replaced; the men to fly them could not. Between 24 August and 6 September, 103 pilots were killed and another 128 severely wounded. Twenty-five percent of the British fighters had been destroyed as well.

Luftwaffe losses in men and planes were even more staggering. However, by early September 1940, German air force pilots began to report a decline in the intensity of the British fighter defense. The success of Göring's strategy to control the skies over Great Britain seemed to be in the offing, but then Adolf Hitler ordered a sudden and disastrous re-allocation of Luftwaffe resources.

As he had already shown, the Führer had no qualms about bombing the citizens of any city if it suited his purposes. London, however, was still marked as a prohibited area on all Luftwaffe charts at the beginning of the Battle of Britain.

But two incidents had already occurred, the repercussions of which hastened the change in tactics. On 15 August, Luftwaffe pilots mistook the civil airport at Croydon for their assigned targets, the RAF stations at Kenley and Biggin Hill. Croydon, less than ten miles from central London, was well within the forbidden zone decreed by Hitler, and an enraged Göring ordered that the pilots who committed the blunder be court-martialed. The order was never carried out, since none of the offenders made it home from the raid. They were either dead or prisoners of war.

A more serious incident occurred on the night of 24–25 August. The assigned targets were the aircraft factories at Rochester and oil storage tanks on the Thames. But a navigational error led two pilots astray, and they dropped their bombs directly on London.

The day after the London raid, the Reichsmarschall, who was following the air war not from the front lines or Luftwaffe headquarters but from his vast estate, Carinhall, fired off another angry message to the Luftwaffe airfields. He reserved "to himself personal punishment of the commanders concerned by mustering them to the infantry," he said. Göring's responses back up the German arguments that the first bombings of London and Croydon were the result of pilot error.

A month before, Churchill had written to Archibald Sinclair, secretary of state for air, "In case there is a raid on the centre of Government in London, it seems very important to be able to return the compliment the next day upon Berlin." Sinclair assured the prime minister that by 1 September the RAF could mount such a raid.

The morning after those few bombs fell on London, Churchill called on Sinclair to keep his promise. That night, 25–26 August, about fifty Hampdens and Wellingtons bombed Berlin. The raid was more symbolic than destructive. Visibility was limited, and only a few bombs fell within the city limits. A summerhouse was destroyed and two people injured in a Berlin suburb, but most of the bombs fell well outside the city on farmland, which prompted the Berliners to joke, "Now they are trying to starve us out."

No German commander disputed that London was to become a target eventually. As their campaign proceeded, the city would have to be bombed as a way of forcing the remaining planes in Fighter Command to take to the air to defend the capital. The British, the argument went, would throw everything into the fight to save London.

Churchill was passionately attached to London, but he was more passionately attached to democracy and destroying totalitarianism. Cities can be reconstructed; the destruction of democracy creates less tractable problems. Unlike Pétain, who saw the destruction of Paris as a desecration, Churchill would have sacrificed London without hesitation in order to fight on against the Nazis.

No doubt to the dismay of at least some of the members, he told the House of Commons during the Blitz that "the law of diminishing returns operates in the case of the demolition of large cities. Soon many of the bombs would only fall upon houses already ruined and only make the rubble jump."

In September 1940 Churchill was concerned chiefly with the protection and continued operation of RAF Fighter Command and its airfields. "Far more important to us than the protection of London from terror bombing," he said after the war, "was the functioning and articulation of these airfields and the squadrons working from them. . . . We never thought of the struggle in terms of the defence of London or any other place, but only who won in the air."

The Luftwaffe raids, accidental or not, and the British retaliatory raid quickly changed the thinking on both sides. Escalation of the air war had come. The British returned to Berlin on 28–29 August and again on 31 August–1 September.

On 3 September, Göring left the safety of Carinhall and traveled to The Hague to meet with his top air commanders. They were informed that henceforth the Luftwaffe was to concentrate on London instead of continuing the attacks on the RAF airfields, aircraft factories, and shipping. The strategy recommended itself for two reasons. First of all, German bombers over the British capital would bring up the rest of the RAF fighters, which would easily be destroyed by the Luftwaffe. Second—for some this was even more important—such raids would pay back the British for the raids on Berlin.

That night (3–4 September) and the next (4–5 September), Bomber Command again raided Berlin. On the night of 5–6 September, the Luftwaffe responded. Sixty-eight bombers dropped 60 tons of bombs on the London docks. The Blitz had begun.

Two days later Göring watched from the French coast as the first massive fleet of German aircraft headed for London. Over 1,200 planes attacked the city in the late afternoon and evening. The armada was almost evenly divided between fighters and bombers, many of which carried a new 3,600-pound bomb.

Churchill was correct that the Blitz was not just an act of inhumanity. It was also an enormous strategic blunder, a view borne out by German accounts as well. Fighter Command was reeling from its losses, and the Luftwaffe's diversion to bombing London was, said Churchill, "a breathing space of which we had the utmost need." The German attacks had damaged not only the airfields and planes; the communications and organizational structure had also suffered extensively. A few more such raids and Fighter Command might have collapsed completely.

"Göring should certainly have persevered," said Churchill. "By departing from the classical principles of war, as well as from the hitherto accepted dictates of humanity, he made a foolish mistake."

Göring would later blame everyone but himself for the disintegrating air war in the west. In the meantime, it was clearly necessary to shift completely to night bombing, and for fifty-seven consecutive nights as many as 200 German bombers a night raided London. The damage was enormous, but, as Churchill put it, "London was like some huge prehistoric animal, capable of enduring terrible injuries, mangled and bleeding from many wounds, and yet preserving its life and movement."

Still, Churchill wondered after the war what the reaction of Londoners would have been if they had been subjected to the heavy bombers

and high explosives that were available to the Allies after 1943—
weaponry "which might have pulverised all human organisation." No
one, he said, "has a right to say that London, which was certainly uncon-
quered, was not also unconquerable."

Fighter Command rose to the battle with stunning success. Evading
or ignoring the roving German fighters, the RAF attacked the bombers
directly. On a memorable day—15 September 1940, celebrated as Battle
of Britain Day—the Luftwaffe lost 56 planes, 34 of them bombers.
Other planes were so damaged that many had to be scrapped. Such
losses, some 25 percent of the entire bomber force, were insupportable.

The British capital held out, and finally, on the night of 3 November,
Londoners had their first night of unbroken sleep in two months. No
sirens sounded and no bombs fell. The Battle of Britain was over. The
Germans had lost 1,389 aircraft and the British 790. The defeat forced
Hitler to do more than just postpone Operation Sea Lion; henceforth, it
played no part in German strategic planning.

Besides, Hitler's attention was now fully focused on a plan that had
long been gestating: Operation Barbarossa, the invasion and subjugation
of the Soviet Union. Afterward, said Hitler, he would revisit the Western
Front.

The bombing continued, of course—England could not be allowed
to rebuild and expand its armed forces and plan a return to the Continent unchallenged—but it became more diffuse. The raids also served
to distract attention from the buildup in the east. However, there was yet
another change in Luftwaffe strategy by Göring. Henceforth the chief
targets were to be the industrial towns and cities of Great Britain.

The new policy was announced with an attack that decisively turned
the British public toward thoughts of total war and retribution. The
Coventry raid, on the night of 14–15 November 1940, provided the
British with a propaganda windfall.

Many so-called historical truths begin life in a propaganda ministry
or a press department, and in World War II not a few of these involved
the air war. Two well-known and much-discussed "facts" have thus
come to dominate any discussion of Coventry. The first is that the city
was leveled and thousands of people were killed, with additional thou-

sands injured. The second is that Churchill and the British high command knew well in advance that the city was targeted but declined to warn the populace so as not to reveal to the Germans that British intelligence had broken their top secret codes.

The first point is easily corrected, but even there the correctors are often at odds. All agree, however, that the death toll was wildly exaggerated for propaganda purposes. The most reasonable and probably most accurate figures are from the weekly résumé of military activity given to the War Cabinet and the prime minister the week of the raid which states that some 380 people were killed and 800 injured. In London that same week, deaths totaled 484 and injuries 1,080.

The physical destruction in Coventry was indeed horrific, but it was limited to the city center. The important Coventry factories, the ostensible reason for the raid, were located out of the main blast areas and were back in business in fairly short order, as were transportation and essential services.

The area of devastation—some one hundred acres—was, however, of historical and architectural importance and included the fourteenth-century St. Michael's Cathedral, only the 295-foot spire of which survived. Photographs of the burned-out church and the visit by King George VI were sent around the world. Coventry became a symbol of Nazi barbarity, alongside another notorious raid earlier that year, the bombing of Rotterdam on 14 May 1940.

While certainly horrible, the Rotterdam raid was nowhere near the tragedy trumpeted by Allied propaganda. Some 800 people died, not the 25,000 or 30,000 alleged to have been killed by the German bombers. But the Allies skillfully exploited the raid to firmly fix the Nazis in the world's mind as a nation of barbarians who wantonly bombed the peaceful and civilized Netherlands, the land of tulips and silver skates.

The rumors of a conspiracy to conceal the fact that the British had broken the German code are less easy to refute. Conspiracy theories take on a life of their own and are generally impervious to refutation, no matter how strong the evidence to the contrary. They will always have their adherents. However, this much seems clear: the British did know by 11 November 1940, via the Ultra decryptions, that an operation called

Moonlight Sonata, in which one of four possible targets was to be attacked, would take place at the next full moon—around the fifteenth of the month.

During the afternoon of 14 November, British radio operators began to pick up powerful concentrated radio beams from the Continent. These were the signals from the German system called *X-Gerät*, or X-Device, which was used by the Luftwaffe to triangulate a target. One beam, the direction beam, was the main flight path. As long as there was a buzzing sound in the pilot's earphones, his plane was on course. Dots and dashes signaled if he veered to port or starboard.

The pilot maintained his course while the aircraft's radio operator listened for a second signal, which crossed the aircraft's path and indicated that it was thirty miles from the target area. A timer was then set that ran until a third signal indicated that the bomber was nine miles from the target. The timer was reset, and the release of the bombs was automatic when it registered zero.

Churchill attended Neville Chamberlain's funeral at Westminster Abbey at noon on Friday, 14 November, then returned to the Annexe, his quarters in the Board of Trade Building, where he had moved on 16 September after a particularly heavy raid had damaged 10 Downing Street. He and his wife lived at the Annexe until the war ended.

Downstairs from their living quarters were the famous War Rooms, where most of the decisions pertaining to the war were made and seen through. This warren of rooms was deep belowground, and the prime minister was carried down the stairs and back up in a chair by three Royal Marines.

At the Annexe on this afternoon, he prepared to leave for a weekend at Ditchley Park, an estate northwest of Oxford, which had been placed at his disposal. Ditchley was much more secure than the official country residence, Chequers, which was just thirty miles from London and well known to the Germans.

Chequers was especially vulnerable during the full moon, when the long drive, which somewhat resembled an arrow pointed directly at the house, was easily seen from the air. And this weekend there was to be a full moon.

As he stepped into his car, Churchill was handed a message. His secretary recalled that the car had reached Kensington Gardens when the prime minister ordered the driver to turn around and return to the Annexe. According to the message, the German radio beams converged over London, and Churchill refused to travel to the country if there was to be a raid on the capital.

By 1500 hours it was clear that the beams converged instead over Coventry. The RAF was alerted, and antiaircraft batteries were readied and fighter planes put on alert. However, no warning was passed to the civil authorities. But there was a good reason for this.

The British had developed a system, called Cold Water, designed to jam or divert the *X-Gerät* transmissions and cause the German planes to drop their bombs well outside any populated areas.

The first German bombers cleared the Channel coast just after 1800 hours, and the RAF unit assigned the electronic countermeasures went into action. Unfortunately, Cold Water failed. Coventry was attacked an hour later. The 449 bombers dropped 500 tons of high explosives and 30 tons of incendiaries on the city center.

Since the final determination that Coventry was the target came through conventional radio signal intercepts, there was no risk in issuing a warning. Ultra would not have been compromised. But myths die hard, especially when conspiracy theories have arisen.

Adding to the controversy was the dismal fact that even though the RAF dispatched 200 fighter planes and there was an antiaircraft barrage, only one German bomber was shot down. Questions were asked in Parliament, and there were demands for retribution.

If there was a bright side to the Coventry raid, it was that the German air force did not follow up with another raid while the city was reeling from the disaster. In this the Germans were not unlike their British and American counterparts. The Germans had bombed London night after night, but the aim there was to bring up the defenders so that the Luftwaffe could destroy the fighter screen and then bomb with impunity and make way for an invasion.

Neither side seemed to grasp the importance of the double or even the triple blow from the air, which, theoretically at least, could prevent a city from recovering for many months, if ever. Neither side seemed to grasp how important this was until late in the game. Two important factors must be considered, however, before one blames either the Allies or the Germans for lack of imagination or planning. While the Allies had more resources available to them in terms of planes and weaponry, the lack of trained air crews often did not allow a follow-up raid. And both sides were subject to the whims of the weather. There were seldom consecutive clear nights over England or the Continent.

Churchill and his War Cabinet ordered Bomber Command to bomb the center of a German city in retaliation for the Coventry raid. Mannheim was the chosen target, but the raid had to await the next full moon. Finally, on the night of 16–17 December 1940, the largest raid of the war up to that time—and perhaps the first instance of pure morale bombing—was launched.

The "fire raisers," the precursors of the Pathfinders, whose job it was to set fires to mark the target, missed the center of the city, and therefore most of the damage was in residential areas. Thus from a military point of view the raid was a failure. But it marked a turning point in the thinking of many in the British high command. Morale bombing was elevated to strategy. If pursued relentlessly, senior officers argued, it could bring Germany to its knees without a single Allied soldier ever setting foot on the Continent.

Later, in defense of the British area bombing of cities, as opposed to the American bombing of precise targets, one document stated, "While the success of [the Americans'] attacks against the aircraft and ball-bearing industries must have undermined the confidence of the German High Command, the civilian population was little affected. Only the RAF bomber command component of the offensive could have been expected to evoke any considerable reaction from the civilian population."

For this to happen, area bombing had to be employed, although the drafters of the report continued to maintain that "the object of the RAF attacks was the destruction of industrial areas. For this purpose the incendiary bombs pay far higher dividend."

Further, they said, "The risk of death from incendiary attacks is comparatively small, save in exceptional cases, such as Hamburg, when enormous conflagrations are set up. In the majority of our attacks the concentrations achieved were not such as to produce those conditions."

The incendiary bomb was a small, rather insignificant-looking device—most of those dropped on Dresden weighed just four pounds—that fire wardens advised they could be extinguished with nothing more than a bucket of sand if an individual reacted quickly. And there were incidences where they were picked up and tossed out a window before they ignited. Such actions were rare in actuality, since incendiaries were dropped by the hundreds of thousands.

In the early bombs, phosphorus was used, but as the war progressed other materials were soon found to be more effective and lethal. Thermite, a mixture of aluminum powder and iron oxide, set alight with a magnesium fuse, could generate temperatures well over twelve hundred degrees Fahrenheit. Such high temperatures coupled with the vast quantities of the weapons dropped on an urban area ensured that firefighters and rescue workers would be overwhelmed.

After Coventry and until the invasion of the Soviet Union, the Luftwaffe repeatedly bombed Manchester, Plymouth, Southampton, and Liverpool-Birkenhead. And London was revisited several times as well. The raid on 29 December 1940 was particularly damaging. Churchill called it "an incendiary classic."

The Luftwaffe first dropped high explosives to sever the water mains, followed by incendiaries, which set more than fifteen hundred fires. This was the raid that destroyed eight Wren churches and the Guildhall and almost incinerated St. Paul's Cathedral. It was also a powerful demonstration of the proper bombing of highly flammable old cities, a lesson duly noted by Arthur Harris and other advocates of area bombing.

As the winter wore on, the Luftwaffe raids decreased in size and ferocity. There were fewer sorties and a dramatic decrease in the bomb tonnage. However, with the coming of better weather in March and April 1941, there was an upsurge. On 16–17 April and 19–20 April, London was hit by the heaviest raids in the long Luftwaffe campaign against the city, which doubtless gave the advocates of morale bombing renewed vigor.

The majority opinion that Bomber Command's resources would be better spent bombing the German synthetic oil plants still held, but the seeds for massive area bombing had been planted. In any event, the oil campaign was thwarted in early 1941. Clear weather and a full moon were the necessary elements for the night raids on these difficult-to-find targets, and the weather was particularly foul in February and March 1941. Fog, wind, rain, and snow, not enemy action, caused the loss of seventy RAF planes in one thirty-day period.

By early March, however, the target priorities had been changed. The German navy threatened to succeed where the Luftwaffe had failed. Between June 1940 and March 1941, U-boats, battle cruisers, and pocket battleships, aided by Focke-Wulf Condor long-range maritime bombers, sank almost 900 merchant ships carrying supplies for the relief of England. From then until the middle of the summer, Bomber Command was ordered to concentrate on the U-boat bases and shipyards, the factories that made submarine components, and the Condor airfields.

There was much carping within Bomber Command about this change of targets, but Sir Charles Portal, chief of the air staff, saw it as an opportunity. He was fully aware that Bomber Command's claims of success in bombing the oil targets were greatly exaggerated. He was only too happy to divert the planes to these easier-to-find and thus more vulnerable targets. He made no effort to have the order reversed.

The 9 March 1941 directive ordering Bomber Command to concentrate on the U-boat menace had a qualifier: "Priority of selection should be given to those [targets] in Germany which lie in congested areas where the greatest moral [sic] effect is likely to result." On 18 March, Arthur Harris, then deputy chief of the air staff, referring to Mannheim and Stuttgart, said, "Both are suitable as area objectives and their attack should have high morale value."

Any talk about the relative merits or morality of area bombing versus precision bombing was just that in the early years of Bomber Command—talk. At most there were only nine nights a month—the time of the full moon—when there was any chance of what was called accurate bombing. And even then the weather had to cooperate. Rivers, coastlines, and other prominent geographical features were useful reference points—when they could be seen. The port cities of Germany, the Netherlands, and France and the industrial cities on the Rhine, the Weser, and the Elbe were therefore bombed consistently.

A method resembling the German system of triangulation of radio beams was being worked out by British scientists but would not become available to Bomber Command until 1942. The major method of navigation remained dead reckoning, that combination of compass course, air speed, and wind velocity and drift which, theoretically, gave the navigator his position. The system was so dependent upon factors that were little more than guesswork, however, that a pilot was fortunate if he was over the right city; it was folly to hope to hit a small target within that city. Until the introduction of advanced navigational aids in 1943, nighttime precision bombing was only a strategic concept. Therefore, " 'area bombing' against German cities with a view to breaking German civilian morale was the most useful means of employing the bomber force."

A fairly simple pattern thus developed. A part of the bomber force was directed at a major industrial or port facility in the target city. Other planes were directed to bomb the city itself, in order to cause maximum disruption among the civilian population. It was area bombing, not precision bombing, although the target was "nominally industrial."

The optimistic predictions of victory through aerial bombardment of Germany and the occupied countries came back to haunt Bomber Command in August 1941 when D. M. Butt, of the War Cabinet secretariat, issued his report on bombing accuracy. Just one-third of the pilots who had said they had successfully attacked the assigned target had come within five miles of it, said Butt. Two-thirds were within five miles of targets on the more visible and closer French coast, but in the industrial and smoggy Ruhr the figure fell to one-tenth. On the nights of a bomber's moon, the optimum condition, only two-fifths of the bombers dropped their loads within five miles of the target, and on moonless nights the figure fell to one-fifteenth.

When two-thirds of the bomber force dropped their bombs five miles or more from the designated targets, the obvious question was how many bombs were actually hitting a worthwhile target. And the person who was asking and answering this question was Winston Churchill himself. Did not this report give the lie to his 1940 prediction that British bombers would bring Germany to its knees?

Churchill's disillusionment was not long in manifesting itself. In response to Portal's plan to "Coventryize" forty-five German cities, the prime minister said, "It is very debatable whether bombing by itself will be a decisive factor in the present war." He cited the British people, who, he said, had been "stimulated and strengthened" by the German raids. "The most we can say," Churchill acerbically remarked, "is that [bombing] will be a heavy and I trust seriously increasing annoyance."

Portal did not let this go unanswered, and as RAF historian Denis Richards said, he "spiked Churchill's guns." Who was to carry the war to Germany if not Bomber Command? Portal forthrightly asked the prime minister. Portal admitted that ground forces would eventually have to be used, but it would be 1943 before any such offensive was possible on the Continent. In the meantime, he said, "The only plan is to persevere." In other words, Bomber Command must continue the attacks on German manufacturing and morale. Otherwise there would be no Allied offensive operation in western Europe until an invasion could be launched across the Channel. Churchill acquiesced.

As for the success of the RAF campaign against the submarine pens, those in Holland were active until February 1945. The ones in France also went relatively unscathed until late in the war. As Admiral Karl Dönitz said, "No dog nor cat is left in these towns. Nothing but the submarine shelters remain."

Portal's contretemps with Churchill resulted in a reprieve for Bomber Command and its head, Air Marshal Sir Richard Peirse, who had succeeded to the post when Portal had been promoted to chief of the air staff. Bomber Command was allowed to resume its attacks on Germany and the occupied countries. The reprieve was a brief one and ended the night of 7–8 November 1941, when 37 planes, out of 392 dispatched, were lost—9.4 percent, which was double the loss rate of any previous night operation.

The raids included Berlin, Cologne, Mannheim, and a few minor targets, but it was the operation against Berlin that caused a storm of criticism. Out of 169 aircraft sent to the German capital, only 148 returned—a staggering loss of 12.4 percent. There were no losses over Cologne, but there was also little damage—even less damage than in Berlin, where it was negligible. Mannheim reported no damage at all. Bomber Command would not return to Berlin in force until January 1943.

The day after the debacle at Berlin, Sir Richard Peirse was driven down to Chequers to meet with an angry prime minister. A week later, Churchill ordered a reduction in Bomber Command operations until new and more effective policies could be developed.

The first order of business was the removal of Peirse himself, which was accomplished on 8 January 1942. There was also to be a new bombing policy—the direct response to the Butt Report, which had been so critical of the so-called precision bombing.

"It has been decided," wrote Air Vice Marshal Norman Bottomley, "that the primary objective of your operations should now be focussed on the morale of the enemy civil population and in particular of the industrial workers." The date of this area bombing, or morale bombing, directive was prophetic: 14 February.

Finally, on 22 February 1942, the third and arguably the most important component was put in place. Air Chief Marshal Sir Arthur Harris assumed his new post: commander in chief, Bomber Command.

Officially, Harris did not have a hand in drafting the morale-bombing directive. He was en route home from Washington when the directive was issued. But he wholeheartedly endorsed it and proceeded at once to implement it, although he chose his words carefully when describing what Bomber Command policy actually was. "Area bombing" became the preferred formulation.

During the three months while Bomber Command was effectively "standing down" on the Continent, the British were being battered elsewhere. General Erwin Rommel and his Afrika Korps successfully counterattacked in North Africa, Singapore was lost, and HMS *Prince of Wales* and HMS *Repulse* were sunk by the Japanese. However, Hitler had already committed the great follies that would bring him and the Third Reich to total destruction. He had drawn both Russia and America into the war on the side of England.

On the night of 28–29 March 1942, Arthur Harris put the new policy into effect and Bomber Command had its first great success of the war. More than 200 bombers attacked Lübeck. Although the city was famous worldwide for its picturesque architecture and as the setting for Thomas Mann's novel *Buddenbrooks,* it was, and is, the most important German port on the Baltic. But Harris was not primarily interested in destroying the docks and piers.

The medieval Altstadt was the target. "Lübeck," said Harris, "was more like a fire-lighter than a human habitation," and with this raid he spectacularly demonstrated his theory of "concentrated incendiarism." As historian Max Hastings wrote, "Lübeck, then, did not attract the attention of the bombers because it was important, but became important because it could be bombed."

The German high command was stunned by the ferocity of the attack. More than a quarter of the medieval heart of the city went up in flames. And Goebbels was quick to bemoan the loss of the great artistic monuments to the "British craze for destruction."

• • •

While the debate over morale bombing versus precision bombing continued among the Allied commanders, there was no debate among the enemy about a policy that was being implemented with increasing ferocity. At five o'clock in the afternoon before the Lübeck raid, Special Train 767 left the Paris suburb of Drancy, where the Germans, aided by French collaborators, had begun to intern Jews in 1941. Aboard were 1,113 foreign-born Jews, mostly Poles. The train arrived at the concentration-camp complex near the Polish town of Oswiecim in Galicia three days later, after a stopover at the concentration camp at Compiègne.

This camp complex, better known by its German name, Auschwitz, would in time become the very symbol of Nazi depravity. Construction at Auschwitz was authorized by Heinrich Himmler in April 1940, and the first, experimental gassings took place in September 1941.

By early 1942, more than 700,000 Jews had already been murdered as the Nazis moved eastward. Word of these atrocities, particularly in Poland and the Soviet Union, had long since reached the West, but there was no acknowledgment by either London or Washington of the crimes being committed.

Now, as the gas chambers at Auschwitz became fully operational, the Nazis were prepared for murder on a truly industrial scale. The men, women, and children on this first French deportation train were among the early victims.

. . .

For the citizens of the cities of both sides, the air war gained in intensity in 1942. Hitler ordered "terror attacks of a retaliatory nature" against Britain for the Lübeck raid. Beginning on the night of 23 April, the Luftwaffe responded with a series of raids on the British equivalents of Lübeck: Bath, Exeter, Norwich, Canterbury, and York. These were the notorious "Baedeker raids." The term was coined by Baron Braun von Stumm in the press department of the German Foreign Ministry. For compiling a list of Britain's historic cities, what better source was there than the authoritative and complete Baedeker guide to Great Britain?

Goebbels was quick to see that the term was causing revulsion in the world. "I censured this in the sharpest terms and took measures for preventing the repetition of such folly," he recorded in his diary. Only the unfortunate choice of words used to denote the operation upset him. He heartily approved of the raids themselves. "There is talk about scenes like those in Coventry," he said. "That's the sort of music we like to hear."

The RAF, meanwhile, did not hold back from destroying another historic German city, although Rostock was also an important Baltic port and home to the Heinkel aircraft factory. On four consecutive nights in late April, a total of 520 bombers attacked Rostock, destroying 60 percent of the city center. A new term began to appear in the German reports of the Rostock raids—*Terrorangriff* ("terror raid")—and clearly terror bombing was a tool to be used as any other weapon would be to carry the fight to the enemy.

New names began to be added to the growing list of wrecked cities in England and Germany, bombed-out symbols of the new warfare conducted by both the Luftwaffe and the RAF. Rotterdam, Coventry, and the Baedeker raids are the most often cited atrocities against noncombat-

ants by the Luftwaffe, but another, much more horrifying example is little known or remarked on. On 6 April 1941 the German air force killed
some 17,000 civilians in a raid on the Yugoslav capital of Belgrade.

As for the British, there seemed no strategic justification for the
bombing of Lübeck—the target was the center of the medieval and
highly incendiary Altstadt, after all—but it did serve to demonstrate the
effectiveness of the fire-raising strategy. Indeed, for the rest of the war,
Lübeck suffered no further concentrated attacks by the RAF. The International Red Cross persuaded Britain to spare the city so the port could
be used for the shipment of Red Cross supplies.

The fire raids on the two old Hanseatic League cities of Rostock and
Lübeck were more than just revenge for the depredations of the Luftwaffe, of course. Harris needed to demonstrate to Churchill and the air
command that his bombers could do what he said they could do: take the
war to the enemy and cause massive destruction, with minimum, or at
least acceptable, losses.

After the Lübeck raid there was a considerable bump in the road.
Harris had come in for severe criticism for a low-level, daylight raid on
Augsburg on 17 April, which, while partially successful in bombing, resulted in a loss of seven out of twelve Lancasters. Rostock partially re-
deemed the error. But Harris was more than thin-skinned; he often
seemed to have no skin at all. He brooked no criticism, not even from
Churchill. His correspondence with the prime minister is peppered with
defensive, self-serving comments.

In a memorandum of 2 May 1942, he dismissed the suggestion of his
chief critic, the minister of economic warfare, that the target should
have been Stuttgart and not Augsburg as "Plain Suicide" and "just silly."
As for the implied criticism that Bomber Command did not cooperate
with other departments, he said he would do so if possible. However, he
added, "I could not in any circumstances agree to discuss projected attacks outside my Headquarters with other Departments. I do not even
tell my crews, to whom security is a matter of life and death, where they
are going until the last moment before briefing."

For the next full moon, Harris put into effect a plan that was to
profoundly alter the future of aerial bombardment. On the night of

30–31 May 1942, he dispatched 1,047 Wellingtons, Stirlings, Halifaxes, Whitleys, Manchesters, and Hampdens—every plane that he could beg, borrow, or steal—on the first thousand-bomber raid. The target was the Rhineland city of Cologne.

Not all the planes reached the target; only 868 did. But two-thirds of the 1,455 tons of bombs dropped were incendiaries, and their effect was devastating. Thousands of buildings were destroyed, 45,000 people were bombed out of their homes, and at least a third of the population fled the city.

Albert Speer was visiting Göring at Schloss Veldenstein on the day after the raid and listened while the Reichsmarschall talked by telephone with Joseph Grohé, gauleiter of Cologne. Göring adamantly refused to believe that so many planes could be put in the air and so many tons of bombs dropped in one raid. He ordered the gauleiter to revise his reports to the Führer to reflect lower figures.

A few days later at the Wolfsschanze (Wolf's Lair), Hitler's headquarters near Rastenburg, in East Prussia, Speer discussed the incident with the Führer. Hitler had already discounted Göring's estimates and chose to rely instead on his own reports, which were based largely on accounts in the foreign press, no doubt provided by Goebbels. Göring suffered no diminution in status, however, much to the chagrin of Speer and the disgust of Goebbels, who despised him. Göring, he said, "has as much to do with the [Nazi] Party as a cow with radiology."

The propaganda minister stayed remarkably well informed about what was happening in the field and in the world's capitals. His interpretations of the intelligence that he received and conclusions that he reached were quite something else. His diaries are filled with keen insights that are immediately rendered worthless when they are refracted through his ideological lens.

For example, he and Churchill were as one in their fear and certainty of Stalin's designs on eastern Europe. The Nazis, after all, had used the issue of Communist expansion and domination in their rise to power. Goebbels, however, saw Communism purely as part of a Bolshevik-Jewish conspiracy to take over the world.

Goebbels was sometimes fairly clear-eyed about the prospects for the war. As early as 8 May 1943, he confided in his diary, "The end is in sight in Africa. . . . In the end the Axis is to be thrown out of Africa entirely. There is tremendous confidence of victory in London, and rightly so. I see hardly any chance for us." The following day he described the debacle in North Africa as a "sort of second Stalingrad."

But Goebbels was also one of the first practitioners, some would say the inventor, of what in years to come would be called "spin." His justification of the African adventure is a masterpiece of the genre. While the struggle went on in the deserts of North Africa, he said, there could be no invasion of Europe proper. Therefore the defenses in western Europe, the so-called Atlantic Wall, could be constructed relatively unimpeded.

Goebbels's ability to rally the German people through propaganda was tested further in the disastrous month of July 1943. The deposition and arrest of Mussolini and the ascension of Marshal Pietro Badoglio—precursors to the end of Fascism in Italy and that country's surrender—was called "the greatest example of perfidy in modern history" by the propaganda minister. His remarks rather oddly echoed Franklin Roosevelt's more famous indictment of Italy in 1940 when Mussolini declared war on France: "On this tenth day of June 1940, the hand that held the dagger has struck it into the back of its neighbor."

Goebbels's ruminations on Italian treachery were interrupted by news that was beginning to come in concerning a disturbing new Allied air offensive. The RAF and the U.S. Eighth Air Force had launched the Battle of Hamburg, a series of raids on Germany's major seaport and one of the Reich's most important industrial centers. Bomber Command led off on the night of 24–25 July 1943. A force of 728 aircraft out of 791 dispatched dropped 2,284 tons of bombs in fifty minutes. The bombs fell over a wide area, some six miles long, but caused considerable damage and 1,500 deaths.

The Americans followed up in daylight raids on Sunday, 25 July, and Monday, 26 July. Dense smoke from the fires caused by the massive British bombardment, combined with cloud cover, made visual targeting nearly impossible. Indeed, only 100 of the 182 U.S. B-17s dropped their bombs, just 195 tons, on the city. The next day the Americans fared even worse. Only 54 bombers out of 121 dispatched were effective, dropping 126 tons of bombs. As the historians Middlebrook and Everitt said in their *Bomber Command War Diaries,* "The Americans quickly withdrew from the Battle of Hamburg and were not keen to follow immediately on the heels of R.A.F. raids, in future, because of the smoke problem."

On the night of 27–28 July 1943, however, the British returned. Seven hundred and twenty-nine bombers dropped 2,326 tons of bombs on the city center in a relatively concentrated pattern. The city was still reeling from three raids in seventy-two hours, and its rescue and firefighting services were overwhelmed. Temperature and humidity were also in perfect alignment to create a cataclysm.

As the fires that raged throughout the city spread and joined together, air from outside the fire zones was sucked in, creating hurricane-force winds, which further fed the flames. The air war's first recorded firestorm was born. Contrary to popular belief, the Hamburg firestorm was not the result of advance planning. It was the result of powerful and unexpected forces, which in the future seldom came together in such a way that it was replicated, although it became a much desired goal of Bomber Command.

Indeed, there were only a handful of true firestorms created during the long Allied bombardment of Germany. But the lessons learned from these incendiary attacks on Germany would prove valuable later in the American bombing campaign against Japan. In the most devastating air raid of the war using conventional weapons, the raid on Tokyo on 9 March 1945, between 90,000 and 100,000 people were killed and half the city was destroyed.

But that lay far into the future. For now, Germany was the primary target, and the night after the firestorm, Bomber Command raided Hamburg again. Another 729 aircraft dropped an additional 2,326 tons of bombs on the crippled city. A severe thunderstorm prevented a third raid, comprising 740 bombers, from reaching Hamburg on the night of 2–3 August. No matter. Much of the city lay in ruins, and two-thirds of the population, some 1.2 million people, had fled to other cities, towns, or the countryside.

Most of Germany's cities now began to witness firsthand the destructive might of Allied airpower. The British by night and the Americans by day. No city was safe from the destruction and death raining from the skies.

Not all successful raids involved massive fleets of bombers. Nor were they all recognized as a great success. On the night of 18–19 November 1943, ten Mosquitoes attacked Essen in a raid characterized as a "minor operation" by Middlebrook and Everitt. *The Goebbels Diaries,* however, reports a different result. The propaganda minister lamented that the Krupp steel works was 100 percent closed down by the Mosquito raid.

While it may not have been the most strategically important of the German cities—in terms of weapons plants, military bases, or oil refineries—the destruction of Berlin carried incalculable psychological weight. Therefore, a devastating series of sixteen raids by Bomber Command began on the night of 18–19 November 1943 and continued for two and a half months. The second raid, on 22–23 November, caused more damage than any other raid in Bomber Command's long campaign against the German capital. Cloud cover kept the Luftwaffe on the ground, setting off a renewed round of criticism of Göring and his pilots.

The poor visibility also meant that the raid was pure blind bombing. But the bombs found the target, falling in a swath some twelve miles wide across the city. Among the destroyed buildings was the Kaiser Wilhelm Church, the blackened ruins of which would become a stark reminder in postwar Berlin of the carnage of war. The ruins were incorporated into a new war memorial church in 1959.

Goebbels admitted, but only in the private confines of his diary, the destructive effect of the Allied bombing. Time and again he lamented the inability of the Luftwaffe to stop the Allied planes, which were destroying one city after another. And while the bombing was nowhere near as precise as advertised by the Allies, it did succeed in bringing the war home to the enemy and causing great disruption.

Of the more than a million residents who fled Hamburg, most filtered back into the city during the next months and tried to resume their lives. The Reich, however, had to divert staggering amounts of supplies, thousands of men, and great effort to protect, house, and feed the beleaguered civilian populace. The effort was a tremendous drain on the German war effort. In Berlin alone, after the great raid of 22–23 November, two and a half divisions, 50,000 Wehrmacht troops, were called in to clear the streets and restore services.

In spite of the destruction and the horror of the raids, Goebbels averred that Germany and the Germans remained unbowed. A diary entry of 25 November 1943 is a fair example of the Nazi mind-set. "Of what avail are all sorrow and pain? They won't change conditions. This war must be seen through. It is better that our workers crawl into cellars than that they be sent to Siberia as slave labor. Every decent German realizes this."

And, in spite of the carnage from the skies, Germany did manage to rally, through the use of a seemingly inexhaustible source of labor. Slaves from the east, prisoners of war, political prisoners, and, of course, hundreds of thousands of Jews from the concentration camps worked around the clock in the factories, mines, and refineries, and in rebuilding the wrecked highways, railroads, and buildings. Historian Daniel Goldhagen has estimated that there were at least 10,000 concentration camps and ghettos in Germany and the occupied territories. In Berlin alone there were no fewer than 645 forced-labor camps.

With such a huge labor force available, it is little wonder that in Hamburg, five months after the raids, industry had recovered 80 percent of its preraid capacity. But no nation could constantly rebuild itself from within, produce arms and armaments for a vast army, and fight a two-front war. The bombing campaign would ensure the ultimate collapse of the Third Reich.

Goebbels and others in the Nazi hierarchy, in spite of some pessimism and barely concealed anger at Göring and his inability to fight back against the British and American bombers, still looked for a miracle in the form of new weaponry, which would not only stem the tide but bring them victory.

Speer was not so sanguine. He doubted that either new weapons or reprisals against Britain would provide the key to victory. In any event, no such weapon could possibly be deployed until March 1944, at the earliest. Thus the Germans could only watch helplessly as their leaders led them further down the road to ruin and the deaths of hundreds of thousands of civilians in the air war, which would increase in ferocity, not lessen, as the Allies closed in on the Third Reich.

CHAPTER FIVE

VERGELTUNGSWAFFEN

The V-Weapons

Less than a week had passed since the successful landings in Normandy when there came a sobering reminder that the final collapse of the Third Reich might not be as close as it had seemed. But the feared Nazi counterattack came not against the Allied forces moving inland from the beaches of France; it was directed against the civilian population in England.

On the night of 12–13 June 1944, thousands of people from the Channel coast to London were roused from sleep by a high-pitched, pulsating sound from the sky—a strange noise that would become all too familiar in the months ahead. A new weapon, a pilotless "flying bomb," had made its debut.

The official German designation was FZG-76. The Allied military called it the V-1. Civilians, however, ignored both designations. To them the new terror weapon was simply the "buzz bomb" or "doodlebug"—a twenty-five-foot-long unmanned aircraft with a wingspan of seventeen and a half feet that carried an 1,870-pound explosive warhead and was powered by a pulse-jet engine that gave it a distinctive sound.

The V-1 was an ingenious device, not only cheap to build—it was made of low-carbon steel and wood—but also easily transported and launched, and its preset course ensured that the weapon was secure against electronic countermeasures such as jamming or interference.

A small propeller in the missile's nose was set to rotate a certain number of times, each revolution representing a fraction of the distance from the launch site to the target. When the proper number of revolutions was reached a signal cut off the pulse-jet engine and the flying bomb dropped like a stone.

It was calculated that some 80 percent of the V-1s would land within a target circle eight miles in diameter, a rather rough target area at best. But its slow speed (a maximum velocity of 350 miles per hour) and low cruising altitude (3,500 to 4,000 feet) made the V-1 vulnerable to both fighter planes and antiaircraft fire. Thus the weapon never approached the 80 percent accuracy figure.

Much of the V-1's effectiveness, however, was psychological. It was a fiendish device that announced its own coming. The throbbing engine sound was immediately identifiable, and as long as one could hear the V-1 engine, one was safe. But when the engine cut out, there was a brief silence followed by a piercing whine as the projectile, with nearly a ton of high explosives, hurtled to earth. To a person on the ground the weapon always seemed to be coming from directly overhead.

On 13 June, at the meeting of the War Cabinet, Churchill was advised of the "attack by pilotless aircraft." The number of the flying bombs was given as twenty-seven. There had actually been only eleven, and the damage was slight. It was therefore decided that there would be no official acknowledgment of this new threat.

On 15 June the danger became much clearer. At least 50 people died that night and 400 were injured. By the end of the week, the death toll had risen to 526 and 5,000 people had been injured, 2,200 seriously. It was obvious to the British public that something new had been introduced, and equally obvious that the government must acknowledge the threat.

Churchill rose to the occasion. In announcing the new German aerial offensive, he praised the people at home and exhorted them to be brave in the face of the attacks. Like the brilliant commander he was, he managed to convince the British public that they should accept this latest outrage with the same stoic courage they had displayed during the Battle of Britain, the Blitz, and the Baedeker raids.

In addition, he said, the people at home should welcome the opportunity to share in the battle with their troops on the Continent and in
Asia. He also pointed out that the German attacks on the British homeland drew resources from the battlefield, which saved Allied lives and
would hasten the end of the war.

In Berlin, Joseph Goebbels lost no time in trumpeting the power and
destructiveness of the new weapon. He broadcast a recording of the
launch of a V-1 from the Channel coast with an eyewitness account.
There followed lurid descriptions of the carnage in London and the
south of England. "England is trembling—London is ablaze," intoned
the announcer.

But while the British were struggling with how to deal with the buzz
bombs and their destructiveness, at Hitler's headquarters the reaction
was quite different. The Führer's military commanders predicted no
miracles from its deployment and did not hesitate to say so, even to the
Führer. Indeed, Albert Speer reported that Hitler was so disappointed at
the initial performance of the V-1 that he was on the point of canceling
the program altogether.

Then, almost as if it were a theatrical production, the reviews from
London came in. The press chief handed Hitler the vivid accounts from
the British newspapers about the flying bombs and their effect on the
capital. His mood changed at once. He ordered the escalation of the V-1
campaign. The wily Goebbels had once again trumped his opposition.

During the week ending 29 June, 650 tons of high explosives were
dropped on London, not much less than the 770 tons that fell on the city
during the worst fortnight of the Blitz in 1940. Total casualties to date
from the flying bombs were 17,328. More disturbing was the report that
although the number of dead was about 2,000, the number of killed and
seriously injured was 7,403—compared with 16,456 for the whole
month of September 1940.

The figures were not released, however, and the government's silence, which was designed to deny the Germans valuable information on
the efficacy of their weapons, only added to the public's fear. After all,
the physical damage could not be concealed. Some 500 houses were
being destroyed each day and 21,000 damaged. Thousands of civilians

were made homeless. But, again, these figures, along with the number of casualties, were kept secret.

While no one believed that the flying bomb was the rumored secret weapon that would turn the tide for Hitler—the kill rate for the V-1 was a low one fatality per bomb, with three more persons injured—both politicians and military strategists had to take any new weapons as a serious threat. It was not known how much more intense the attacks might become or what deadlier weapons might be in the offing. Nothing, it seemed, was too outlandish to contemplate. There was even talk of a mysterious "death ray."

The War Cabinet was also faced with the question of whether to provide misinformation to Germany about where the flying bombs were actually falling. The designated ground zero was clearly Charing Cross, and it was argued that if the enemy could be convinced that they were overshooting the mark, they might adjust their aiming so that many of the bombs would fall in the open country. Opponents of misinformation argued that it could backfire. The Germans might very quickly ascertain that they were being fed false data and correct their aim so that even more bombs might fall on central London. More to the point, no one, civilian or military, wanted to take responsibility for redirecting the German fire from one area of England to another.

Therefore Churchill and the War Cabinet stayed with the devil they knew, and there was no doubt by now that it was, indeed, Satan they were dealing with. By 1 August, 3,407 of the flying bombs had appeared over England, and 1,594 had landed on London—killing 4,175 people and injuring 12,284. By the end of September, a total of 5,890 of the weapons had eluded flak and Fighter Command to kill 5,835 people and injure 16,762 others, almost all of them in London or its suburbs.

After the war, it would be revealed that there had been at least one source feeding misinformation to Berlin about the accuracy of the V-1 weapons. Eddie Chapman, a British safecracker, went to work for the Germans when they captured the Isle of Jersey, where he was imprisoned. In June 1944, he parachuted into England to report to his supposed new masters on the flying bombs. Chapman, whose code name was Zig-Zag, was loyal to his country, however. He immediately volunteered his services to British intelligence and became a double agent. His false reports resulted in many of the buzz bombs landing harmlessly in the countryside.

• • •

The V-1 was by no means a surprise to Churchill and the War Cabinet. British intelligence had first become aware of the development of the vengeance weapons in January 1943. During an interrogation, a German Luftwaffe captain shot down in Africa revealed that he had once landed at a place called Peenemünde. The report was forwarded to England and the intelligence service at once turned its attention to the site, which lay at the tip of an isolated peninsula on the island of Usedom, just off the Baltic coast.

In the spring of 1943, the RAF began a two-month series of reconnaissance flights over Peenemünde. The aerial photographs revealed what was clearly a manufacturing and test facility, and the product was all too visible as well—rockets and a rather strange-looking smaller craft with short wings. One of the test vehicles had crashed on the Danish island of Bornholm, and a sketch, which resembled those spotted in the reconnaissance photos of Peenemünde, was smuggled out to British intelligence.

The RAF was ordered to destroy the base, but Bomber Command had to await a full moon. Finally, on the bright night of 17–18 August 1943, Peenemünde was attacked by nearly 600 planes from Bomber Command. The crews were not told what the target was, only that it was important. Nearly 1,800 tons of bombs were dropped, 85 percent of them high explosives.

Also in the summer of 1943 Allied reconnaissance flights revealed suspicious construction sites in the Pas-de-Calais and the Cherbourg Peninsula. A French agent, Michel Hollard, enlisted a workman at the installation at Bois Carré who was able to obtain drawings of one of the buildings. Intelligence experts realized these strange ski-shaped structures must be the launch platforms for the flying bombs.

In December 1943 aerial bombardment of the French sites began, and by the time of Overlord, 103 of the 140 identified sites had been destroyed. While this campaign, labeled Crossbow, delayed the launching of the V-1s, it by no means eliminated them as a threat. The Germans simply changed their tactics. Instead of building large, easily spotted concrete ramps for the launching of the missile, they made the launch sites smaller and thus more easily camouflaged.

Few weapons of war have had such a powerful effect, out of all proportion to their real toll in terms of physical destruction, deaths, and injuries. The Germans miscalculated, however. The vengeance weapons' greatest effect was to raise the stakes in the retaliatory war against civilians. Residents of the cities of the Reich would soon be targeted as never before. But first it was felt that a massive aerial campaign—Crossbow redux, as it were—had to be launched to neutralize the V-1 launch sites.

Just four days after the first V-1 landed in London, Churchill dispatched 405 aircraft of Bomber Command to attack the flying-bomb sites in the Pas-de-Calais. This raid, on 16–17 June 1944, was the beginning of a massive three-month bombing campaign, which Churchill urged on Bomber Command and the U.S. Army Air Forces.

Over the objections of those military advisers who saw the V-1 as a deadly nuisance but not one that could affect the outcome of the war, Churchill appealed to Supreme Commander Dwight Eisenhower to give top priority to destroying the launch sites, which—on paper, at least— seemed to be a simple matter. The range of the flying bomb was only 130 miles, which put the launch sites in easy target range of planes based in England.

Carl Spaatz, especially, objected to the bombing campaign against the V-weapon sites. He said that the long summer days—over sixteen hours of daylight in midsummer—should be used to maximize the American daylight bombing of strategic targets, such as the synthetic oil plants.

Spaatz argued that while the H2X radar then in use enabled bomber crews to locate cities, it was of little use in finding these all-important targets, which had been built away from the cities. These plants had to be located and bombed visually.

Spaatz was overruled, but it became clear after the war that his so-called oil plan was more strategically sound than any other. Chief among the critics of the Allies' not pursuing the systematic destruction of the Nazi's oil supply was none other than Albert Speer, the Nazi armaments czar.

According to Speer, a great turning point in the war occurred on 12 May 1944. "On that day," wrote Speer, "the technological war was decided." Even as the Allied air forces were preparing to support the invasion of the Continent, the Eighth Air Force, in a massive raid, attacked fuel plants in eastern and central Germany. Daily production was immediately reduced by 20 percent. Two weeks later other devastating American raids, which included attacks on the oil fields at Ploesti, Romania, resulted in a loss for the month of 50 percent of production capacity. And in the summer of 1944, when both the Eighth Air Force and Bomber Command were allowed to return to their preinvasion strategics, a series of crippling blows was launched against the German oil fields, refineries, and storage facilities.

However, in his diaries Speer repeatedly returned to what he called the Allies' "lack of consistency." Why, he wondered, did the RAF and the USAAF switch target priorities instead of following up immediately on these successful raids?

Instead, in a reprise of the Luftwaffe's actions during the summer of 1940, the Allied command did not immediately revisit the sites of raids that had seriously damaged critical industries. Speer maintained that they could have put the sites permanently out of commission by a second or perhaps a third raid. If they had done so, he said, the Allies could have completely halted German war production. Instead, both the RAF and the USAAF often diverted their forces to less worthwhile targets.

In late July 1944, for example, according to Speer, a series of massive raids knocked out 98 percent of the aircraft fuel plants. But almost immediately the bombers were diverted to Crossbow targets, tactical support of troops, and the area bombing of cities. Speer was quick to take advantage of the lull. By November 1944 production had risen to 28 percent of the July levels.

The repair and rebuilding of the production facilities, bridges, rail lines, and highways was not the miracle of Nazi organization and the Aryan work ethic trumpeted by Goebbels and the other Nazis, including the armaments minister himself. There was a darker explanation. The German war machine had a workforce that made no demands as to food, housing, or wages. Millions of slave laborers worked around the clock to meet the goals set by Speer.

. . .

The V-1, as British intelligence had warned, was the forerunner of a much more dangerous weapon. Two months after the first buzz bombs hit London, word came from the Continent that the Germans had launched another, very different form of missile. Two of these had been fired against Paris on 6 September, and although both had exploded in midflight the new threat was clear.

At the noon meeting of the War Cabinet on 9 September, it was announced that two of the new weapons, "of the type expected," had landed the evening before, one in Chiswick, at 1843 hours, and one near Epping just a few seconds later.

Some knowledge of the V-1 had been gleaned from the sketches of the downed test vehicle made by the Danish underground, but British intelligence knew a great deal more about this new weapon, which was dubbed the V-2. The Polish underground had been able to recover a test vehicle that had failed to explode, and an RAF Dakota was dispatched to Poland to bring the pieces of the rocket to England, where it was reassembled.

But the knowledge was of little use in defending against the weapon. The rocket traveled at supersonic speed, more than a mile per second, and thus there was no radar trace and no advance warning.

Three more of the rockets fell over the weekend, but again there were few casualties and little damage. Indeed, for the entire week only five people were killed in all of England from enemy action. However, the next week was a frightening one: 56 people died in rocket attacks, another 13 from flying bombs, and 22 in the coastal areas from long-range shelling from the French coast.

Churchill decided not to go public with this second new German weapon. He saw no reason to alarm the people further, and besides, he reasoned, why do anything that could buttress morale in the Reich? Also, to the mystification of the War Cabinet, the Germans themselves were not trumpeting this latest achievement and would not do so until the first week of November, when Goebbels broke his silence. The earlier campaign, he said, "has now been intensified by the employment of another and far more effective explosive."

Three weeks later the propaganda chief's threat was borne out by a particularly appalling incident. On Saturday, 25 November 1944, a V-2 ripped into a Woolworth store in Deptford, killing 157 people and injuring 178.

· · ·

The launch of the V-weapons, the feverish preparations for repelling the Allied landings in France in 1944, and the fearsome efforts against the Soviet armies in the east in no way interfered with another vast Nazi program, which continued apace.

Nothing was to be allowed to halt or interfere with the cornerstone of Nazi ideology and strategic planning: the total eradication of European Jewry. Indeed, the threats from without accelerated the program. Incredibly, on 15 May 1944, the greatest single deportation of the war began.

Most of the 750,000 Jews of Hungary had been rounded up and interned, but the Hungarian leader, Admiral Miklos Horthy, refused repeated requests, at least one delivered in a stormy meeting by Hitler himself, to turn them over for deportation to the labor or death camps.

When the Germans, who had become increasingly unsure of their putative allies, took matters into their own hands and occupied Hungary, the long-sought deportations finally began, supervised by Adolf Eichmann, who had set up headquarters in Budapest. By mid-July, more than 435,000 Hungarian Jews had been crammed aboard trains, a hundred to a boxcar, and shipped to Auschwitz, where all but a handful were murdered.

Horthy, invoking the international outcry from the International Red Cross, the Vatican, and others, was able to stop the deportations, but it was not because the Germans had had a change of heart. Trading Jews for military equipment was one of the odious parts of the bargain that was struck.

In any event, the reprieve was temporary. Horthy was forcibly removed by the Nazis and imprisoned in Bavaria, and most of the 300,000 Hungarian Jews who were still alive were now conscripted as slave laborers. They were worked to death in mines and factories in the Reich proper or were murdered by Hungarian Fascist collaborators, who regularly assaulted them in the ghetto in Budapest. It was estimated that when the Red Army entered the city in February 1945, the bodies of 10,000 murdered Jews lay unburied.

• • •

In July and August 1944, one-fourth of the total bombs dropped by the U.S. Army Air Forces were directed to eliminating the V-weapons sites. Whether they hit their targets became a much-debated and much-disputed point. What was not disputed was the fact that the V-1 attacks continued unabated.

Indeed, there was no appreciable letup until ground forces began to overrun the launch sites in the Cherbourg Peninsula and the Pas-de-Calais, which led to an announcement in early September that the V-1 campaign had been defeated.

The announcement was premature. The Germans still had V-1 launch sites in Belgium and the Netherlands, and the Luftwaffe had developed the capability to launch the flying bombs from Heinkel bombers. Eleven V-1s hit London during the week of 18 September.

As we have seen, the damage done by the V-1s was relatively minor and the casualties relatively light, but there was no convincing the British public that this was so. The *V* was shorthand, after all, for *Vergeltungswaffe*, "vengeance weapon."

Vengeance was in the air, and while in less turbulent times revenge might be a dish best eaten cold, no such sentiment intruded on Churchill and the Chiefs of Staff. There would be increasing numbers of reprisal raids against the German civilian population.

Retribution as a weapon was not a novel idea or a new option. It was

always part of the arsenal of war for Winston Churchill. Two years earlier, in June 1942, in response to the Nazi massacre and destruction of
the Czech village of Lidice—itself an act of retribution for the assassi-
nation by Czech partisans of Reinhard Heydrich, SS Deputy Reich Protector of Bohemia and Moravia—the prime minister had instructed
Arthur Harris to launch Operation Retribution. Bomber Command was
ordered to obliterate three German villages comparable in size and population to Lidice.

Harris responded that it would take a force of 100 bombers for each
village, attacking low and dropping two-thirds incendiaries and one-
third high explosives to do the job. Since the targets were small and not
easily distinguishable, a full moon was necessary.

Harris, a loyal soldier who had the confidence of the prime minister,
pointed out to Churchill that the "justification of giving up one of our
rare fine moonlight nights to this task can only be judged on political
factors." It is clear from the memorandum that it was not retribution
that bothered Harris; his concern was that the operation would take
Bomber Command away from bigger and more important game.
Churchill acquiesced to the air marshal's argument, and Operation Retribution never came off.

What was left unsaid in the Harris memo was that in 1942 such precise bombing was beyond the scope of Bomber Command. Indeed, such
a surgical strike was probably beyond the scope of Bomber Command or
the Americans throughout the war.

• • •

The thirteen-month Crossbow campaign, which began with the August
1943 raid on Peenemünde, was, from its inception, the subject of intense
debate, and the argument continued long after the war. The *United
States Strategic Bombing Survey*, for example, concluded that the Peenemünde raid had little or no effect on development or production of the
V-weapons.

There was also the question of the cost in men and planes of the
Peenemünde raid. Bomber Command lost 40 aircraft—23 Lancasters, 15
Halifaxes, and 2 Stirlings—and 243 airmen. Since most of the losses were

in the last wave of the attacking aircraft—which fell victim to the late-arriving German night fighters—the total losses were judged to be an acceptable 6.7 percent. In this last wave were the Canadian 6 Group, which lost 12 out of 57 planes, or 21 percent, and the British 5 Group, which lost 17 out of 109 planes, or 15.6 percent. Such losses as these were staggering.

Bomber Harris and RAF historian Denis Richards reached a very different conclusion from the American postwar investigators. They defended the raid and the losses at Peenemünde, claiming that the action cost the Germans an estimated two months in lost manufacturing and deployment time—two months that proved crucial in the summer of 1944. They had an unlikely ally in Joseph Goebbels, who recorded in his diary that the raids on Peenemünde and the launch sites in the Pas-de-Calais "have thrown our preparations back four and even eight weeks."

And the director of the rocket base, Walter Dornberger, in his self-serving memoir, titled *V-2*, said that although the damage was nowhere as great as the British believed, the first RAF raid caused a delay of four to six weeks in the development program, which was passed on to the production stage. Four weeks off the schedule meant that the V-1s were not ready until mid-June 1944 instead of mid-May—when the invasion fleets were being readied in the Channel ports—and the V-2s not until September.

Thus it is clear that the Crossbow raids did have an important effect. If the V-weapons had been operational in the months preceding Overlord, they might well have caused it to fail, as the supreme commander himself, Dwight Eisenhower, said.

• • •

The raid on Peenemünde had other ramifications besides the destruction of the physical plant. Several of the key scientists who had developed the rocket program were killed. And on the very day of the raid by Bomber Command, Dornberger had reassured his restive staff that the rocket program now had the highest priority in Berlin. "Personnel is streaming in," he recalled telling them. "In the last fortnight over twelve hundred men have arrived." In his memoirs he was still employ-

ing the circumlocutions and euphemisms of the Third Reich. The "personnel" that were "streaming in" were slave laborers.

"Losses were particularly heavy among foreign construction workers
at Trasenheide camp," said Dornberger matter-of-factly. Between five
and six hundred of the dead—about 75 percent of the total—were these
slave laborers, another sobering reminder that even the victims of the
Nazis were as likely to be killed in air raids as their tormenters.

The raid also served notice that the site was in reach of Allied heavy
bombers, which forced the Germans to move production to vast underground factories that were carved out in the Harz Mountains near Nordhausen. The excavation was done by slave laborers from concentration
camps, and when the factories were completed still others worked
around the clock under the most barbaric conditions to produce the
V-weapons.

The testing of the V-weapons was transferred to southeast Poland,
deep in the forests of the triangle formed by the Vistula and San Rivers.
Thousands of Poles were forcibly removed from the villages in the area
to make way for the vast test site, which was served by the rail line that
ran through Dresden. And there would be no shortage of labor. In addition to the Poles, who could be pressed into service, the Auschwitz-
Birkenau and Majdanek camps lay in close proximity.

In one of the most tragic incidents of the war, Bomber Command attacked the Nordhausen camp on 3 and 4 April 1945, believing that the
buildings in the aerial photographs were military barracks. Hundreds,
or perhaps thousands, of the inmates were killed.

. . .

As the Germans continued their retreat back into the Reich, they
threw everything they had left into the V-weapons arsenal against England. The first week in March 1945, 68 V-2s hit England, 41 landing in
London. It was the worst bombardment since the campaign began.
Three hundred and four people died that week. The next week saw some
drop-off in the casualties, but for a jittery populace it was only marginally better; 200 people were killed, 125 in one incident.

By the third week of March, the V-weapon campaign was nearing its end, although twenty V-2s and two V-1s hit the capital. Finally, on 29 March 1945, what would be the last of the flying bombs, eleven in all, were launched from the Continent. Only five got through. There were no deaths, and just five people were wounded. But earlier in the week, seven V-2s had hit London and four had landed in Essex, killing a total of 137 people, bringing the toll for the month to almost 600.

Along with the V-1 and V-2 attacks, the Luftwaffe also managed to stage a few last-ditch bombing raids. One such raid, on 17–18 March, killed twelve people in Hull. Three nights later, Norfolk was bombed.

But at last the ten-month *Vergeltungswaffen* campaign was over. The V-2s had killed 2,754 people and seriously injured 6,523. Flying bombs had killed 6,184 and seriously injured 17,981.

However, it was not until 26 April 1945, just eleven days before the surrender of Germany, that Winston Churchill reported to the House of Commons, with relative certainty, that the V-weapon attacks against England had ended. But Churchill knew too much of his military history not to hedge his bets. More than 30,000 Londoners had died as a result of Luftwaffe raids, flying bombs, and rockets, and more than 130,000 had been injured.

"It is my duty," he said, "to record facts rather than indulge in prophecy, but I have recorded certain facts with a very considerable air of optimism which I trust will not be brought into mockery by events."

As for who should be credited with stopping the attacks, the prime minister was willing to congratulate the RAF and the antiaircraft gunners, but, he said, "[We] should not forget it was the British Army that took the sites."

. . .

Another campaign, indeed the longest German campaign against the British civilian population, was one that has received relatively little attention: the artillery bombardment of the English Channel ports. The first shells from the German batteries on the French coast fell on Folkestone in August 1940 and the last on Dover on 26 September 1944. It took only a minute for a shell to cross the twenty-two-mile strait that separates England from the Continent. Therefore, when the Germans opened fire, sirens warned the people that they had sixty seconds to find cover. Thousands hid in the caves and tunnels that honeycombed the famous chalk.

The bombardment was sporadic—2,226 shells landed on Dover, killing 109 people in four years—but it was a siege nevertheless, one that lasted longer than Stalingrad. Some 17,000 homes were damaged or destroyed. At the end of the siege, the Germans, anticipating the immediate capture of the coastal batteries—Calais surrendered to Canadian troops on 1 October 1944—began to fire everything in their arsenal at the British coast, including 16-inch armor-piercing shells. That last day 63 shells (50 in one hour) hit Dover.

· · ·

The V-2 has enjoyed great fame, but it was one of the most inefficient weapons ever devised. Each rocket carried less than a ton of explosives, and every launch was a one-way trip. Therefore, if every V-2 built had landed on London, the total amount of high explosives delivered would have been less than 10,000 tons. By way of comparison, in just one raid on Cologne, on the night of 30–31 October 1944, Bomber Command dropped 4,000 tons of high explosives and incendiaries on the city.

Perhaps a more resonant indictment of the wasteful V-2 program is the contrast between it and the development of the Mosquito bomber by the British. Each of these 400-mile-per-hour planes was capable of carrying a 2,000-pound bomb, which was the rough equivalent of the payload of a V-2 rocket. And every Mozzie could make flight after flight over Germany, practically at will, returning to its home base to rearm and fly again.

But in reality the Allied response to the V-weapons was almost as misguided as the development of the weapons themselves by the Germans. Operation Crossbow is a textbook example of the danger of political solutions being given priority over military matters in wartime—thus extending the hostilities. Thousands of sorties were flown against the

V-weapons sites—one Bomber Command raid comprised 1,114 planes—instead of the more important targets in Germany and eastern Europe espoused by Carl Spaatz: the oil fields and refineries.

In spite of its failure, the German rocket program has since its inception engaged the imagination of the public. Much of its fame, of course, is tied to its role as the precursor of the intercontinental ballistic missile and the giant rockets of space exploration. However, it was the less glamorous but far more deadly weaponry of the Allies that decided the issue and destroyed the Axis powers.

As Bomber Harris observed, Germany put its faith in the weaponry of the First World War—the U-boat—and the unproved and ultimately futile weaponry of the next war—the rocket program. To quote A. J. P. Taylor again: "The decisive difference between the British and the Germans is the British . . . knew what they were doing and the Germans did not."

Albert Speer might have agreed. The Allied bombers were effectively doing the job of pulverizing Germany, which, Speer maintained, could have been halted if there had not been the lamentable waste of men and matériel in developing the V-weapons. But Hitler, enraged by the increased bombing of German cities, chose to concentrate on terror weapons.

The chief losers in this misallocation of resources were the *Wasserfall* (Waterfall), a large surface-to-air missile, which was developed as early as 1942, and the new jet plane, which was in production but too late to make a difference. Speer was confident that these weapons could have beaten back the Allied air offensive against German industry in 1944 if development had been started earlier.

The Waterfall was guided by remote control to its target and was capable of destroying bombers at altitudes as high as 50,000 feet. The ground controller had to see the plane, however, which meant that the rocket could not be used in heavy cloud cover or at night; but this problem could have been solved in perhaps eighteen months. Only about 220 scientists were assigned to work on the Waterfall, as opposed to the more than 2,000 who were involved in the development of the V-weapons.

Instead of focusing on the Waterfall, the Führer ordered Speer to increase V-2 rocket production to 900 per month. Speer later derisively pointed out that this would have been thirty rockets a day, which, assuming they all reached their targets, meant delivering a payload of just twenty-four tons of high explosives, the equivalent of the bomb load of twelve B-17s. As he said, it would have taken 66,000 rockets—more than six years' production—to match the explosives dropped by the Allies on just one city, Berlin.

Speer ruefully recalled that he had ignored an urgent appeal from Professor C. Krauch, the commissioner for chemical production, to concentrate on the antiaircraft missile. In a memorandum to the armaments minister, Krauch condemned those who argued that terror must be answered with terror.

The only sensible course, Krauch argued, was to develop the Waterfall surface-to-air missile. Speer, who differed from the other Nazi satraps in that he at least sometimes went his own way, this time followed his Führer. He ignored Krauch's appeal, and the Allied bombers continued to devastate the cities of Germany and terrorize its citizens.

Professor Krauch was correct. The chief effect of the rocket and flying-bomb attacks against Great Britain was to still the minor but vocal segment of the British population that had begun to question the bombing of civilian populations and to strengthen the position of the advocates of the terror bombing of German cities.

CHAPTER SIX

OPERATION

THUNDERCLAP

Run-up to
the Inferno

N o politician can ignore the rumblings of a beleaguered citizenry, and Winston Churchill was a master at judging public opinion and the psychology of the people. Once, in response to praise for his oratory from his personal physician, Lord Moran, Churchill said, "I don't know about oratory, but I do know what's in people's minds and how to speak to them." Lord Moran offered the explanation that the war and the threat to the nation had given Churchill this insight.

Winston Churchill, the son of Lord Randolph Churchill and the grandson of the 7th Duke of Marlborough, knew nothing of the lives of common people, but beginning in May 1940 he became their voice. He wonderfully articulated the hopes and dreams of the entire British people, a remarkable achievement for a man who had never ridden a public bus and whose one excursion on the London Underground, during the General Strike in 1926, ended with his getting lost and having to be rescued by friends.

Churchill's reading of the popular will told him, correctly, that foremost in the thoughts of the British people in the summer of 1944 was revenge. Although accepting of their role of "frontline soldiers" in the V-weapons attacks, Englishmen believed that equal punishment should be meted out to enemy civilians. There was thus much agitation for the reprisal bombing of German cities—no matter that most of the larger German cities had already been destroyed.

The call for vengeance knew no class boundaries. Most of the residents of South London had probably never heard of either Vita Sackville-West, the writer, or Knole, the great house in Kent where she grew up. Sackville-West, like Churchill a member of the upper reaches of British society, reacted in precisely the same way as bombed-out tenement dwellers when she heard that her ancestral home had been hit.

In an angry letter to her husband, Harold Nicolson, Sackville-West spoke for most of her countrymen. "Those filthy Germans!" she cried. "Let us level every town in Germany to the ground! I shan't care."

Churchill, whose own grand boyhood home, Blenheim Palace, was also damaged by bombs, doubtless agreed with the formidable Vita, and he had both the authority and the will to "level every town in Germany."

He also had the means at hand. The prime minister was as much soldier as politician. He was a graduate of Sandhurst and had served with some distinction in India and Egypt as a young man. And he also knew something of airplanes.

While he was first lord of the Admiralty, he had become so enamored with flying that in 1913 he began lessons at the Eastchurch naval air station on the Isle of Sheppey, flying as many as ten times in one day. He was thus an early and enthusiastic proponent of airpower; it may be apocryphal or not—his biographer Martin Gilbert says not—that he coined the term "seaplane."

Only the entreaties of his wife and friends and the deaths of two of his instructors, one in a plane in which Churchill had just flown, convinced him to give up flying. But soldiering was never very far beneath the surface. At the age of forty-one, he went back into the British army, serving in France from November 1915 until May 1916.

Now, his natural reaction was a military one: strike back. On 1 July 1944, after two weeks of flying-bomb attacks, the prime minister asked the Chiefs of Staff to restudy the question of reprisal raids. As for himself, Churchill had already made up his mind. The Germans would pay heavily for this latest outrage.

However, during all the carrying on about vengeance weapons and London, Chief of Air Staff Charles Portal observed, rightly, that the city was a legitimate military target. It was not only the seat of the British government but an important center of war production and communications.

Churchill was adamant. There must be reprisals. The people would accept no less, he argued. In the War Cabinet meeting on 3 July, he reported receiving a large number of letters from the general public urging him to take strong countermeasures against Germany for what he termed an "indiscriminate form of attack." Terror bombing was at last on the table.

In calling for reprisals, Churchill first suggested that the Germans be warned that if they did not halt the V-1 attacks, Bomber Command would systematically raze smaller German cities in retaliation. General Walter Bedell Smith, Eisenhower's chief of staff, supported the prime minister. It is therefore reasonable to assume that both Eisenhower and Roosevelt did, or would, as well.

His plan called for the systematic destruction of small towns of populations of 20,000 people or so. To destroy such small targets, it would be necessary to drop 600 tons of bombs on each target in daylight, which meant that the Americans would have to do it. The planners admitted that somewhere on the order of 900 tons would actually be necessary to ensure a raid's success.

It was estimated that five such towns could be destroyed in one good-weather operation. Since there were only three or four days a month when weather conditions, less than 2/10 to 3/10 cloud cover (20 to 30 percent), were favorable for such an operation, the Americans could be expected to destroy fifteen to twenty small towns per month.

While the destruction of small towns would no doubt have serious effects on morale, such a campaign could not be planned in advance to produce the desired devastating effect. News of the bombings could be controlled locally, for one thing, and the weather could never be relied upon. Besides, said the planners, even if a hundred towns of 20,000 people were destroyed, only 3 percent of the population of Germany would be affected.

Acting Major General L. C. Hollis, senior assistant secretary, Office of the War Cabinet, wrote to Churchill that for the Germans to change their policies in the light of such a threat would be militarily foolish. What, after all, were a few small towns to the German high command when weighed against the success of the flying-bomb campaign against England, which was not only slowing production owing to a jittery populace but also tying up 50 percent of Bomber Command in Operation Crossbow?

The first sea lord, Sir Andrew Cunningham, took the opposite view. He felt that such a threat might well have the desired demoralizing effect on the people and that the Nazi military leaders might well call off the V-weapons attacks.

Charles Portal and Air Chief Marshal and Deputy Supreme Allied Commander Arthur Tedder opposed any plan that would divert Bomber Command from what it saw as its primary mission. Oil and communications should remain the primary targets for Bomber Command. Besides, Hitler cared nothing for the cities of Germany, large or small—he never toured a bombed-out city—and would willingly sacrifice any or all of them. Indeed, he remarked more than once that the Allied air raids actually made his dream of building a new Germany that much easier by destroying the old.

Another form of attack that was discussed was the widespread strafing of civilians by fighters, although everyone knew that this action could not be done on the scale that would produce a widespread catastrophe.

Everything, it seems, was on the table for discussion, including the use of poison gas, not only against the Crossbow installations but also in Germany itself. Other actions against civilians included the proposal that Germany be warned that from a certain date all movement by road or rail was forbidden and subject to attack.

The use of poison gas was eliminated as an option, even though Churchill argued strongly for it, and wholesale bombing and strafing of all occupied Europe was impossible. There were nowhere near enough men or planes available to carry out such an ambitious plan.

Churchill clearly had come some distance in the four years since he had sent a memorandum to Alfred Duff Cooper, minister of information, on how to handle the reporting of air raids on England. "Press and broadcast should be asked to handle air raids in a cool way and on a diminishing tone of public interest," he wrote. "The facts should be chronicled without undue prominence or headlines. The people should be accustomed to treat air raids as a matter of ordinary routine. . . . It must be remembered that the vast majority of people are not at all affected by any single air raid, and would hardly sustain any evil impression if it were not thrust before them. Everyone should learn to take air raids and air raid alarms as if they were no more than thunderstorms."

This rather Olympian pronouncement could well have been issued by leaders of any of the Axis powers or their propaganda ministers. But statistical analysis was certainly on Churchill's side. The odds of being killed by a flying bomb were only one in thirty thousand.

On 5 July 1944, the Chiefs of Staff met to discuss Churchill's call for reprisal raids against Germany for the V-1 attacks. Afterward they reported "that the time might well come in the not too distant future when an all-out attack by every means at our disposal on German civilian morale might be decisive." Further, the Chiefs of Staff recommended to Churchill that "the method by which such an attack would be carried out should be examined and all possible preparations made."

Thus began intensive planning sessions by a committee that included not only representatives from the American and British air staffs but also the British Foreign Office and the Ministry of Economic Warfare. The representatives from these various groups began to develop a new policy with a new name. Henceforth the planners would talk of "morale bombing."

According to the committee's top secret report, entitled "Attack on German Civilian Morale," Berlin was to be the target of a four-day, three-night round-the-clock bombardment by Bomber Command and the Eighth Air Force. During the raids, 20,000 tons of bombs would be dropped. Many things recommended the German capital as the target, not the least of which was its vast size. Even in bad weather it could be found.

Berlin was also the premier population and administrative center of the Reich, as well as a vital industrial and communications center. And, of course, the most important Nazis, including the Führer himself, were in residence. In these particulars, Berlin differed not at all from London—although not even Portal offered this analogy publicly.

Since a daylight raid on Berlin would produce the greatest number of casualties because of the population density during working hours, the specialists in daylight bombing, the Eighth Air Force, would have to lead the way. Under visual conditions, 2,000 American bombers would drop 5,000 tons of bombs on a 2.5-square-mile area of central Berlin. At that time of day, the area, which would absorb a bomb density of 2,000 tons of bombs per square mile, was estimated to contain some 375,000 people.

The effectiveness of the initial raid would be compounded by an "all-incendiary attack by Bomber Command, on the heaviest scale, on the remainder of the city." Bomber Command, in a departure from standard operating procedure, would attack in daylight, which would necessitate the Americans' providing a large force of escort fighters. If necessary, Bomber Command would follow up that night with another incendiary attack.

Not so incidentally, such a raid would have postwar ramifications as well. Churchill always viewed the Soviet allies with suspicion and had few illusions about the extent to which they could be expected to cooperate after the defeat of Germany.

"The total devastation of the centre of Berlin would, moreover, offer incontrovertible proof of the power of a modern bomber force; it would convince our Russian allies and representatives of other countries visiting Berlin of the effectiveness of Anglo-American air power," said the drafters of the report. Further: "A spectacular and final object lesson to the German people on the consequences of universal aggression would be of continuing value in the post-war period and would appreciably ease the task of policing the occupied areas by means of air forces."

Officially, RAF policy was to destroy industrial areas, which, as Harris often observed, were located in the cities of the Reich. So, naturally, his bombers attacked cities. And for his purposes, incendiaries were more effective and paid a larger dividend than high explosives. So the ratio of incendiary bombs to heavy bombs was very large. It was also argued, somewhat disingenuously, that incendiaries caused fewer casualties among civilians than did high explosives.

Further, the British pointed out, the RAF raids had caused much greater disruption among the civilian populace than did the American raids, which were ostensibly against precise targets—oil refineries, aircraft plants, railroad yards, and the like. Since these targets were in outlying areas, civilians were little affected, or so it was officially stated. In reality, the truth was otherwise.

In chilling detail, the report reveals how far planners on both sides had descended after five years of warfare. There would be, it was projected, approximately 275,000 casualties—137,500 dead and 137,500 seriously injured. The name chosen for this massive raid connoted both its suddenness and its deadliness: Operation Thunderclap.

As the report stated, "The main purpose of [Thunderclap], which may be carried out in the closing stages of the war, is to precipitate the capitulation of the German High Command. If the operation should succeed in curtailing the duration of the war by even a few weeks it would save many thousands of Allied casualties and would justify itself many times over." The memorandum also said forthrightly, "The operation would not, necessarily, cause any sudden breakdown in German administration." After all, most of the government had already left town or was dispersed. The postal system, for example, was being administered from Dresden.

But the destruction of the administrative apparatus was not the goal of Thunderclap. As the drafters of the plan said, "The essential purpose of the attack however is to deliver an overwhelming blow to German national morale. . . . The whole population of Berlin would be spectators of the catastrophe, and, in the state of war, which has been postulated, the effect might well be decisive."

On 13 August, John Strachey, director of bomber operations, received a memorandum advocating the Thunderclap plan. "I still feel there is a strong case," wrote the unidentified correspondent, "after the virtual collapse of the [German] Army in Normandy, for laying on a 'Rotterdam' on the centre of the Capital." The terror bombing of Berlin and killing or injuring of hundreds of thousands of civilians would cause a national panic that "at the best may prove the last straw."

The air staff had consulted with the Foreign Office, the Ministry of Economic Warfare, and an "unofficial representative" from General Spaatz's headquarters. There was general consensus about Thunderclap, but there were still deep divisions among the principals about diverting men and matériel from destroying the German armed forces and bombing strategic supplies, particularly oil. But everyone regretted that Thunderclap had not been in place to take advantage of the attempt on Hitler's life on 20 July 1944.

After all suggestions were discussed and most eliminated, one target still recommended itself for a Thunderclap-type raid: Berlin. A genuine crisis could be effected by destroying the government communications and public services of the center of Nazi power. Although some two million people, half the city, had been evacuated, there were as many people, some 3 percent of the population of Germany, still living in Berlin. A catastrophic raid on the capital would thus have the greatest possible effect on the civilian population of Germany, since no attack of such magnitude could be covered up or disguised.

Harris and Spaatz were in agreement that their two commands would be able to drop a total 20,000 tons of bombs on Berlin over a period of four days and three nights. With that added to the 48,000 tons of bombs that had already been dropped on the German capital, the estimate of destruction and death seems accurate enough.

A first draft of the report went so far as to suggest that a large raid might even trigger revolt in Berlin, which had, it was said, "some traditions of anti-Nazi activity." This last projection was a bit too roseate. It was dropped from the final version.

In the final report, issued on 22 August, under the heading "Other Large Towns," the planners discussed the alternatives to Berlin. "In the main the tactical factors governing the attack on other large towns such as Hamburg, Cologne, Frankfurt or Munich, are similar to those of attack on Berlin."

While Allied losses would be less since at least three of these targets were near the German border and thus the penetration would be not as deep as with Berlin, they were also harder to find in bad weather. But, more important, there would be less destruction in each of these cities per ton of bombs dropped. The original report thus clearly and unmistakably called for the Thunderclap target to be Berlin.

The report acknowledged that "immense devastation could be produced if the entire attack was concentrated on a single big town other than Berlin and the effect would be especially great if the town was one hitherto relatively undamaged." This is the sentence often cited in reference to the Dresden raid as evidence that the planners had Dresden or a similar city in mind in 1944. Not so, it seems. The very next sentence reads, "The political effect would however be less than that of comparable devastation in Berlin." For the planners, Thunderclap meant the bombing of Berlin, which was not only "unmissable," even in the worst weather, but would also allow for a "banquet raid," offering something for everyone and every taste.

The main impetus or ingredient necessary for launching Thunderclap was less easily defined or recognized. What would be the actual flash point, the crisis that when fully and quickly exploited by a devastating raid could bring down the Reich? No one was certain, but until then, said the report, "it is essential that we should devote our maximum effort to attacks on the German war economy and on the German army and its essential supplies."

The planners—whose report was, after all, for Winston Churchill, who was calling for vengeance for the V-weapons—left themselves an out. "There may, however, be a moment," they wrote, "at which the balance can be tipped by an attack directed against the morale of the High Command, the army and the civilian population rather than against objectives immediately related to the battle."

In other words, Bomber Command and the U.S. Army Air Forces would together so devastate the Reich and terrorize the populace that

Hitler and his cohorts would either capitulate or be overthrown. There were three main factors to be considered:

1. The morale of the political and military leaders could be affected by heavy attacks on government and military centers and by "well judged propaganda."
2. The morale of the armed forces could be affected by conditions in the field, by interdiction of supplies and weapons, and by the conditions at home.
3. While admitting that riots, strikes, uncontrolled looting, or other civil disorder might occur in "an extreme case," the report concluded that "this is not in any circumstance a probable contingency except among foreign workers."

There was, however, some chance of absenteeism, shirking off at work, and general hostility toward government and administration if civilian morale deteriorated—a very big "if." But, the report continued, an attack on morale "may force the authorities to divert increasing resources to the maintenance of morale at the expense of other vital commitments." In other words, thousands of field guns would have to be used to defend cities from air attack instead of being deployed as artillery at the front. Civil defense measures would cause additional diversion of large numbers of men and huge amounts of matériel to aid the civilian populace. In particular, hundreds of thousands of people made homeless by the raids would have to be cared for, causing further disruption.

If anyone still had doubts that the chief target in any civilian bombing campaign would be women and children, this report resolved those doubts. "It must be remembered that there are few able-bodied male Germans between 17 and 45 left in Germany outside the Army and the Police." As for foreign workers, they might be more sensitive to air attack, but the report admitted that they were subject to total police control. These workers were, after all, mainly slave laborers. The report continued:

In this situation it is unlikely that fluctuations in civilian morale will have any decisive influence upon the High Command until its authority has already been greatly weakened by other causes and the machinery of repression has begun to break down. The occasion for an attack on civilian morale as such will not arise until it is generally believed even in Germany that the Nazi system is collapsing and that total defeat is imminent. This opportunity to enforce surrender may be a fleeting one; if it is not seized either the extremist elements may succeed in rallying the army for a further stand or the collapse may spread so rapidly that central government ceases to exist.

It is generally agreed that the greatest effect on morale will be produced if a new blow of catastrophic force can be struck at a time when the situation already appears desperate. The blow should be such that it cannot be concealed or minimised, and it should if possible imply a threat that it will be continued and intensified if surrender does not follow. The German attack on Rotterdam in May 1940 was made in somewhat analogous conditions, and illustrates the effect which may be produced. Carefully coordinated propaganda is of course essential.

The report admitted that the "available evidence suggests that German civilian morale is at present negative rather than positively good or bad." The average person was concerned only with getting by from one day to the next and was under no illusion that resistance to authority or protest against the war would improve his or her lot.

The hopeful but guarded note that foreign workers might become restive reflected the view of Goebbels himself. As early as April 1942 he wrote in his diary, "It is now also becoming evident that the great successes of the English with their air raids are due to sabotage on the part of foreign workers." British intelligence was doubtless made aware of the Nazi chiefs' fear of the foreign workers in their midst and the police investigations of their alleged sabotage and aid to the enemy. In reality, of course, there was little to hope for among the British and little to fear from the foreigners on the part of the Germans. The slaves remained quiescent.

Clearly, in a short time, British and American planners had learned the craft and the importance of propaganda. Joseph Goebbels himself could not have phrased it better.

Neither Arthur Harris nor Carl Spaatz sat in on the sessions that devised the Thunderclap plan. Although the American commander was in agreement with the final draft, he asked that no mention be made in the report of "the concurrence of his unofficial representative at the Meeting."

As for Harris, it can be surmised that he had no qualms about such a massive raid on Berlin since he had planned a similar Anglo-American operation against the German capital for 21 June 1944 in retaliation for the flying-bomb attacks.

According to Harris, Doolittle, the Eighth Air Force commander, came to Bomber Command headquarters the day before to confer with the British staffs and go over the final plans. The discussions were proceeding amicably and the operation seemed feasible to everyone until Harris asked about the long-range American fighter support necessary to protect the British bombers. Not only would it be an unusually deep penetration into the Third Reich, but the British would be raiding in daylight, an unusual move for them. Bomber Command would thus require an extraordinarily large number of fighter escorts.

Neither Doolittle nor his boss, Carl Spaatz, commanding general of the U.S. Strategic Air Forces, was anxious to deploy the American fighter squadrons over such a vast area. The bomber stream would run some sixty miles in length. When they told Harris that he could have nowhere near the number of fighter planes that he demanded, he withdrew from the plan forthwith.

Harris, in his memoirs, maintained that his withdrawal forced the cancellation of the entire operation, which was not so. A thousand American B-17s and B-24s did raid Berlin on 21 June 1944, dropping almost 1,400 tons of bombs on the German capital and its environs.

Spaatz was very much troubled by the bombing of civilians as outlined in the Thunderclap plan. He wrote to Eisenhower on 24 August that the Eighth would participate in the raid against Berlin, but the American goal would remain attacking targets of military importance. "U.S. bombing policy, as you know," he reminded Ike, "has been directed against precision military objectives, and not morale." Eisenhower reassured Spaatz, telling him, "We will continue precision bombing and not be deflected to morale bombing."

• • •

The V-1 terror attacks on the British cities, the calls for reprisals, and the drafting of the Thunderclap plan were part of the backdrop of the Octagon Conference in Quebec on 12–16 September 1944. At the conference, Churchill and Roosevelt provided a resonant example of the odium in which Germany was held and the desire for revenge that permeated the thinking of otherwise rational beings. The two leaders approved and initialed the Morgenthau Plan, a scheme concocted by Roosevelt's secretary of the treasury, Henry Morgenthau.

The Morgenthau Plan called for the elimination of Germany as an industrial power. Any successor state to the Third Reich was to be reduced to an agricultural and pastoral society. British Foreign Secretary Anthony Eden and U.S. Secretary of State Cordell Hull were appalled at the idea that postwar Germany would be so crippled and prevailed on Churchill and Roosevelt to disavow their actions. The plan was scrapped.

• • •

Concurrent with Thunderclap, it was also proposed that bombers attack SS and Gestapo headquarters and, in an effort to stop the murder of the remaining Jews of Europe, the concentration camps themselves. However, in a tacit admission that bombing was not all that accurate, the planners had to reject these addenda.

The headquarters were too scattered throughout urban areas to be bombed effectively. As for the concentration camps, by far the largest number of deaths would be among the inmates—a supposition that was borne out by the raids on Peenemünde and Nordhausen, in which great numbers of slave laborers and very few Nazis were killed.

This last decision would later fuel charges that in spite of knowing of the persecution and murder of the Jews, Churchill, Roosevelt, and their military advisers passed up opportunities to save them by destroying the rail lines leading to the death camps.

An examination of the map of the largest camp, Auschwitz-Birkenau, clearly points up the difficulty of accurately bombing an area approximately two by five miles in area, when it was considered good bombing if the bombs fell within half a mile of the target. The factories that were staffed with slave labor, the barracks for the inmates, and the grisly machinery of extermination were in such close proximity that bombs would have killed many thousands of the people that any such raids were supposed to save. As for the rail lines—there were four serving the camp—the Germans had millions of slave laborers, and until the very end of the war they were quickly able to repair damaged rail lines, often within hours of their being bombed.

Since at least August 1941, it had been known what was happening in the Nazi-occupied areas in eastern Europe. Neutral governments, intelligence sources, and émigrés were reporting the German atrocities in frightening detail. A week after returning from the meeting with Roosevelt in Newfoundland, Churchill declared in a broadcast speech, "Since the Mongol invasion of Europe . . . there has never been methodical, merciless butchery on such a scale, or approaching such a scale. . . . We are in the presence of a crime without a name."

Churchill had spoken out even earlier, on 21 December 1937, against Hitler's persecution of the Jews. During a debate in the Commons over Lord Halifax's visit to Hitler in Berlin, Churchill described the visit as appeasement of the Führer and tacit approval of his racial policies.

Debate has long centered on whether in his "crime without a name" speech Churchill was referring to what became known as the Holocaust or calling the world's attention to the murder of Russian noncombatants. Certainly, it was known that Jews were being rounded up, interned, and deported. After all, Churchill received weekly reports on German police activities.

Many explanations have been put forth as to why these facts were not made more of by the British government. The press was certainly reporting the atrocities. One construction is that old standby: to have done

Visitors to prewar Dresden often referred to the city as "the Florence on the Elbe." The Zwinger Complex, the cathedral, Theaterplatz, the royal palace, and the Semper Opera House, built over three centuries in styles ranging from Renaissance to Baroque to rococo to neoclassical, constituted one of the most beautiful and harmonious architectural assemblages in the world.
WALTER HAHN

The twentieth century revealed a darker side of Saxon society. Dresdeners were early and enthusiastic supporters of the Nazi party and German expansionism. TOP: The Sturmabteilung, the SA, parades in honor of Hindenburg and Hitler on February 1, 1933. BOTTOM: With Germany triumphant in Europe, Dresdeners turned out in August 1940 to salute the military at a parade through the Schlossplatz. WALTER HAHN (TOP); HEROLD (BOTTOM)

The Altmarkt, the great square in the Altstadt, was for centuries the epicenter of Dresden commercial life. TOP: *The square as it appeared in 1943.* BOTTOM: *The Altmarkt with the tower of the Kreuzkirche, the oldest church in Dresden (right); the Rathaus, or town hall (left); and the statue of Germania, the symbol of German pride and nationhood.*

WALTER HAHN (TOP)

Reconstruction of
the Altmarkt into a
semblance of its prewar
aspect took almost
twenty years after its
destruction on the night
of February 13–14, 1945.
The square as it
appeared in 1956 (top),
in 1951 (left), and
in the 1960s (above,
right).

W. MÖBIUS (LEFT)

The wreckage of
the Grosse
Meissner-Strasse,
on the right bank
of the Elbe in
Dresden Neustat,
graphically illus-
trates the vast area
covered by the
firestorm.

W. PETER SENIOR

Gr.Meissner-
Strasse.

The Wallpavillion, or Rampart Pavillion, the most beautiful of the three great Baroque entrances to the courtyard of the Zwinger, Augustus's pleasure palace and museum. The Zwinger was completely destroyed in the three-part raid.
W. MÖBIUS (TOP);
R. PETER SENIOR (BOTTOM)

The Frauenkirche, built 1726–1734 by Protestant Dresdeners in part to protest the conversion to Catholicism of the Augustuses, became the symbol of the city for over two hundred years. It withstood the bombing of February 13–14, but collapsed February 15 when the intense heat melted its sandstone supports.

MARTIN LUTHER

The extent of the devastation caused by the firestorm
as seen from the tower of the Rathaus in the Altstadt.

The firestorm
temperatures ranged
as high as 1,500
degrees centigrade,
which twisted steel
girders and melted
street lamps.
R. PETER SENIOR

Nothing could survive in the inferno that swept across Dresden during the night of the raid. These two incinerated, shrunken corpses were found in the ruins.
R. PETER SENIOR

Overwhelmed by the number of unburied bodies and faced with the threat of a catastrophic outbreak of disease, the authorities were forced to burn the victims instead of transporting them out of the city for burial in a mass grave. A giant pyre was erected in the Altmarkt, and the burning of the corpses began on February 25, 1945.

WALTER HAHN

Bodies were brought by wagon to the Altmarkt, where they were stacked, doused with gasoline, and set afire in the very shadow of the statue of Germania.
WALTER HAHN

The ruins of Frauenkirche, seen here, in the winter of 1965, served for half a century as a reminder of the horrors of war and the suffering of the people of Dresden. R. PETER SENIOR

In February 1990, just four months after the fall of the Berlin Wall and the first moves toward German reunification, a worldwide campaign and appeal for funds was launched to rebuild the Frauenkirche. Work began in 1993, and in October 2005 the reconstructed church, incorporating thousands of blackened stones from the original structure, was finished. MARSHALL DE BRUHL so would have compromised the Ultra program. Historian Richard Breitman takes a different view. He cites a July 1941 Ministry of Information caveat that propaganda must be handled very carefully so as not to seem too extreme. If filled with seemingly fantastical reports of atrocities, instead of rousing the British people to action it might have the opposite effect.

Even allowing for a half century of retrospection, reading the now declassified reports and memoranda one is sometimes almost overcome by whiffs of the unmistakable anti-Semitism of the British Foreign Office and Ministry of Information in the 1930s and 1940s. What else can one make of a memorandum that says that information and propaganda "must deal always with treatment of indisputably innocent people. Not with violent political opponents. And not with Jews"?

Harold Nicolson, that pillar of the diplomatic establishment, confided to his diary in June 1945, well after the Nazi genocidal policies and atrocities had been publicized around the world, "The Jewish capacity for destruction is illimitable. And although I loathe anti-Semitism, I do dislike Jews."

By the time of Churchill's speech, hundreds of thousands of Jews were already dead—starved to death or victims of disease in the concentration camps that had sprung up all over Europe; beaten or shot to death by camp guards; or murdered by the Einsatzgruppen, the killing squads that followed the troops and executed the civilian populace as the Wehrmacht moved across eastern Europe and into the Soviet Union. In the first three weeks of Barbarossa, some 50,000 Jews were murdered by the Einsatzgruppen.

Poland, with the largest concentration of Jews in the world, some three million, had already been under the Nazi terror for almost two years. The Warsaw Ghetto was home to over 400,000 people, each of whom had a food allotment of 183 calories per day, about the number of calories in two slices of bread. By the end of 1942 most of Poland's Jews had been liquidated.

The program of transporting the Jews to the east and certain death was highly classified, and the operation was carried out in all of Europe by relatively few people, considering its vast scope. As Hitler had foretold in *Mein Kampf,* "If propaganda has imbued a whole people with an idea, the organization can draw the consequences with a handful of men." The German people had for over a decade been barraged with the anti-Semitic propaganda of the Nazis and had become inured to the suffering of their neighbors and fellow citizens.

The term *Sonderbehandlung* ("special treatment") was devised by Himmler and his staff to describe the deportations and killing. Even this euphemism became troublesome, so by April 1942 the program was changed to "Transportation of the Jews to the Russian East."

Sonderbehandlung was applied to other groups as well. Hundreds of thousands of non-Jews—Catholic priests and nuns, Communists, Polish prisoners of war, homosexuals, and Gypsies—were rounded up and sent to the camps or murdered where they were found. By the end of the war three million non-Jewish Poles had also been killed.

Jewish leaders in Britain and America repeatedly tried to apprise the world of the enormity of the Nazi crimes against their coreligionists. Influential newspapers, in particular the *New York Times,* joined in the chorus of horror. In England, the archbishop of Canterbury wrote a letter to the *Times* of London. Finally, on 17 December 1942, an Allied declaration condemning the systematic murder of European Jewry was issued; but, significantly, it offered no plan for saving those millions still alive.

The official line was that victory over the Germans was the first order of business and everything else must be subordinate. There were many underlying issues as well. One was the fear of a massive influx of Jewish refugees, which was of especial importance to those such as Anthony Eden. Another concern was the reaction of the Arab world. How would the inevitable introduction of huge numbers of Jews into their ancient homeland in Palestine affect relations with the Arabs, who controlled much of the world's oil supply?

In late 1942 and early 1943, however, there were no Allied ground forces in Europe except the Russians, who were fighting a purely defensive war for their very existence. The only way to take the war to the Germans was by air; but the RAF was still hesitant to venture too deeply into Germany because of the unacceptable losses over the heavily defended Fatherland, and the U.S. Army Air Forces was still feeling its way. Its operations were more or less restricted to bombing French and German ports.

The campaign to save the Jews was thus limited to a war of propaganda, although it was not a war of lies and deceptions. All of the horrors were true. And it may have resulted in the saving of some of the persecuted by lending encouragement to the brave souls who hid their unfortunate countrymen and by convincing those Jews who could still do so to go into hiding or to flee.

Nothing can spare those civilian and religious and military leaders from the judgment of history that they did not at the very least speak out against the atrocities being perpetrated against the Jews. At the same time, credit must be given the military for moving as rapidly as possible to destroy the Nazis and bring down the system responsible for the atrocities.

As for precision bombing of the camps or the rail lines leading to them: that was never a real option. The technology that could ensure the pinpoint bombing of such small targets was never available. It is estimated that anywhere from 50 to 75 percent of the bombs being dropped by Bomber Command were not even hitting the cities they were intended to, which were large targets indeed. And when the American bombers entered the war in force in 1943, they quickly learned that their bombing tactics and accuracy were also sadly deficient. In the first half of 1943, they managed to drop only 14 percent of their bombs within 1,000 feet of the target. By the end of the war the figure had improved considerably but was still just 44 percent. Some 73 percent still fell within only 2,000 feet of the target—nearly half a mile. As for the rail lines, the Germans demonstrated again and again that they could repair bombed rail lines in just a few hours.

Hitler's victims were locked up in a vast Continental prison or death camp. In 1942, moral suasion was the only weapon the Allies had against an enemy without morals. Therefore, the world watched helplessly, and for the most part silently, as the remaining Jews of Europe were slaughtered.

For Hitler, Göring, Goebbels, Himmler, and the other top Nazis, there was no turning back from the course they had set. They would fight on no matter what. They knew full well that a German defeat and surrender meant a hangman's rope for them. Each of them might say, with Shakespeare's Macbeth, "I am in blood / Stept in so far that, should I wade no more, / Returning were as tedious as go o'er."

· · ·

In Washington, the Thunderclap report and its clear endorsement of terror bombing was greeted with some alarm by many members of the air force staff, in particular Major General Laurence S. Kuter, assistant chief of staff for plans.

Kuter was one of Hap Arnold's so-called boy generals. This characterization was not always applied kindly, at least by the senior officers in the other services and, indeed, in the U.S. Army itself. The public and press delighted in the appellation, however. In any event, the classification was born of necessity. The army air chief had had no choice but to promote a group of young officers to senior rank. The air services were so new that there weren't enough old-timers to fill the slots. Arnold never had any cause to regret raising relatively youthful men to positions of prominence. Many of them went on to positions of great power in the military and defense establishment.

The dashingly handsome Kuter was both an articulate spokesman for the military and a man of strong convictions. "It is contrary to our national ideals," he wrote, "to wage war against civilians." Kuter doubtless believed this, but as Spaatz biographer Richard C. Davis points out, it was directly counter to what he had written three years earlier when he helped draft AWPD-1. That directive promoted morale bombing as a viable policy. However, AWPD-1 also warned that bombing of civilians might very well have the opposite effect. It could stiffen the people's will to resist—a point no doubt much influenced by the example of the British during the recent Blitz.

The 1941 directive also specified that there must be definite signs that the enemy's morale and will to fight on had declined and, further, that there must be signs that the people were losing faith in the military. In addition, all psychological conditions for such a campaign must be in place—a very big caveat. Now, three years later, Kuter was clearly disturbed by what he saw as a strategic wrong turn. "Our entire target policy," he said, "has been founded on the fact that it was uneconomical to bomb any except military objectives and the German productive capacity."

Kuter identified a simple fact that was invariably overlooked or ignored by the advocates of morale bombing. "The bombing of civilian targets in Germany cannot be expected to have similar effects to those which can be expected in a democratic country where the people are still able to influence national will," he said. The objects of civilian terror bombing had no way to communicate their misery, fear, and anger to the government in power. And even if they did, their protests would be ignored or stamped out. Only Hitler himself decided the course of action.

His compunctions about morale bombing notwithstanding, Kuter was compelled by duty to draw up a plan for the bombing of population centers. His suggestion in some ways paralleled or supplemented Thunderclap, but it had one significant difference. Why not, Kuter said, concentrate on a smaller city, one that was "ancient, compact, historic" but also had "as much industrial importance as possible."

A dozen such cities should be chosen and announced to the Germans. However, to cause maximum chaos, the Germans should be warned that just one of the designated targets would bear the brunt of the massive attack by a thousand or more bombers. After that, if necessary, another city would be targeted, until all twelve were obliterated.

Kuter's "death by a thousand cuts" had little chance of causing the collapse of the Third Reich for the very reasons he had put forth himself. The people's misery would not sway the Nazis, who ruled their lives. As the war came closer to home, the vise of the police state closed ever tighter. Then, too, the German people were clearly in no mood to capitulate. Consider the adulation of Goebbels when he toured bombed-out cities: he was cheered as a hero by the survivors.

Hap Arnold proposed yet another plan. The air force chief suggested a full week of round-the-clock bombing throughout the Third Reich by all available fighters and bombers. No area was to be spared. Arnold's plan was the least viable and must have disappointed his many admirers.

There were nowhere near enough crews, planes, or escorts to implement such a mission. As the top-ranking airman, Arnold should have known this.

Early in 1944, the American ambassador in London, John G. Winant, had written to Roosevelt objecting to the bombing of civilians. As Winant pointed out to the president, it was understandable that the British might be justified in their nighttime raids on populated areas because the Germans had done the same thing to them. The American reluctance to bomb civilians was therefore understandable, since no Americans cities had been bombed. But, Winant told the president frankly, many of the target selections made by the British and then passed on to the Americans for execution were political judgments and not based on military needs.

"In the European area I believe that British political considerations are integrated in military decisions and that they do not conform necessarily with United States long term interests," said Winant. The Americans should concentrate on aircraft factories, ball-bearing plants, and other such targets, he argued.

The ambassador was particularly disturbed by the American attacks on Budapest, Bucharest, and Sofia, which theoretically were supposed to destroy the railway marshaling yards but were also directed at the morale of the civilians. He said such raids were ineffective since railroads could be repaired very quickly but the political ramifications would be severe. The Soviets had not bombed the cities, but the Americans had. Winant was no doubt looking to the future and the by then clear Soviet role in the makeup of postwar Europe.

The State Department also weighed in, saying that the bombing of civilians was causing diplomatic problems. The Joint Chiefs replied that only military targets had been bombed and that, besides, the targets had been picked not by Washington but by the chief of the air staff of the Royal Air Force.

. . .

In spite of the lip service being paid to precision bombing, everyone knew that the almost constant cloud cover over Europe ensured that targets were obscured most of the time. Civilian deaths were inevitable. But the euphemistic "precision bombing" at least provided some sort of moral fig leaf.

While Eisenhower promised to respect Spaatz's scruples about morale bombing, he clearly left himself a way out. The agreed-upon bombing priorities would be observed, he told Spaatz, "unless in my opinion an opportunity arises where a sudden and devastating blow may have an incalculable result." The supreme commander soon seemed ready to invoke his proviso. On 9 September 1944, he notified Spaatz that he should be ready to launch Thunderclap at any time. Spaatz accordingly instructed Doolittle to be prepared to reorder the bombing priorities. The Eighth must be ready to bomb Berlin "indiscriminately."

Spaatz's biographer Davis speculates that Eisenhower's order perhaps was prompted by the upcoming Operation Market Garden, which was designed to capture bridgeheads on the Lower Rhine in the Netherlands and open the way for a rapid advance into the Reich itself. The crossing by Allied troops of the great river, with its mythic connection to the German people—it flows through the nation's psyche—combined with a devastating air raid on the capital might be the one-two punch so long sought by the Allies.

Market Garden (17–25 September 1944) was a disaster, a stunning reversal for the Allies. Not only were the Rhine bridges not captured, but troops that should have been used to clear the Scheldt Estuary and open the port of Antwerp had been diverted to Holland. Antwerp, although it was in Allied hands, was not opened to traffic until the end of November.

Thunderclap was thus delayed, but only temporarily, and it stayed in the forefront of the strategic bombing plans. In a matter of just a few weeks the "crisis" necessary—the imminent collapse of the Third Reich—seemed at hand.

· · ·

The Germans staged one more massive ground offensive: the attempted breakout in the Ardennes on 16 December. The Battle of the Bulge, which was designed to split the Allied armies and recapture the port of Antwerp, was a sobering warning to the Allies, but the 27 December 1944 War Cabinet Joint Intelligence Sub-Committee Report, "German Ability to Maintain the Present Counter-Offensive," was right on target with its assessment of the German breakout. It could not be sustained since Germany could not move the substantial numbers of reinforcements needed into the Ardennes because of the expected massive Soviet push in the east.

As predicted, the German counterattack was short-lived, and the Wehrmacht retreat into the Reich resumed. Eisenhower, however, never underestimated the enemy, a sound rule for all commanders. In a dispatch dated 7 January 1945 he said, "There seems to be a kind of fanaticism or 'German Fury' behind the present operations and I have no doubt but that the Germans are making a supreme and all-out effort to achieve victory in the West in the shortest possible time. The Ardennes battle is in my opinion only one episode and we must expect attempts in other areas."

There would be no other major German land offensive, but Eisenhower would have been most unwise not to have considered the possibility and planned accordingly. His assessment was made even more difficult because of the reticence of the Soviets to show their hand or confide in their British and American allies.

The supreme commander and his colleagues had long chafed at the lack of information about Soviet movements in the east and the Russians' almost paranoid hesitance to put anything important in writing. Someone always had to be dispatched to Moscow to deal with them directly. Winston Churchill, Anthony Eden, Harry Hopkins, and Cordell Hull, among others, had all made the pilgrimage, some more than once.

Now, as the war seemed to be heading into its final stages, some news from the Russians about an offensive would be welcome. In turn, Eisenhower would be glad to exchange information with his Soviet counterparts. It would thus be necessary for another face-to-face meeting to work out a more coherent strategy between the two uneasy Allies.

On 14 December, American ambassador Averell Harriman met with Stalin to assure him that Eisenhower "was very anxious to operate in concert with the Russians and to help the Russian armies whenever such support might be needed."

Eisenhower, naturally, had to remain at his headquarters in France, but on 23 December 1944, Roosevelt cabled Stalin that Eisenhower would be sending a representative to the Soviet Union "to discuss with you the situation in the West and its relation to the Russian front in order that information essential to our efforts may be available to all of us." Eisenhower's choice was Air Marshal Sir Arthur Tedder, deputy supreme Allied commander and head of all Allied air operations.

On 15 January 1945 Tedder met with the Soviet premier. The wily Stalin said that even though there was no Soviet-Allied treaty it was in the self-interest of the Allies to ensure that the Soviet Union was not annihilated by the Nazis, just as it was in the self-interest of the Soviet Union to ensure the survival of the West in the struggle against Nazism.

Stalin was particularly concerned that the German communications system was such that it was an easy matter to move troops between the two fronts. Even now, Stalin said, the Germans must be moving forces from the west to the east, and although there was no specific mention of Dresden, it was clear to all that Wehrmacht men and matériel would have to pass through the Saxon city to reach the Eastern Front.

According to the Air Force Historical Office, "Tedder outlined to Stalin the 'application of the Allied air effort with particular reference to strategic bombing of communications as represented by oil targets, railroads and waterways.' There was also specific discussion of the problem that would face the Russians if the Germans attempted to shift forces from the West to the East and of the necessity of preventing this possibility."

• • •

The bad weather of January and February 1945 kept many of Bomber Command's planes grounded, but any break in the weather was seized upon by Harris, who had already begun to look farther east for targets.

Bomber Command had made several deep penetration raids, one as early as October 1940. The first was an unsuccessful effort to bomb the

Škoda arms works at Pilsen, in Czechoslovakia. Other small raids followed, but they were chiefly calling cards, part of the plan to force the Germans to scatter their antiaircraft defenses all over Europe. In April 1943 another attempt was made to destroy the Škoda works, but the bombers mistakenly bombed an asylum seven miles from the target. Other raids on the Škoda factory were equally unsuccessful.

Bomber Command had also ranged as far as Italy in 1943, bombing both Turin and Milan. These major northern Italian industrial cities were legitimate targets, but the most notable casualty of the raids was the famous Milanese opera house La Scala—not the primary target, the Fiat factories.

To the end, Harris believed wholeheartedly that his avowed plan to destroy all of the cities of the Reich was the surest way to end the war. But he now had to give way to Portal, who directly ordered him to commence attacks on the oil targets, raids that Speer would characterize as fatal blows to the German war machine.

The first Bomber Command raid on a major eastern German oil facility was at 'Leuna, near Leipzig, on 6–7 December 1944. This RAF raid was seven months after the first American raids on oil facilities in eastern Germany—the series of raids on 12 May that Speer said had decided the technological war.

But there were no further major British raid on oil targets until 14–15 January 1945, when Bomber Command returned to Leuna. This was partly because of the foul weather and partly because planes were diverted to pound the Germans who had broken out in the Ardennes.

However, directives from Portal or no, Bomber Harris never lost sight of his chief goal, as his detractors point out. On the night of 2–3 January he staged one of the great area raids of the war. Nuremberg—the city of the Meistersingers, with its two thousand medieval houses—was obliterated by over 500 Lancasters.

Harris was careful to satisfy Portal's demands, however, and the RAF resumed deep penetration raids into eastern Germany and western Czechoslovakia in search of oil targets. Pölitz, near Stettin, and Zeitz, near Leipzig, and Brüx, fifty-five miles from Prague, were all heavily bombed and largely destroyed. If there was any possibility of flying, Harris launched his bombers. But after the Pölitz raid on the night of 8–9 February, the weather was again uncooperative. Bomber Command mounted no more serious offensives until Dresden.

· · ·

The debate as to which policy was more effective—more-or-less blind bombing as practiced by the RAF or the much touted precision bombing of the Eighth Air Force—has raged since the bombing campaigns began. The British, under Bomber Harris, felt no reason to explain or apologize for their form of aerial warfare. The Americans, while taking the moral high ground (or so it seemed to many of their colleagues in the RAF), never returned with their bomb loads if they could not find the designated target. They simply bombed what they could find. If it was a city, so be it.

Great claims for American precision bombing were made during World War II. "Our bombers can drop a bomb in a pickle barrel!" trumpeted the Americans. "Of course we can," one airman wryly observed. "We just have to find the barrel."

Here was the crux of the problem: how to find the target and bomb it when the pilot and the bombardier could not see it. Neither the Americans nor the British ever came close to achieving pinpoint or precision bombing. Even the Norden bombsight, which has been much celebrated as having ushered in a new and more effective bombing policy, was accurate only in direct proportion to the visibility of the target on the ground.

Thus began the search for navigational systems that would provide a solution to the problem, and as each new one was unveiled it was hailed as the answer. But their drawbacks became apparent almost as soon as they were deployed.

The first was the system called Gee. Using this system the navigator relied on radio signals transmitted from a master station and two slave stations to plot his course. Theoretically, the plane's position was at the intersection of the lines on a special Gee chart. It was hoped that the device would be able to direct the planes to within a mile or so of the city to be bombed. Heretofore, only one in ten Bomber Command planes had bombed within five miles of the target.

The major drawback to Gee was that its range was only 350 to 400 miles. Further, once the frequencies had been worked out by the Germans it could be easily jammed. The limited range still put the cities of the Ruhr in reach, as well as many cities beyond. Although the Germans could devise jamming techniques—after all, they had used similar systems to bomb England—there would be at least a five-month window of opportunity.

Gee did not prove to be as effective as predicted. There were glitches in the transmission of the radio signals, and visual landmarks still were necessary to guide the bombers after Gee had brought them to the supposed target.

But the system was helpful in other ways. With the aid of Gee it was easier to concentrate the bomber streams, making them more defensible against night fighters. Even more important, the return flight home was no longer a nightmare that could end in fiery death or in the freezing waters of the English Channel or the North Sea, as these flights often did. The signals became stronger as the planes neared their home bases, making the landing fields easier to locate.

As predicted, by August 1942 the Germans were jamming the Gee frequencies, shortening its effective range by at least a hundred miles. But something new was already waiting in the wings: again, a device not unlike the system used so successfully by the Germans during the Blitz. This was Oboe, which sent radar signals from two ground stations to an aircraft and thus plotted its course and position. When the aircraft reached a preset position, the target, a signal was sent for it to unload the bombs.

The drawbacks of the Oboe system were obvious. Like Gee, the range was fairly short because of the curvature of the earth. And the bombers had to fly a steady course, with little or no deviation, which made it impossible for them to take evasive action when attacked by the German fighters or when they ran into heavy antiaircraft fire.

As Arthur Harris observed in his memoirs, the limitations of both

Gee and Oboe necessitated yet another change in strategy. Instead of hundreds of bombers finding the target individually, a few planes—Halifaxes, Lancasters, and, best of all, the new high-speed Mosquitoes—equipped with the latest navigation systems could lay out a path to the target, dropping aerial route-marker flares to guide the way. Once the target was located, marker aircraft dropped massive incendiary bombs, which showed the bomber fleets where to release their ordnance.

This elite group that was formed to lead the way was christened the Pathfinder Force, and if it was not quite the longed-for turning point for Bomber Command, its actions did indeed improve the accuracy of aerial bombardment and herald the imminent destruction of most of Germany's cities.

By early 1945 a yet more advanced navigation system, loran (long-range navigation), was made available to Bomber Command. The navigator was able to determine his position by locating the point where a ground wave and a sky wave intersected. The sky wave was not dependent on the curvature of the earth, since it was bounced off the ionosphere, and the ground wave had a much longer range than other systems, 600 to 900 miles. The loran system was employed by the Pathfinder Lancasters and the marker Mosquitoes for the first time on the Dresden raid.

Another step forward in actual bombing practice came with the introduction of H2S (called H2X by the Americans), a self-contained radar navigation system that could project an image of the ground below on a cathode-ray tube in the plane itself. It was, admittedly, a rough image of the terrain, but H2S did afford a view of the proposed target—assuming, of course, that the bomber stream was over the designated target.

· · ·

By the end of January 1945, with the Russians advancing rapidly in the east, the time seemed ripe for the revival of the plan known as Operation Thunderclap—a massive raid on Berlin. Bomber Command had not staged a major raid on the German capital since the disaster of 24–25 March 1944, when 72 bombers were lost, 8.9 percent of the total force.

The British Mosquito bombers had continued to take the war to the citizens of the German capital, and during one period, they attacked Berlin on thirty-six consecutive nights. These were not solely harassing raids. The plane, which could carry a 4,000-pound bomb, was capable of doing real damage, and one measure of its effectiveness is a telling entry in Joseph Goebbels's diary. "In the evening we have the regulation Mosquito raid on Berlin," he wrote. "During the night the cursed Englishmen return to Berlin with their Mosquitoes and deprive one of the few hours' sleep which one needs more than ever these days."

Large-scale bombardment of Berlin had been delegated to the Americans, who averaged one major daylight raid a month. No city was as well protected and thus more feared than the city known to the bomber crews as "the Big B." On 29 April 1944, the Americans lost 63 planes and another 432 were damaged out of a total effective force of 618 aircraft.

As the Germans withdrew from the west, the removal to the Fatherland of antiaircraft batteries was one of their highest priorities. The major cities were ringed with more and more of these deadly weapons. Thus the cities of Germany, in particular Berlin, became more, rather than less, dangerous as the Western Front contracted. In a series of raids throughout northern Germany on 6 August 1944, for example, 531 out of 929 effectives were damaged by enemy fighters or flak. In raids on 7 October 1944, over half of an effective force of 1,400 bombers was damaged and 40 were shot down.

■ ■ ■

Ten days after Tedder's meeting with Stalin, on 25 January 1945, the Joint Intelligence Sub-Committee of the War Cabinet had ready a proposal for closer Soviet-Allied cooperation on the Eastern Front. Entitled "Strategic Bombing in Relation to the Present Russian Offensive," the report recommended a four-day raid on Berlin in which 25,000 tons of bombs would be dropped on the German capital.

No one thought that this new version of Thunderclap would lead directly to surrender, but it was expected to generate such numbers of refugees fleeing from Berlin along with the millions fleeing the Russians that it would "create great confusion, interfere with the orderly movement of troops to the front, and hamper the German military and administrative machine." Further, the raid would "materially assist the Russians in the all important battle now raging on the Eastern Front and would justify temporary diversion from attacks against communications or indeed any targets other than oil plants or tank factories."

Churchill, in a 25 January meeting with Sir Archibald Sinclair, secretary of state for air, asked during a general discussion of the RAF what the plans were for "basting the Germans in their retreat from Breslau." The prime minister was concerned about the upcoming Yalta Conference, at which an important issue would be how the British and American air forces were planning to support the now-rapid Russian advance into the Third Reich.

The next day Portal told Sinclair that oil was still the number one priority. After that the RAF could assist in harassing the retreating German troops. This would move such actions up the list, above the previously decided targets, the jet-engine factories and the submarine yards.

After meeting with Portal, Sinclair replied to the prime minister. He recommended that the tactical air forces and not the heavy bombers be used to attack the Germans retreating from Breslau.

Sinclair felt that the heavy bombers should continue the attacks on the German oil industry. Such attacks, he pointed out, would benefit all the Allies, including the Russians. However, since attacking small targets depends very much on good weather and attacking large targets does not, he advocated the bombing of Berlin and other large east German cities such as Leipzig, Dresden, and Chemnitz.

All of these cities, Sinclair pointed out, were not just administrative centers but also the centers of vital rail and highway networks through which most of the enemy's men and matériel had to pass.

Churchill's response was immediate and Churchillian. "I did not ask you last night about plans for harrying the German retreat from Breslau," he testily wrote to Sinclair. "On the contrary, I asked whether Berlin, and no doubt other large cities in East Germany, should not now be considered especially attractive targets. I am glad that this is 'under consideration.' Pray report to me tomorrow what is going to be done."

Sinclair immediately called Bottomley about the matter, and the next day, 27 January, Bottomley wrote to Arthur Harris about Bomber Command attacking Berlin, Dresden, Chemnitz, and Leipzig.

Harris's biographer Dudley Saward was hardly a disinterested party—he worked closely with Harris throughout the war—but he is certainly right that the Dresden decision did not originate with Harris but at the highest levels of command, and Harris was provided with a paper trail to explain his actions, particularly in the final paragraph of Bottomley's message: The chief priority remained German oil production, but next in order came attacks on Berlin, Leipzig, and Dresden, designed to create chaos among the refugees that had flooded into those cities and to disrupt troop movements and reinforcements to, or retreat from, the Russian front.

Bottomley enclosed a copy of the 25 January Joint Intelligence Sub-Committee report, which he said had not yet been considered by the Chiefs of Staff. In his note, he said that while Portal did not feel that Thunderclap would be effective in Berlin, subject to the "overriding claims of oil and the other approved target systems, there should be one large attack on Berlin and related attacks on Dresden, Leipzig, Chemnitz, or any other cities where a severe blitz will not only cause confusion in the evacuation from the East but will also hamper the movement of troops from the West."

While the priorities (oil and other approved target systems) were to be observed, enough leeway was built in to satisfy everyone, and on 27 January Sinclair wrote reassuringly to Churchill. While oil would remain the chief priority, the Air Staff had put into effect plans to bomb Berlin, Dresden, Chemnitz, and Leipzig and other cities in the east where massive air raids would destroy roads and railways and thus disrupt or halt both the massive movements of civilians and any reinforcements from the Western front.

The next day, 28 January, Churchill acknowledged without comment the receipt of Sinclair's memorandum. That same day Portal, who was to accompany Churchill to Yalta, met with Bottomley and Spaatz to discuss the plans.

Everything was now in place for Thunderclap. When Churchill left for Yalta, via Malta, on 29 January, he was assured that his call for "basting the Germans in their retreat from Breslau" had been heeded by the air barons, and on 31 January, Bottomley sent a cable to Portal, in Malta, outlining for Churchill the "order of priorities for Strategic Air Forces."

The chief targets remained the synthetic oil plants. Next in order came the attacks on Berlin, Leipzig, and Dresden, designed to disrupt civilian evacuation and hamper all troop movement. Attacks on communications—rail lines, marshaling yards, highways, bridges, and the like—were third in importance.

The new jet planes were causing increasing anxiety in Bomber Command, and thus attacks on jet-aircraft plants and airfields and communications in southern Germany were added to the list.

Other targets (tank factories, submarine yards) were to be considered marginal, although these might be "substantial" since they constituted convenient tactical "filler" targets in those areas of priority oil targets when the primary target could not be attacked.

The report also included a directive that would turn out, in the event, to be used as evidence to support the accusations of Allied barbarity during the Dresden raid. The escort fighters were to attack all rail movement after their primary task of escorting the bombers had been carried out.

There was nothing unusual in this further assignment for the fighters, if it can be called an additional duty. A primary function of fighter planes was and remains the strafing of enemy troops and rail and road traffic. And since all rail lines in and out of Dresden paralleled streets and roads and ran through heavily built up areas, it was to be expected that civilians would be exposed to the fire from the American fighters.

With an eye toward Yalta, Bottomley concluded by pointing out that the Russians "may wish to know our intentions" concerning the targets as outlined and which lay just a few miles to the west of their lines.

Meanwhile, discussions continued between the Americans and the British about how best to support the Soviets. On 1 February 1945, "Strategic Bombing in Relation to the Present Russian Offensive" was promulgated by Air Marshal Sir Douglas Evill, vice chief of the air staff. Of particular interest was the following:

Evacuees from German and German-Occupied Provinces to the East of Berlin are streaming westward though Berlin itself and through Leipzig, Dresden and other cities in the East of Germany. The administrative problems involved in receiving the refugees and redistributing them are likely to be immense. The strain on the administration and upon communications must be considerably increased by the need for handling military reinforcements on their way to the Eastern Front. A series of heavy attacks by day and night upon these administrative and control centres is like to create considerable delays in the deployment of troops at the Front, and may well result in establishing a state of chaos in some or all of these centres. It is for these reasons that instructions have been issued for heavy scale attacks to be delivered on these centres at the earliest possible moment, in priority immediately after that of the important oil producers. The justification for the continuance of such attacks would be largely reduced if the enemy succeeded in stabilising his Eastern Front. Successful attacks of this nature delivered at once, however, my well prevent him from achieving this aim.

In other words, with the Russians moving rapidly westward, everything that could be done by Allied airpower to prevent reinforcements from the west must be done. Events were rapidly overtaking the planners. Something approaching a total breakdown might be brought about by day and night bombing of the eastern German cities that were already overwhelmed by the hundreds of thousands of refugees fleeing the Russian advance.

On this same day, 1 February, the Russians were only fifty miles from Berlin and the capital was declared a fortress city. It was to be defended to the death.

This air staff note, code-named Fleece 75, was sent out to the Chiefs of Staff at Malta on 2 February. This message was to be used to coordi-

nate the Allied air offensive with the Russian ground offensive on the
Eastern Front. The bombing priorities were listed as follows:

1. Oil
2. Communications—particularly "focal points of
   communication in the evacuation areas behind the Eastern
   Front, namely Berlin, Leipzig, Dresden, and Chemnitz or
   similar areas"
3. Tank factories
4. Jet fighter production
5. U-boat construction and assembly

Kuter, who in spite of his two-star rank and relative youth had been
deputized by Arnold to represent him at Malta and Yalta, had already
cabled acting air force commander Barney Giles from Malta, listing the
targets in order of priority as agreed to by Portal, Bottomley, and Spaatz.
The second component of the target list was described a bit more fully,
however: "Attack of Berlin, Leipzig, Dresden and associated cities where
heavy attack will cause great confusion in civil population from East and
hamper movement of reinforcements from other fronts will be next in
order of priority for air forces operating from the United Kingdom."

Also on 2 February, in a message to Spaatz marked "Top Secret—Personal," Major General F. L. Anderson, Spaatz's personal representative
at Malta, told his boss that General Marshall wanted to be sure that no
Russians were inadvertently attacked by American bombers on the missions to eastern Europe. In addition, said Anderson, Marshall had suggested that "in conjunction with our attacks on Berlin and associated
cities attacks on Munich would probably be of great benefit because it
would show the people that are being evacuated to Munich that there is
no hope. Perhaps the Fifteenth Air Force could take this on in conjunction with the Eighth's attacks on Berlin."

Spaatz immediately sent a message to Generals Twining and Eaker
of the Fifteenth Air Force, informing them that the British were continuing their nightly Mosquito raids on Berlin and that Bomber Command
planned to attack Leipzig and Dresden. The Eighth would attack Berlin

when weather permitted. The Fifteenth, meanwhile, was "to attack [Munich] when tactical and other conditions are appropriate and within your transportation priority."

This promised massive strike against Berlin was scheduled by the Eighth Air Force for the afternoon of 2 February, but it was scrubbed because of the weather. If the weather had been clear some 120 miles to the southeast in Saxony, the entire Dresden controversy would perhaps have never engaged the attention of military historians to quite the degree it has. For Dresden was an alternate target of the planned thousand-bomber raid by the Eighth Air Force on 2 February. There would have been massive destruction to be sure, but the city would have been spared the firestorm.

The next day, 3 February, the weather was more cooperative, and Carl Spaatz, who had for the most part stuck to the policy of bombing oil targets and military installations, did Bomber Harris one better in the category of area bombing. Although the target was officially categorized as "marshalling yards," the purpose of the raid was to create maximum chaos in Berlin, which was overrun with refugees from the east. More than 1,000 B-17s, with 600 P-51 escorts, dropped 2,267 tons of bombs on the center of the city.

· · ·

The thousand-bomber American raid on Berlin was the heaviest raid of the war on the German capital by either the RAF or the U.S. Army Air Force. A vast swath of the city was destroyed, including Hitler's headquarters.

But oil-production facilities were not forgotten on this day by the Americans. Another 434 B-24s were sent against the oil refineries at Magdeburg. Two-thirds of the planes failed to find the oil targets, but with the aid of H2X radar they located the city and emptied their bomb loads blindly through the cloud cover.

On 5 February, Spaatz cabled Kuter in Yalta: "All out effort will be placed against targets mentioned whenever weather conditions permit. Necessity for liaison party with various Russian Armies becomes increasingly apparent. On recent attack in Berlin our fighters were practically over Russian lines and destroyed a number of German airplanes taking off from an airdrome east of Berlin."

The Eighth returned to its appointed rounds, the oil plan, on 6 February, with a massive raid directed at production facilities at Lützkendorf, Böhlen, and Magdeburg. The expected good weather did not materialize, and the bombers were unable to find the primary targets. The secondary targets and targets of opportunity were obscured as well, and the raids were conducted using H2X. Hardest hit were Chemnitz and Magdeburg.

Although the Yalta Conference was being convened to plan for a postwar Europe, the date of the end of the war was by no means certain. Indeed, Spaatz wrote to Arnold on 7 January, "Our estimate of the situation concerning the whole German war proposition does not lead up to the conclusion that German strength will crack in the near future."

The Germans had pulled one great surprise with the Ardennes offensive; and Allied leaders, with good reason, were much concerned about two new German weapons: the snorkel U-boat and the jet fighter.

The snorkel device allowed the submarine to bring in and exhaust air without surfacing, which made it far less vulnerable to detection and greatly increased its range. The new U-boats were also faster and could be turned out relatively quickly. If sufficient quantities could be produced, the transatlantic shipping lanes would again be at risk and the end of the war delayed by many months.

The Me 262 jet fighters were appearing in increasing numbers and were having some success against Eighth Air Force bombers. They were clearly a formidable weapon. Moreover, unlike the Fw 190s and the Me 109, which required high-grade aviation fuel, the Me 262 burned low-grade fuels such as kerosene, which was in ample supply.

Therefore, Spaatz began to argue in January 1945 that the heavy bombers should return to their primary role of strategic bombing and that the bombing of jet-aircraft production facilities be accorded as much importance as other targets—in particular, oil. Eisenhower, who still very much had the German breakout in the Ardennes on his mind, felt that the bombers should continue to support the ground troops at this time. Spaatz, with the help of Doolittle and Bedell Smith, had his way, and Eisenhower reluctantly agreed.

· · ·

At Malta, there surfaced one of those plans that are the bane of serious military strategists. Although unlikely to work, they take up much energy and time but must be attended to for political reasons. This one, however, was first proposed by Carl Spaatz, a serious military strategist indeed.

The Americans floated the idea of flying radio-controlled, unmanned "war-weary" bombers loaded with 20,000 pounds of high explosives into industrial targets (that is, cities) in Germany. This was actually a dusted-off plan, called Aphrodite or Weary Willie, that Spaatz had devised in June 1944 as part of the Crossbow campaign against the V-1 and V-2 sites.

At one test of such a weapon, at Shoeburyness, a pilotless B-17 carrying 20,000 pounds of Minol-2, or Torpex, was crashed. It showed that a B-17 so loaded with high explosives could do nine to twelve and a half times the damage of a 4,000-pound bomb. If it was crashed into a built-up location, the damage would be catastrophic, destroying everything within a radius of 145 yards—a total area of 66,000 square yards, or more than 13.5 acres.

Both the air force and the U.S. Navy had been involved in testing and launching several missions against various sites on the Continent, using worn-out B-17s and B-24s. A pilot and copilot would get the plane airborne, set the remote controls, and bail out. Escort aircraft would then guide the plane by remote control to the target.

A half dozen or so Aphrodite missions using war-weary planes took place in 1944, but none was successful and several of the pilots were killed, most notably a navy lieutenant named Joseph P. Kennedy Jr., the son of the former ambassador and the older brother of the future president. He took off in a navy B-24 loaded with 21,000 pounds of high explosives on 12 August 1944. Before he and his copilot could turn the plane over to the two control planes that would guide it to the target, a V-2 launch site in France, and bail out, the bomber exploded.

At Malta, Aphrodite was scuttled by the British, who were still being bombarded by the V-weapons and who worried that the Weary Willies might embolden the Germans to use their own war-weary bombers to stage reprisal raids against British cities, particularly London.

The plan would not die, however, and its most important advocate turned out to be the American commander in chief himself, Franklin Roosevelt. On 29 March, the president cabled Churchill that his Chiefs of Staff had assured him that technological advances in remote control would make the planes more accurate, thus presumably sparing civilians.

Further, said the president, "many lucrative targets in the industrial areas in Germany can be leveled and the German war effort correspondingly weakened." The Germans, said Roosevelt, did not need the impetus of drone bombers filled with high explosives to attack England. "In addition," he mused, "combat experience with this type of weapon on the Continent will make possible the most effective use of this type of weapon in the battle against the highly concentrated areas of the Japanese homeland."

Churchill felt he had to refer Roosevelt's cable to the British Chiefs of Staff for a decision, or so he said. He did not respond until 14 April 1945, by which time Roosevelt, who had died suddenly, had been succeeded by Harry S. Truman. The message is pure Winston Churchill.

"If the United States military authorities really consider this practice necessary to bring about the end of the German war we will not dissent," he said. However, he pointed out that the war situation had turned decidedly in favor of the Allies and "these great explosions in German cities" no longer had their former importance.

And the retaliatory argument was still strong with the British. As the prime minister said, if the Germans also had a number of "war-weary bombers that could make the distance, London is the obvious and indeed the only target, and even a few very big explosions in London would be a very great disappointment to the people."

He reminded Truman that so far 1 in 131 Londoners had already died in air attacks, a figure higher than that of any other locality on the Allied side. Presumably, he was not counting the Soviet Union.

Churchill closed by saying, "Having put the facts before you I leave the decisions entirely in the hands of your military advisers, and we shall make no complaint if misfortune comes to us in consequence."

The Weary Willie concept compared favorably, if one can use that word, with a brainstorm of Lord Selbourne, of the Ministry of Economic Warfare. On 28 July 1944 he bypassed all chains of command and wrote directly to Eisenhower. He recommended that fifty Lancasters be sent to the Ruhr that week to drop a half million incendiary devices known as the Braddock. This was an extremely small bomb attached to a card that served as a parachute. Printed on the card were directions in eleven languages as to how to use it. All the finder had to do was plant the bomb in some flammable place and press a red button. The would-be saboteur then had half an hour to escape before the bomb went off and everything went up in flames. The idea was that slave laborers and left-wing opponents of the Nazi regime, as well as hundreds of thousands of ordinary Germans who were disillusioned by the Nazis and the Reich's declining military fortunes, would use the small firebombs to commit wholesale sabotage and help bring down the regime.

Eisenhower preferred to drop real bombs rather than Braddocks and turned down the idea, but the supreme commander did leave the door open if the time ever became ripe.

Selbourne tartly commented, "This is again 'jam tomorrow.' " He also made no attempt to hide his scorn for "certain distinguished officers who have never concealed their disbelief in 'BRADDOCK.' "

But in February 1945, the Braddock plan was dusted off and given a try. There were no reports of arson or sabotage, although the police chief of Mannheim did note that some of the incendiaries had been dropped in his area and warned about their danger to "children at play." He also said that anyone who let one fall into the hands of foreigners or did not report it to the police would be punished.

. . .

At Yalta, General Aleksei I. Antonov, chief of staff of the Soviet army, briefed the American president, the British prime minister, and their staffs on the situation on the Eastern Front and the Russian operational plans for the succeeding months.

After a long and discursive account of the ground campaign, Antonov turned to the question of the air war in the east and how the Allies could best support the advancing Soviet armies. He asked the British and Americans "in particular to paralyze the junctions of Berlin and Leipzig."

The Russians were naturally keen to have Allied air support, but they were equally anxious to avoid friendly fire as their troops moved westward into Germany. While the accuracy of the bombers had marginally increased, no one believed that lines of troops 25,000 feet below heavy cloud cover were not in great danger of being wiped out unless protected by a fairly wide safety zone.

Now, with the Soviet troops so close to the target cities, a so-called bomb line would have to be created to protect Antonov's troops from being killed by errant bombs from the British and American planes, which could in just a matter of minutes stray over the Soviet advance lines.

The Americans, British, and Soviets agreed on the bomb line, and the operational date set for it to go into effect was 8 February. This limit line or prohibition zone would run from Stettin to Berlin to Dresden and on to Pardubitce, Brno, Vienna, Maribor, and Zagreb. All of these points were to be "inclusive to the Allied Strategic Air Forces." The line also extended to Sarajevo, Pécs, the eastern border of Albania, and the southern border of Bulgaria.

"Inclusive" meant, of course, that all of these cities were to be considered suitable bomb targets. The line was to be adjusted as the Soviets moved west, and the Allies could bomb in the east in exceptional circumstances—but with not less than twenty-four hours' notice to the Soviets. The zone as refined was to be sixty kilometers in advance of the forward troops of the Soviet army, about thirty-five miles.

The limit-line agreement was signed by Sir Charles Portal, marshal of the Royal Air Force, S. A. Khudyakov, marshal of aviation of the Red Army, and Laurence S. Kuter, major general of the U.S. Army Air Forces. The two-star was not only very young, but he was outranked by three full grades by most of the men he had to deal with it at Malta and Yalta, and he was made painfully aware of it. "Without you," he wrote to Hap Arnold, "we are just tolerated from bottom to *top.*"

But he rose to the occasion. He did, after all, have the backing of Arnold, a five-star general who could hold his own with any military grandee from Great Britain or the Soviet Union. Then, too, there was the overwhelming might of the American air arm behind Kuter. Thus he did not hesitate to speak his mind.

On 8 February, Khudyakov sent along the agreement to Kuter "as confirmed by the Soviet High Command." Kuter quickly realized that there were changes "concerning the announcement of the limiting line, and the agreement required to operations by the British and U.S. Army Air Forces to the east of the designated line." He rejected the changes and informed Marshal Khudyakov that "the U.S. Air Forces will continue to operate under the arrangements in effect prior to the 6th of February 1945." He pointedly concluded, "This represents the views of the United States Chiefs of Staff."

Also on 8 February, Major General S. P. Spalding, acting chief of the U.S. military mission in Moscow, sent to Major General H. V. Slavin, assistant chief of staff of the Red Army, "a list of strategic targets subject to bombardment by the 8th Air Force."

Oil still headed the list, but the communications targets were second. Of these, Berlin was first, Leipzig was second, and Dresden was third. It thus seems clear that Dresden was considered to be if not the equal of Berlin and Leipzig, an important, even vital, military target. The only remaining question was how soon Thunderclap or some variant could be put into effect. In the event, it was only a matter of a few days.

As the earlier Thunderclap report put it, "Immense devastation could be produced if the entire attack was concentrated on single big town other than Berlin and the effect would be especially great if the town was one hitherto relatively undamaged."

Heavy cloud cover, snow, and winter storms hampered both the British and the Americans for the ten days after the large American raid on Berlin on 3 February, although both Bomber Command and the Eighth Air Force had two notable successes. The Americans staged a massive raid on Chemnitz, just forty-five miles from Dresden, and the

British put the synthetic oil plant at Pölitz, near Hamburg, permanently out of commission.

Then the weather picture changed. Meteorologists reported that favorable conditions beginning on 13 February might finally ensure that the long-planned triple blow against a large German city—Thunderclap—might be possible at last.

Spaatz had already notified the American military mission in Moscow that Berlin, Leipzig, Chemnitz, and Dresden were on the priority list of communications targets. Berlin had already been devastated by the Eighth Air Force on 3 February and would not be bombed again by the Americans until two weeks after Spaatz cabled the Russians his intentions. Leipzig had also suffered heavy raids and was bombed hardly at all for the remainder of the war by either the Eighth Air Force or Bomber Command. And Bomber Command would not revisit Chemnitz, albeit with a massive raid, until early March 1945.

Of the cities mentioned by Spaatz, only Dresden would appear to be a serious target in mid-February 1945. Therefore, on 12 February, he cabled the American military mission that "weather permitting, Eighth Air Force will attack Dresden Marshalling Yard on 13 February with a force of 1,200 to 1,400 bomber planes." The Americans would lead off with a massive daylight raid at midday and the British would follow it up that night with two more assaults, about three hours apart. The message was passed on to the Russians.

· · ·

The picture-book capital of Saxony, which was relatively untouched by the ravages of a war that was now in its sixth year, would now join its sister cities of the Third Reich as a prime target of Allied airpower. The narrow streets, the flammable ancient buildings, and the enormous congestion caused by half a million refugees had created a potential bonfire on the Elbe that was waiting to be lit.

CHAPTER SEVEN

THE TARGET

Florence on
the Elbe

One of Germany's grandest cities had the most humble of beginnings. Dresden began life in the Middle Ages as a Slav fishing settlement. The fishermen founded their little village, originally known as Drezdany—meaning "forest dwellers on the plain"—on the left bank of the Elbe at a natural crossing of the river.

The first historical mention of Dresden is in a document dated 31 March 1206, signed by Heinrich, margrave of Meissen. Another document, dating from 1216, refers to Dresden as a *civitas*, a town.

On the right bank, or the north shore, of the Elbe another settlement was founded. It became somewhat confusingly known as Altendresden, perhaps signifying that it was even older. A wooden bridge was soon built across the river to link the two settlements, but in 1287 it was replaced with a stone bridge, which became something of a medieval tourist attraction.

Altendresden, which did not receive a charter until 1403, burned to the ground in 1491, and the newly built town became known as the Neustadt. The original settlement across the river then became known as the Altstadt. The two separate towns became one in the sixteenth century.

Dresden was ruled not by kings but by electors—so called because they were one of the seven rulers entitled to elect the Holy Roman Emperor. Two of the electors, through treaties, war, and outright bribery, served simultaneously as elector of Saxony and king of Poland. The electors were, in the main, devoted to the arts and sciences, and through their patronage Dresden became a city unrivaled for art and culture in Germany and, indeed, throughout much of Europe.

Elector Friedrich the Wise, who ruled from 1486 until 1525, was a true Renaissance man. Not only did he found the University of Wittenberg, he earned everlasting fame as the protector and patron of Martin Luther. Many of Friedrich's successors continued the Saxon tradition of humanism and support for the arts.

Moritz, called the savior of Protestantism, was also a great patron of the arts. His lasting contribution was the founding, in 1547, of the court orchestra that is today the world-renowned Dresden Staatskapelle.

August, who became elector in 1553, was the first of the electors to begin to amass the collections that would make the city a cultural mecca. He began the great collection of books and manuscripts that in time would become the Sächsiche Landesbibliothek, the Saxon State Library.

But August had other interests as well. He collected lavish examples of the jeweler's, goldsmith's, and silversmith's art. This collection eventually grew so large that it was necessary to house it in a series of vaulted rooms in the *Schloss,* the royal residence. In time, the collection became world famous as the Grünes Gewölbe, the Green Vault. August also started the royal picture collection. Thus, by the end of the sixteenth century, Dresden was already the envy of Europe for its collections of books, paintings, manuscripts, and decorative objects.

Succeeding electors added to their patrimony, but it was Augustus II, called Augustus the Strong (1670–1733), who ushered in what became known as Dresden's Augustan age. Although it spanned less than a hundred years, it imparted to Dresden the look and reputation that has endured to the present day.

For centuries, Germany was ridden with princes who vied with one another to have a personal Versailles, complete with ballet, theater, and even the occasional harem. These petty princes ruled supreme in their small worlds, with little regard for the common people. As historian

Robert B. Asprey so aptly put it, Europe "belonged largely to emperors, kings, nobles, and priests. They made war as they made love: Scarcely one affair ended before another began."

Augustus resembled his fellow nobles in many respects. German historian Leopold von Ranke, in his *Memoirs of the House of Brandenburg and History of Prussia*, said that Augustus went "from pleasure to pleasure, without the least regard to duty or to dignity." The king, said von Ranke, "delighted in a mixture of power and licentiousness." Dresden was a "voluptuous court in which the relations of the sexes were emancipated from all restraint and decorum."

Augustus was, indeed, a man of great appetites. He allegedly fathered three hundred children, one of whom, by one of his mistresses, Aurora von Königsmark, was the celebrated French soldier the maréchal de Saxe.

He was not, however, just a voluptuary. His many additions to the royal picture collection were of the finest quality, as were his acquisitions of sculptures, porcelains, books, and manuscripts. Augustus was also a patron of music and theater. Under this elector of Saxony and king of Poland, Dresden was the most glittering court in Germany, and in Europe second only to Versailles.

Augustus the Strong also saw one of his passions—the collection of porcelains—translate into an economic boon for his kingdom. The process for making porcelain had been known in China for over a thousand years, but no one in the West had been able to unravel the secret of its manufacture.

The mystery was solved in 1708 by the Dresden alchemist Johann Friedrich Böttger. The technique for making porcelain was soon wedded to the Saxon penchant for the fanciful, and one of the major industries of Saxony, indeed of Germany, was born. Figurines, dinner services, vases, and all sorts of decorative pieces in the most ornate and whimsical shapes began to appear from the royal porcelain works.

Although porcelain and fine china are inextricably linked in the popular mind with Dresden, in 1710 the Royal Saxon Porcelain Manufactory was moved nine miles down the Elbe, to the Albrechtsburg, the medieval fortress castle overlooking Meissen.

Augustus the Strong died in 1733. "I have not at present strength to name my many and great sins," he told his confessor.

Augustus's son and heir, Augustus III (1696–1763), who was also King Frederick-Augustus II of Poland, spent his thirty-year reign in Dresden, content to let Count Heinrich von Brühl, the prime minister who had served his father, run the affairs of state. The elector's interests lay elsewhere.

In January 1742, Frederick the Great came to Dresden to persuade Augustus to join him against Austria during the First Silesian War. Augustus did not join the meeting until it was well under way and, according to Frederick "answered yes to everything with an air of conviction mixed with a look of boredom."

Diplomacy was not on Augustus's mind. The Saxon was anxious to get to the opera, and the overture was about to begin. Frederick was also a music lover, but war was an even greater passion. "Ten kingdoms to conquer would not keep the King of Poland one minute longer," sniffed the Prussian.

Augustus III may have slighted politics and diplomacy, but such cannot be said about his artistic endeavors. Under his aegis, the royal picture collection grew into that assemblage of paintings, drawings, and sculpture that ranks among the finest in the world and is the reason that Dresden became a primary destination for art lovers.

The centerpiece of the collection, *The Sistine Madonna*, Raphael's most famous work, was acquired by Augustus in 1754. In addition, there were many of the greatest paintings of the greatest masters: Titian, Correggio, Veronese, Giorgione, Tintoretto, Poussin, Watteau, Lorrain, Carracci, Rubens, Van Dyck, Vermeer, Botticelli, Caravaggio, Tiepolo, Velázquez, Zurbarán, Murillo, Dürer, Holbein the Younger, Cranach the Elder, van Eyck, and Rembrandt. Augustus III appointed Bernardo Bellotto the court painter in 1747. This nephew and student of Canaletto's produced many fine views of the city in the style of his famous uncle, and fourteen of them were installed in the Gemäldegalerie at the Zwinger.

Count von Brühl's diplomacy and Augustus's lack of interest in diplomatic affairs eventually brought great suffering and destruction to

Dresden. In the Seven Years' War, Saxony allied itself with the wrong side, and its erstwhile ally Frederick was merciless.

Augustus III and Brühl fled to Warsaw after the defeat of the Saxon army at Pirna in 1756. When they returned to Dresden after the cessation of hostilities in February 1763, two-thirds of their city lay in ruins. The Prussian cannons had done their work well, and what was left of the fortifications was dismantled.

The king and his minister were both broken by the defeat of Saxony and the humiliations they suffered at the hands of Frederick, and they died within weeks of each other in October 1763. The brief but glittering Augustan age was at an end, and Dresden was no longer the capital of an important German political entity. Prussia was now the great German power and would remain so.

Dresden did regain its importance as a cultural and artistic center, however. Subsequent rulers repaired the ravages of warfare, and once again Dresden beguiled the visitor with its dazzling assemblage of the baroque, rococo, neoclassical, and German Renaissance, which blended into a startlingly beautiful cityscape and served as architectural stage set before which all civic activities were played out.

The Brühlsche Terrasse, the esplanade above the Elbe in the Altstadt, had been a special place for Dresdeners since 1738, when it was laid out along the former ramparts in front of his palace by Brühl, then at the height of his powers as prime minister. Celebrated as the "balcony of Europe," it afforded a sweeping view of the river and the grand buildings on the opposite shore, the most impressive and recognizable being the Japanisches Palais, so called because of its upturned roof corners, reminiscent of Japanese temple architecture.

Built in 1715 to house the royal porcelain collection, the Japanese Palace became, in 1786, the Royal Library, the repository for hundreds of rare medieval illuminated manuscripts: the works of Martin Luther (including his German translation of the Bible), illustrated works by Albrecht Dürer and Lucas Cranach, Persian and Chinese illuminations, a thirteenth-century Jewish holy day prayer book, and, of course, the Dresden Codex, one of only three extant Mayan manuscripts. Other treasures included two sections of Johann Sebastian Bach's great Mass in

B Minor, the Kyrie, and Gloria. Bach enclosed the music in a letter of 27 July 1733 to Augustus III that was a petition for the position of court composer. He was turned down because he was a Protestant.

Near the Japanese Palace stood a more utilitarian circular building just as dear to the fun-loving Saxons as its more imposing cousin. This was the Zirkusgebäude, the amphitheater on the Carolaplatz that was the home of a Dresden institution, the Sarrasani Circus.

Not far away, also in the Neustadt but visible from the Altstadt, across the river, stood, as it had since 1736, the *Goldener Reiter,* the gilded equestrian statue of Augustus the Strong—Dresden's greatest ruler.

· · ·

Behind the Brühlsche Terrasse lay the Altstadt, or the Old City, that assemblage of baroque and German Renaissance buildings and parks that had so impressed visitors for over two hundred years.

Among these buildings, the most immediately recognizable was the Frauenkirche, the Church of Our Lady. Dresden was overwhelmingly Lutheran, and although the Dresdeners were always loyal to the electors, they had never accepted the Augustuses' conversion to Roman Catholicism, which they had done in order to gain the Polish throne. The church, it was said, was erected by the Dresden town council only three hundred meters from the Royal Palace as a monumental Lutheran rebuke.

Construction of the Frauenkirche began in August 1726 and the church was dedicated in 1734, although it was not finally completed until 1743, five years after the death of its architect, the German baroque master Georg Bähr. On 1 December 1736, Bach gave a two-hour organ recital there with much of the royal court in attendance.

The Frauenkirche at once became the most famous building in the city and arguably the most important example of eighteenth-century Protestant ecclesiastical architecture in the world. Its height was 312 feet from the base to the top of the lantern, and some four thousand worshippers could gather inside what became known as the "Stone Bell" because of its distinctive shape.

Augustus III, to appease his Catholic subjects, rose to the Protestant challenge of the Frauenkirche. In 1738 he commissioned the Italian Gaetano Chiaveri to build the enormous Katholische Hofkirche, the largest Catholic cathedral in Saxony, on a site adjacent to the Royal Palace.

Dresden's oldest church, the Kreuzkirche, just a few streets farther on, was founded about 1200. It became a Lutheran church during the Reformation and the official church of the court when the electors embraced Protestantism. In 1760, during the Seven Years' War, it was destroyed by Frederick the Great's artillery and was rebuilt in the baroque style.

The fourth of the great churches of Dresden was the Sophienkirche, which also adjoined the Royal Palace. Like the Kreuzkirche it was originally a medieval Roman Catholic church, but with the Reformation it too became a Lutheran church. Johann Sebastian Bach's eldest son, Wilhelm Friedmann Bach, was the organist at the Sophienkirche, and his father gave a concert at the church on 14 September 1731. As a Dresden periodical reported, the great master performed "in the presence of all the Court musicians and virtuosos."

The Royal Palace, or *Schloss*, in its various forms, was home to the rulers of Saxony from the Middle Ages until 1918. Immediately adjacent to the *Schloss* and connected by a covered passage, Augustus the Strong built the luxurious Taschenberg Palace for his mistress Constantia, the Countess Cosel.

The Royal Palace faced one of the most beautiful urban complexes in the world: the Theaterplatz. Around this massive square were arranged not only the Royal Palace and the cathedral but also the Semper Opera House, the luxurious Hotel Bellevue and its gardens on the Elbe, and the great museum complex called the Zwinger. Particularly at night, the Theaterplatz presented a glittering array of water, light, and architectural exuberance unmatched anywhere.

Few places bear a name that so belies their purpose and splendor as the Zwinger. The vast ornate complex is so called because it was built on the outer court of the medieval fortress that had stood on the site and also was the site of the royal kennels. Matthäus Daniel Pöppelmann was commissioned by Augustus II to build an orangery, which would wrap around a racecourse and festival site for the court. But the brilliant architect soon won over the king to a more ambitious design. Between 1711 and 1722 Pöppelmann, who was heavily influenced by his travels in Italy, translated his designs into one of the greatest examples of the German baroque.

He enclosed an immense courtyard with carved stone-and-glass one-story galleries and two-story pavilions of the most exquisite refinement. Every cornice, pilaster, and column was covered with nymphs, cherubim, seashells, and flowers. Hundreds of statues from the studio of the Bavarian master Balthasar Permoser adorned the ramparts, stairways, and columns.

In this splendid group of buildings, which Sir Nikolaus Pevsner called "the product of an inexhaustible creative power," Augustus installed his collection of paintings.

The architect most associated with Dresden, not excluding those masters of the baroque Pöppelmann and Bähr, is Gottfried Semper, who was a professor of architecture at Dresden and the court architect from 1843 until 1849. It was Semper who completed Pöppelmann's grand design for the Zwinger. The northeast side of the compound remained open to the Theaterplatz and the riverfront until it was enclosed by Semper's Renaissance-style picture gallery.

But neither the Hofkirche nor the Zwinger dominates the Theaterplatz. That honor goes to the monumental Semper Oper, the home of the Sächsische Staatsoper. Semper's first opera house burned in 1869, but his son Manfred, who was designated to rebuild it, used plans drawn by his father for the new building. The rebuilt house, a grand neo-Renaissance structure, opened in 1878.

The Semper Opera House, in its several incarnations, played host to some of the world's greatest composers and artists—many of whom were resident in Dresden. The post of *Hofkappelmeister*, or conductor, which entailed oversight of both the opera and the orchestra, the Staatskapelle, was held at various times by Heinrich Schütz, Carl Maria von Weber, and Richard Wagner. In addition, Hans von Bülow, Johannes Brahms, and Richard Strauss had close associations with the Semper.

Although Johann Sebastian Bach did not get the longed-for post, he gave numerous recitals in the Saxon capital, and one of his most celebrated works, *The Goldberg Variations,* was commissioned by the Russian ambassador to the Saxon court, Count Keyserlingk, and first performed at the Russian embassy in Dresden.

Bach's great contemporary Antonio Vivaldi also spent time in Dresden, where he produced several works for patrons. Bach, an admirer of the Italian virtuoso, transposed for other instruments some of the Vivaldi concertos.

Wagner's *Rienzi, The Flying Dutchman,* and *Tannhäuser* had their world premieres at the Semper. His next work, *Lohengrin,* was written in Dresden but did not premiere there because of the Revolution of 1849. Dresden also was the birthplace of *Der Ring des Nibelungen* and *Die Meistersinger von Nürnberg.* Wagner began to sketch out the great tetralogy as well as his comic masterpiece while he was in residence in the city, and the composer conducted the premiere of his *Love Feast of the Apostles* at the Frauenkirche in July 1843.

Robert Schumann did not fare as well in the city as his counterparts. The mentally troubled composer eked out a living as a poorly paid choir director. He did record an interesting historical footnote for posterity. While composing the song "Des Sennen Abschied" ("The Cowherd's Farewell"), he was interrupted by the beginning of the Revolution of 1849. The manuscript of the piece, which is in the Dresden State Library, has the notation "interrupted by the alarm bells on May 3, 1849."

A German Requiem, which established Brahms as a great new voice in music, was first presented in Dresden in 1868. And an acolyte of Brahms's—Richard Strauss—would become the leading German composer of the twentieth century.

Strauss had a lifelong affection for Dresden, and the premieres of nine of his operas were held at the State Opera, beginning with *Salome* in 1905 and ending with *Capriccio* in 1942. During rehearsals he shuttled back and forth across the Theaterplatz between the Semper Oper and the Hotel Bellevue, where he lived during rehearsals.

Other great composers who lived and worked for a time in Dresden were Sergei Rachmaninoff, Paul Hindemith, and Ferruccio Busoni.

Hindemith's *Mörder, Hoffnung der Frauen, Das Nusch-Nuschi,* and *Cardillac* and Busoni's *Doktor Faust* were all staged first at the Semper.

· · ·

The two giants of German literature, Friedrich Schiller and Johann Wolfgang von Goethe, were frequent visitors to Dresden. It was Goethe's close friend and mentor, the philosopher-theologian Johann Gottfried von Herder, who first compared Dresden to Florence. His appellation "Florence on the Elbe" was happily expropriated, with some justification, by the Dresdeners. Schiller wrote much of *Don Carlos* in the summerhouse of the villa of friends in Loschwitz.

Heinrich von Kleist lived in Dresden from 1807 to 1809, and novelist and critic Ludwig Tieck lived there twice, the second time from 1819 to 1841. And the greatest musical romantic of the nineteenth century, Frédéric Chopin, lived in a flat on the Seestrasse in 1835.

But perhaps the works that most evoke the Romantic era in Dresden are the lush, moody, darkly mysterious paintings of Carl Gustav Carus, Caspar David Friedrich, Johan Christian Dahl, and Adrian Ludwig Richter. Friedrich's *Two Men Contemplating the Moon* and Richter's *The Crossing of the Elbe at the Schreckenstein* are the visual definition of the term and the era.

As the Romantics rebelled against eighteenth-century classicism, so did the movement called Die Brücke rebel against nineteenth-century forms. This short-lived advance guard of German Expressionism, which was born in Dresden in 1905, drew its name from the Augustusbrücke, the bridge that spans the Elbe near the Academy of Fine Arts, where many of its practitioners either studied or taught.

Their works featured deformed nature, landscapes, and figures; and their brilliant, even garish colors created a sensation. The group eventually comprised Ernst Ludwig Kirchner, Karl Schmidt-Rottluff, Erich Heckel, Emil Nolde, and Max Pechstein. Die Brücke lasted only until 1913, but its influence was felt throughout the twentieth century.

The Expressionist Oskar Kokoschka taught at the academy from 1919 to 1924, and Otto Dix, a leading figure in the Neue Sachlichkeit movement, was a student there and later a teacher.

• • •

Dresden, of course, was not alone among German cities as a bastion of civilization and high culture. It was not alone when, like other areas during the turmoil of the Weimar Republic, it embraced National Socialism and its promise of social order and German rebirth. Nor was it alone in ignoring the dark side of the Nazi movement. Indeed, Dresden firmly embraced National Socialism, and Hitler, whenever he visited the city, was received rapturously by the populace.

The Dresdeners, like most of their countrymen, endorsed the restrictive laws and the curbs on their own liberties, and many of them also endorsed the racial laws that curtailed the rights of the Jews.

• • •

Jews are first recorded in Dresden in the early fourteenth century, and their history was a replication of that of all the Jews of Europe and England. The Dresden Jewish community was destroyed during the Black Death persecutions of 1349. But by 1375, Jews were again resident in Dresden, and they had even built a synagogue. This community lasted only until 1430, however; it fell victim to another pogrom and was expelled.

There is no further mention of Jews in Dresden until the 1690s, when Augustus the Strong's lust for the Polish crown and the money needed to fulfill his dream overrode any religious prejudice. Had he not himself cast aside Protestantism for Catholicism to gain the crown?

He turned to Jewish bankers, who were eager to help the elector. Augustus, partially out of gratitude but mainly because he had further need of their favors, allowed a small group of Jews to settle in Dresden in 1708—about a hundred in all.

In Bismarck's empire, Jews were allowed to attend the German universities and live in previously forbidden areas, and this emancipation led to more rapid growth in the Jewish population and to assimilation, although there were still only 23,000 Jews in all of Saxony in 1925—less than one-half of 1 percent of the total population. Indeed the number of Jews in all of Germany was never more than 1 percent of the population.

When Adolf Hitler came to power on 30 January 1933, he immediately moved to put into place the racial program he had expounded since he'd founded the Nazi Party and had so forcefully advocated during his rise to power.

The burning of the Reichstag building by a young Communist on 27 February was used as a pretext for a decree for the "Protection of the People and the State," which suspended all civil rights. On 24 March the Reichstag voted in the Enabling Act, which turned over all legislative functions to Hitler and his ministers. Within a week, the Law for the Reestablishment of the Professional Civil Service was passed. It eliminated all non-Aryans—anyone with a Jewish parent or grandparent—from the civil service.

Further restrictions followed with sickening regularity. On 25 April 1933 came the Law Against Overcrowding of German Schools, which limited the number of Jews admitted to 1.5 percent.

It was soon forbidden for anyone with Jewish blood to pursue a profession that had any influence on the German *Volk*. This, in effect, put all Jews out of work except those who dealt only with their coreligionists.

As Hitler and his cohorts tightened their grip on the nation, more decrees against the Jews were issued. They were forbidden to farm land. The German citizenship of Jewish immigrants was revoked, which meant expulsion. Jews were forbidden to serve in the military.

At Nuremberg on 15 September 1935, the Reichstag met and endorsed a series of decrees—the Nuremberg Laws—that further codified the status of German Jews. They were stripped of their citizenship and their rights. Marriage between Jews and Aryans was forbidden, and existing marriages were ruled invalid. Extramarital intercourse between Jews and Aryans was a criminal act. Anyone who had one Jewish grandparent was considered a Jew, as were offspring of any liaison between Jews and Aryans and anyone married to a Jew. No one of German or kindred blood under forty-five years of age could be employed by Jews as a domestic. Jews were no longer allowed to drive automobiles. And Jews, who had already been forbidden to borrow books from libraries, were now barred from the buildings altogether.

A visitor to prewar Dresden might have asked what the ruins were just to the east of the Brühl Terrace—just steps from the Frauenkirche, the Academy of Fine Arts, and the Albertinum Museum. These fire-blackened stones were the remains of another Gottfried Semper building, the nineteenth-century Romanesque-style Jewish synagogue. On 9 November 1938, during the Nazi rampage called Kristallnacht, the building was burnt to the ground and dozens of Dresden's Jews were assaulted and arrested.

The traveler to Dresden in 1939 would have looked in vain for another famous site in the city center—the ancient Judenhof, or Jews' Courtyard. The name had survived even though the synagogue that had stood there had been destroyed in the pogrom of 1430. But in 1936 the Judenhof disappeared from guidebooks and city maps—another victim of the Nazi purge of all things Jewish in the Third Reich. The space officially became an extension of the adjoining square, the Neumarkt.

· · ·

The official RAF target description of Dresden, which was first drawn up in 1942, made no mention of china, porcelain figurines, or great works of art. There was a passing reference to the city's medieval origins. But the emphasis was, rightly, on the fact that Dresden was at the center of a vital transportation network. While the individual defense establishments were not the equal of the vast armaments factories in such areas as the Ruhr, in the aggregate they were important indeed.

DRESDEN is the historical capital of Saxony and an administrative centre of considerable importance. It is the eight[h] largest town in Germany but at the same time has a very low overall density of population. Apart from the central area, which has narrow streets and many ancient domestic and public buildings, the town is mainly modern, with a preponderance of large single villas with spacious gardens.

There are a large number of industries, and collectively these are of considerable importance, but individually none are of outstanding value. The principal industrial activities are repairs to rolling stock, aircraft and aero-engines, and the manufacture of machine tools, small arms, optical instruments, medicinal preparations and poison gas.

Transportation: DRESDEN is the centre of an extensive railway system and main lines radiate from here in all directions.

There were nineteen priority targets listed for Dresden, including the Zeiss-lkon optical factory, power stations, water- and gasworks, a gun factory, and small electrical shops. Strategically, however, the important targets were the Friedrichstadt and the Pieschen railway marshaling yards and repair shops. The four railway stations—the Central Station, Dresden-Neustadt, Wettinerstrasse, and Friedrichstadt—were but a short distance from the marshaling yards.

The target map also indicated that most of the ancient heart of Dresden, the Altstadt, was well within the second of the concentric circles drawn at one-mile intervals from the central aiming point, the Friedrichstadt train yards. All the major museums, monuments, churches, and historic buildings were thus within the acceptable target zone.

From the photographs and the briefing it was clear that Dresden would be easy to find, nestled as it was within the serpentine curves of the Elbe. The image on the H2S radar screen should easily match up with the photographic maps and charts. The rail lines snaking out from the passenger and freight stations and marshaling yards stood out boldly.

Hospitals were denoted by red crosses, and at the top of the map was the enjoinder that hospitals were clearly marked and "must be avoided." Hospitals, of course, were as vulnerable as any other structure to the vagaries of visibility, wind, airspeed, and bomb drift. Three hospitals were within a mile of the designated central aiming point. The red crosses and warnings on the maps were designed chiefly to pacify international relief agencies and organizations. No one familiar with bombing practices could guarantee that they could be heeded by air crews flying at 25,000 feet in 10/10, or total, cloud cover or at night.

Another Dresden landmark, but of quite another variety, was also within the inner aiming circle. Immediately north of the Friedrichstadt yards, in a bend of the Elbe in the Grosses Ostragehege, lay the municipal slaughterhouses. These *Schlachthoffen* housed Allied prisoners of war in 1945. In *Schlachthof* No. 5, an American soldier listened as Allied bombers destroyed the city outside the protective walls of his prison. Kurt Vonnegut would later transmute the experience into art in his famous novel *Slaughterhouse-Five.*

Leipzig was the major manufacturing city in all of Saxony, but in February 1945 Dresden had at least 110 factories and industrial enterprises that employed 50,000 workers in turning out arms and other military equipment. Scattered around the city were aircraft-components factories, a poison-gas factory, an antiaircraft and field gun factory, and other factories for producing small arms, X-ray equipment, electrical apparatus, gauges, and gears and differentials. The plants and the number of workers involved constituted a considerable defense industry, which, transportation and communication aside, would have made the city a legitimate military target.

For example, before the war Seidel & Naumann, AG, manufactured typewriters, sewing machines, and bicycles. The company was converted to the manufacture of high-precision testing equipment. A Herr W., in an interview long after the war, said, "Only a few knew what the finished product would look like and what it was to be used for. It was important enough, however, that it had repeatedly protected me from being drafted into the Armed Forces."

Bomber's Baedeker: Guide to the Economic Importance of German Towns and Cities gave the population of Dresden in 1944 as 640,000 and reported that in peacetime the production of tobacco products, chocolate, and confectionaries were a large component of the city's industrial activity. With the coming of war, small factories and light engineering had become important, particularly of electric motors and precision and optical instruments.

North of the river and the Neustadt, there was a large military complex containing barracks, an old arsenal, and a museum. Immediately to the east lay a vast natural preserve, the Dresdner Heide, or heath, where it was reported the Germans were storing large quantities of munitions.

In fact, the arsenal had been converted into munitions workshops, and these and other industrial sites abutted the railway that ran northeast to Görlitz on the Polish border and on the Eastern Front.

The stations and marshaling yards in Dresden were vital components of the rail system connecting northern and central Germany to Poland, Czechoslovakia, Bavaria, and Austria. As such, Dresden was a major transport center for moving supplies and reinforcements to the east. It would also be integral for the transfer of men, and particularly panzer divisions, from the collapsing Western Front to the east.

Conversely, when the Eastern Front finally collapsed, which was imminent, Dresden would be a major center on the line of retreat for the Wehrmacht back into Germany. The city was an important strategic target, the crippling of which would help support the Russian offensive; and the Russian front line was less than two hours away, by rail or road.

An examination of contemporary railway maps clearly shows that Dresden was an integral junction of three of the most important long-distance routes of the German railway system: Berlin–Prague–Vienna; Munich–Breslau; and Hamburg–Leipzig–Prague. The railway system in Saxony, while seventh in mileage in the Third Reich, was third in the amount of tonnage carried. The Dresden stations and marshaling yards were vital components of this system. The Dresden-Friedrichstadt marshaling yards had "a maximum capacity of 4,000 trucks per 24 hours."

These rail lines had become even more important to the German war effort as the industrial regions in the west were being destroyed by the Allied raids. Meissen, Radebeul, Coswig, and Freital, with its steel mills and lubricating oil plant, were all nearby, and as the 1942 targeting report made clear, "Dresden is one of the few direct links through the Erz-Gebirge, between Czecho-Slovakia and Germany. In view of the exploitation of Czech industry, damage to the railway here would cause considerable confusion to rail transit." In 1945, Germany relied heavily on Czech industry, which was still churning out war matériel.

In addition to its importance as a rail center, Dresden was an important river port and the center of freight traffic on the Elbe, which was still, as it had been for centuries, one of the major waterways of Europe.

Worthy as all these targets were, in February 1945 the Soviets were more concerned with interdicting troop movements and reinforcements from the west to the east and disrupting any streams of retreating troops from the east to the west.

And there was yet another reason for destroying Dresden as a rail center—one that strongly recommended itself to the Allied high command. If the Germans were planning a last stand in a redoubt in the Bavarian Alps, as was strongly believed by Eisenhower and other Allied leaders, Dresden lay on the direct line to Bavaria from Berlin. Men and matériel would have to pass through the city to either establish or reinforce such a stronghold in southern Germany.

The alpine redoubt was as chimerical as the death ray and other schemes that were supposedly being concocted by the leaders of the collapsing Third Reich. But military planners must take into account the many possibilities open to a determined and fanatical enemy, no matter how far-fetched they might seem.

And as for any future reaction to the destruction of one more German city, no matter how beautiful and culturally important, that did not loom large among the air barons and their nominal civilian masters in February 1945.

CHAPTER EIGHT

SHROVE TUESDAY,

1945

Dresden on the Eve
of the Apocalypse

By the evening of 12 February, meteorological data indicated that the major air operations in eastern Germany that Spaatz had cabled Moscow would take place the next day would not be possible. The cloud cover that had obscured the Continent for most of the past week had once again moved in, and snow was falling on the Saxon capital. The daylight raid, the massive American first strike, was called off. The Americans would not be going to Dresden on Shrove Tuesday, 13 February. The Eighth Air Force bomber crews and fighter pilots were ordered to stand down.

The Russians were notified of the cancellation, but they also were put on notice that if the weather cooperated, the Americans would go the following day, 14 February. Presumably, in line with the agreement concerning bomb lines and prior notification, the British were also keeping the Russians abreast of their own preparations.

At 0900 the next morning, 13 February, the weather scouts, the aircraft that penetrated far into Europe and relayed meteorological data back to the weather centers in the United Kingdom, reported that the weather had changed for the better over central Europe. The three-part mission was back on, but it would be in reverse order. Bomber Command would lead off that night with the first two waves and the Americans would follow the next day. Harris gave the order to proceed.

By that afternoon, at the 1600 weather conference, the meteorologists at High Wycombe were forecasting even more improvement in the weather conditions over Europe for the next twenty-four hours. There would be approximately four to five hours of clear weather over Dresden beginning at about 2200 hours, which would guarantee the success of a double blow. Further, by delaying the forces for just an hour, it was predicted, the Allies could further increase the possibility of visual sightings.

There was other welcome news from the weather forecasters. Conditions would be favorable over the United Kingdom for the return of the British planes during the early-morning hours of 14 February and for the launch of the American third wave.

· · ·

In Saxony, six hundred miles from Bomber Command headquarters, Dresdeners had awakened to a cold and overcast day. All of central Europe was covered by a thick layer of clouds on this Shrove Tuesday morning. The snow that had fallen in the night had given the buildings and monuments of the Augustuses a light frosting, which further softened their baroque and rococo embellishments and gave them an even more fanciful air.

A disheveled figure shuffled through the quiet, confectionary streets of the city on this chill morning. The man bore little resemblance to the esteemed professor of French literature at the Dresden Technical University that he had once been. After fifteen years in his post, Professor Victor Klemperer had been dismissed in 1935. The distinguished scholar was now dressed in a tattered and patched coat emblazoned with a yellow Star of David and the word *Jude,* which marked him as a pariah in the Third Reich.

Like many assimilated Jews, Klemperer saw himself as completely German. Indeed, he was so far removed from the faith of his birth that he was fifty-nine years old when he attended his first Orthodox funeral and set foot in a Jewish cemetery, although his father had been a rabbi, first in Landsberg on the Warthe, in Brandenburg, then at the Reform synagogue in Berlin. But Victor and his brothers had abandoned Judaism for Christianity, and he had married Eva Schlemmer, a German Protestant.

Klemperer's view of religion is summed up in a remark he made in 1937: "Pity that I have one screw too few or too many to be a good Catholic." For him Zionism was as threatening to assimilated Jews as Nazism, a distorted idea that was as fallacious as his belief that his Protestantism, his marriage, and his heroic service in World War I set him apart from his former coreligionists. His folly was not an unusual one, although the fate of most of Europe's Jews was slower in overtaking him.

His errand today was not unlike many other rounds he had made, delivering announcements from the authorities to Dresden's 198 surviving Jews.

The Jewish community in Dresden had never been a large one, as in Berlin, and when emigration was halted in late 1941 there were just 1,265 left in the city, most of them in the protected category. These were men and women of Jewish birth who were married to Aryans or were the children of mixed marriages. But protection was capricious and arrest was an ever-present danger.

Like all their compatriots who had remained in the Reich, the Dresden Jews were the victims of a relentless campaign whose end was their destruction. Many had been murdered by the Gestapo in the grim cells of the headquarters on Schiessgasse, their deaths listed as suicides. Hundreds had been deported, either directly to the labor or extermination camps or to Theresienstadt, some sixty miles up the Elbe in Czechoslovakia.

Theresienstadt, or Terezín in Czech, was set up by the Nazis in 1941 as a showcase concentration camp and did serve for a while to hide the enormity of their crimes from the world. The small town and fortress, which was famous as the prison of Gavrilo Princip, the assassin of Archduke Francis Ferdinand in 1914, was not an extermination center but a way station for some 120,000 Jews. Nevertheless, more than 30,000 internees died there while awaiting deportation to the labor or death camps, mainly to Auschwitz-Birkenau.

. . .

The circulars distributed by Klemperer this cold morning stated that the recipient or recipients were to gather at the Jewish Center, at 3 Zeughausstrasse, in three days' time, on Friday, 16 February. They were to wear work clothes and bring hand luggage—which, the notice advised, would have to be carried for a considerable distance—and enough provisions for a journey of two or three days.

Klemperer had no illusions about the messages he carried, even though the wording was rather benign. "On this occasion," he wrote in his diary, "there is to be no confiscation of property, furniture, etc.; the whole thing is explicitly no more than outside work duty—but without exception is regarded as a death march." His own name was not on the list, but he had little doubt that he too would soon be following the others.

Age, physical condition, and marriage to non-Jews all meant nothing. There were to be no exceptions to the order. Mixed marriages no longer were to be tolerated. "The most cruel separations are taking place," wrote Klemperer. The Aryan half of a couple was to stay behind, but the Jewish partner and any children, since they were considered Jewish, were to be deported.

Jews had long since been forbidden to move about the city unless they were on prescribed missions, and then they were allowed only on narrowly defined routes. Star-wearing Jews were further prohibited from walking along or entering the Bürgerwiese, the long narrow park adjoining the Grosser Garten. Jews were allowed to cross the park only by way of the Lüttichstrasse, a detour so circuitous that it effectively ruled out doing so. Therefore Klemperer's melancholy task took him until well after dark.

As Klemperer called at the private houses or tenements that had been set aside as residences for Jews—the so-called Jews' houses, some of them in sections of the city that he had not visited in years because of the restrictions—to a person, the people on his list knew that they were being summoned to their deaths.

At each house, the reaction was despair, but he was particularly

moved by a young woman, a Frau Bitterwolf, who lived in the Struves-
trasse.

"Again a shabby house," he wrote. "I was vainly studying the list of
names in the entrance hall when a blond, snub-nosed young woman
with a pretty, well-looked-after little girl, perhaps four years old, appeared. Did a Frau Bitterwolf live here? She was Frau Bitterwolf. I had
to give her an unpleasant message. She read the letter, several times, said
quite helplessly: 'What is to become of the child?' then signed silently
with a pencil. Meanwhile the child pressed up against me, held out her
teddy bear, and, radiantly cheerful, declared: 'My teddy, my teddy, look!'
The woman then went silently up the stairs with the child. Immediately
afterward I heard her weeping loudly. The weeping did not stop."

At another of the Jews' houses lived a Frau Koch and her mother.
The older woman was on the list of deportees, but the daughter had received a postcard to report to the employment office for a medical examination to determine if she should be sent along on the work detail as
well. The daughter later related, "Now we were examined and, of
course, we were all fit to work. . . . So my mother had her deportation
order and I was given a slip of paper that I had to show up for work away
from the city, also on the 16th of February."

There were other Jews in Dresden on this day as well. But these un-
fortunates had already felt the full impact of the Nazi deportation and
extermination program. They were slave laborers sent to Dresden from
concentration camps to work in the various electronics, optical, aircraft
parts, or munitions plants scattered throughout the city.

One group, Jewish women from the camp at Ravensbrück, had been
roused from its makeshift barracks well before dawn and was at work as-
sembling precision instruments at the Zeiss-Ikon factory in Striesen.
Zeiss was the largest employer in Dresden. Some fourteen thousand people, which included thousands of laborers from the occupied countries
and Jews from the concentration camps, worked in its factories.

· · ·

The non-Jewish Dresdeners, in spite of the usual deprivations of war,
had suffered far fewer hardships than the citizens of other cities of the

Third Reich or in many cities of the occupied territories. Their city had seen no great physical damage in almost six years of war. Indeed, the eighteenth-century court painter Bernardo Bellotto would have had no trouble recognizing the subjects of his many paintings of Dresden. The city was as before. No exploding bombs had marred the famous prospect from the Brühl Terrace along the Elbe. No fires had blackened the churches, the museums, or the other great monuments of the rococo.

Dresden had been designed by the Augustuses as a stage set for the court and for their entertainments, and while the sets were physically intact, no Dresdener could pretend that the city reflected much of its glittering prewar image as a great cultural center. Bellotto's paintings had long since been removed, along with the porcelains, the statuary, the bejeweled objects in the Grünes Gewölbe, and the works of the old masters, to safer locales. The art treasures were stacked in cellars below medieval castles or deep in salt mines.

For the ordinary Dresdener, there were still some amenities, and life, although difficult, continued in many ways as before. There were cafés and coffeehouses; mail was delivered; the trains and streetcars, although delayed, operated. The telephone system worked.

The Semper Opera was dark, but another famous Dresden attraction was open for business. At the Zirkusgebäude, the amphitheater on the Carolaplatz in the Neustadt, the Sarrasani Circus, in the best tradition of that ancient form of entertainment, was continuing with performances. Indeed, there would be one that evening.

Even the animal keepers at the Dresden Zoo in the Grosser Garten had managed to keep their charges relatively healthy. Their task cannot have been a simple one, with the human population suffering such shortages of food. Although butchers were selling sausages made of cabbage, somehow food was found for these wild animals, no matter how exotic or in need of pampering. In Berlin one of the animal keepers kept his charges, some flamingos, alive in the tub in his bathroom.

Besides the removal of art treasures, few other wartime precautions had been taken, and the habitual confidence of the Dresdeners was undiminished. Strict blackout procedures were enforced, but unlike in other Reich cities, there was no ring of antiaircraft batteries. The 88-

millimeter antiaircraft guns had been removed to where they could be of greater use—as artillery pieces and antitank weapons on the Eastern Front, against the advancing Red Army.

Dresdeners were not unaware of air raids, although they had no experience of prolonged aerial bombardment. They had spent hours and sometimes entire nights in cellars and air-raid shelters since the British had begun the bombing of Germany.

In his diary, Victor Klemperer reports hearing explosions and antiaircraft fire as early as 20 November 1940. On that night the RAF raided the Škoda arms works in Pilsen, Czechoslovakia, and five targets in Germany. Dresden, where the air-raid sirens went off at 0200, was not targeted, but since only seventeen of the sixty-three Bomber Command aircraft dispatched found the primary target, perhaps some of the planes jettisoned their bombs near the city.

The city had been the target of two raids within the last four months, but they had gone largely unnoticed by the general populace. On 7 October 1944, 333 American B-17s of the First Bomb Division were dispatched to attach the oil installations at Ruhland. Only 59 of the 318 aircraft found the primary target. The remaining 259 headed for targets of opportunity, one of which was Dresden.

At about 1140 a preliminary air-raid warning was issued when planes were detected heading toward the city. Twenty minutes later, at noon, a full-scale air-raid alarm was sounded.

Thirty B-17s dropped 72.5 tons of bombs on the area around the Friedrichstadt station and marshaling yards. At 1330, when the all clear sounded, people began to emerge from the shelters. The physical destruction was minimal, but 435 people had been killed. The raid itself was such a rarity that people actually went to look at the damage.

On 16 January 1945, 364 B-24s from the Second Air Division took off from England to raid the oil installations at Magdeburg and Ruhland. The bad weather played havoc with the mission, and on the return 70 B-24s had to land in France because of the fog in England. But 138 of the B-24s bombed Dresden, a secondary target, beginning at around 1200. Again the marshaling yards were hit, this time with 341.8 tons of bombs, and another 376 people were killed.

Still, the Dresdeners saw the second raid as an anomaly as well. A young woman who lived with her newborn baby in a fourth-floor apartment on the Weisseritzstrasse reported that a crowd of people had come to see the damaged Wettinerstrasse Bahnhof after the October raid. Pieces of the station roof lay in the yard of her building; the blast had blown out the windows of her apartment, and the glass shards had cut her new draperies. Otherwise, she paid little attention to the uproar.

But the war seemed very far away on this February day, and the Dresdeners, in spite of the menacing signs, continued to trust in their good fortune. The two air raids, even with over 800 deaths, were minor incursions compared to what had befallen Berlin, Hamburg, Munich, Essen, Stuttgart—indeed, every other major city of Germany, with their hundreds of thousands of dead, injured, and homeless.

The militarily sophisticated of the city's inhabitants speculated, correctly, that in the October and January raids their city had really been the secondary target. It had been attacked only because the Allied bombers had failed to locate or reach their primary targets—the oil refineries or one of the important industrial cities of eastern Europe. They had released their bombs almost by accident, or so it was argued.

In any event, this was the day before the beginning of Lent, and many Dresdeners, in spite of the exigencies imposed by war, looked forward to celebrating the Teutonic version of the rowdy and raucous Mardi Gras. Since 1933 and the rise of the Nazis, extreme forms of behavior had disappeared from the celebration, but it was still popular, particularly with children, who looked forward to the games, costumes, and masks.

The Dresdeners did not have a compelling reason to celebrate this year—too many of the men of Dresden would never return to the city—but they could be grateful that their elegant city, with its terraces, palaces, art museums, and parks, had been spared.

In the west, the Allied ground forces were moving slowly but inexorably toward the Rhine. In the east, in three short weeks, the Russian army had advanced across Poland and had reached the east bank of the Oder—only seventy-five miles from Dresden and just thirty-five miles from Berlin. And night after night, day after day, hundreds of British and American bombers systematically went about their task of reducing the Third Reich to rubble.

But in Dresden, the old Germany was still alive. The Frauenkirche, the Semper Opera House, the cathedral, and the great public buildings still rose majestically into the Saxon sky. And the continued, almost undamaged existence of their beautiful city imparted a confidence to the populace.

However, Dresden's miraculous survival also spawned and fed dozens of rumors. Two of the more common were that a relative of Winston Churchill's lived in the city or that the Allies had agreed among themselves to spare Dresden so that it could serve as the capital of a new Germany. This latter rumor was bruited about carefully. To talk of a new Germany was to talk of defeat, and defeatism was a capital offense.

While Dresden had suffered few of the physical effects of war, other damage was evident. Like all German cities in early 1945, Dresden was a city of women, children, and old men. Any young men there were attached to the police and civil defense or were disabled veterans. In addition, there were thousands of forced civilian laborers from western Europe, along with American, British, French, and Russian prisoners of war. There were also scattered all over Germany many thousands of men from the occupied countries who had volunteered for work in Germany.

A small monument on the Hamburgerstrasse honors six Belgian and two French workers who were killed in the October raid. Were they unfortunate foreigners who had been transported to Germany as slave laborers? Or were they workers who had willingly taken up the Nazis' offer of jobs and high wages in the Third Reich?

There was also another group of young German men—hidden, furtive, living on the edges of society. These were the military deserters who were becoming a commonplace in the cities of the Reich. As the Allies tightened the vise, their numbers soared. Men on leave simply did not return to the front.

Joseph Goebbels estimated that there were tens of thousands of such fugitives hiding out in Germany. He therefore forbade civilians to give food or lodging to soldiers, any one of whom could be a deserter. He had

nothing but praise for Colonel General Ferdinand Schörner, an ardent
Nazi who was a commander in the east. Schörner employed the most
brutal methods to deter desertions, malingering, and absenteeism.

"Schörner is decidedly a personality as a commander," Goebbels
wrote. "The details he gave me about the methods he uses to raise
morale were first-rate and demonstrate not only his talents as a commander in the field but also his superb political insight. He is using quite
novel modern methods." A particularly effective method devised by
Schörner was to hang miscreants "on the nearest tree with a placard announcing: 'I am a deserter and have declined to defend German women
and children.' "

Goebbels made no distinction between military and civilian duty.
Later in the war, when bread riots erupted in the Rahnsdorf area of
Berlin, the ringleaders, two women and a man, were arrested after they
helped loot a bakery. Goebbels pardoned one woman, but, as he wrote in
his diary, "the other two who were condemned to death I shall have be-
headed during the night." Their grisly deaths were announced on plac-
ards placed throughout Rahnsdorf and broadcast over the radio to the
city at large.

There are no reliable estimates of the number of soldiers who joined
up with the refugee columns headed west or who were hiding out in the
crowded city, but the Reichsminister's fulminations indicate that the
problem was a serious one. Hundreds of deserters were picked up by patrols in Dresden alone.

Above all, there was one compelling and unmistakable sign that the
war was going badly, a sign that could not be hidden from the public or
disguised by the propaganda from Berlin—the vast influx of refugees
from the east. The stream swelled from the hundreds to the thousands to
the millions. Every road, highway, and railway from the east was
clogged with humanity, trying to escape being caught between the Soviet and Nazi forces clashing on the constantly contracting Eastern
Front. A more compelling reason for the exodus was the fear of being
left behind to suffer the barbarities of the advancing Soviets.

Millions of ethnic Germans from East Prussia and Silesia were fleeing before the advancing Red Army, and their flight to the west was already causing enormous disruption on the rail lines and highways. Almost the entire population of East Prussia fled to the Baltic Coast for transport to the Reich proper. Over 450,000 refugees were evacuated from Pillau in January alone. In the harbor at Kiel, the *Wilhelm Gustloff*, arriving with 8,000 soldiers and civilians, was torpedoed by a Soviet submarine. More than 6,000 of the passengers drowned in the icy waters.

With such suffering, it is easy to understand the public's outrage over an act of Göring's that Joseph Goebbels called a Marie-Antoinette gesture. When a column of refugees from the east passed by on the road near his vast estate northeast of Berlin, the Reichsmarschall shot a bison from his herd and gave them the meat. Göring was crucified in the press for the incident, and Hitler was furious. The uncontrite air marshal soon abandoned Prussia altogether. In March, he commandeered two trains to transport his artworks and left for the relative safety of the Obersalzburg.

Others had no way to escape except on foot. Nearly a million people walked to Danzig in the bitter cold. The same sad tale was playing itself out farther south as well. Hundreds of thousands of refugees passed through or around Dresden. Thousands of German soldiers willingly turned from their primary duties to aid the refugees, who could have been their own wives, parents, or children. They often exhibited great bravery and ingenuity in protecting the civilians from certain murder by the Russians who, as they overtook the refugee columns, did not hesitate to gun them down.

As historian John Keegan said, "The flight of January 1945 was an episode of human suffering almost without parallel in the Second World War—outside the concentration camps." The Germans themselves created the climate of revenge. During their advance in the opposite direction, toward Moscow, Stalingrad, and Leningrad, beginning in the summer of 1941, they committed unspeakable atrocities. It made no difference who did the killing—Gestapo, SS, or ordinary Wehrmacht soldiers. Millions of Russian civilians were slaughtered as the Germans made their way across the Soviet Union.

• • •

The crumbling Western and Eastern Fronts, the destruction of their cities, and the desperate measures necessary to rescue their own people from the bombers and invaders did not deter the Nazis from continuing to pursue one of the primary aims of National Socialism: the destruction of the Jews. In the vast catalog of Nazi horrors, these last acts of barbarism are perhaps the most appalling.

As the Soviets advanced in the east, the Nazis murdered the concentration-camp inmates who were too ill or too weak to move. They then began the transfer of the surviving prisoners to the west. Vehicles, ships, and trains were diverted from transporting troops and ammunition to transporting Jews back into the Reich. Many thousands of the evacuees traveled on foot, however, and on these death marches few of the Jews survived.

Of the 29,000 Jews in the Stutthof camp, near Danzig, only 3,000 survived the transfer by ship to Stettin and then on by train to Ravensbrück and Sachsenhausen. In a satellite camp farther east of Danzig, 3,700 Jewish slave laborers in Königsberg were marched to the Baltic coast, where they were told they would board ships bound for Germany. Seven hundred were killed on the march; no ships awaited the others. Instead, the 3,000 survivors were gunned down by their guards when they reached the sea. Almost all of these wretched victims were women.

At Neusalz on the Oder, another thousand Jewish women were marched from the camp to Flossenburg, near Marienbad—a distance of almost two hundred miles. Eight hundred died or were murdered en route. The remaining 200 were then shipped to Bergen-Belsen by train. More died inside the closed boxcars as the train traveled north in the dead of winter.

These scenes of sadism and murder were played out all over the Reich and the occupied territories as the Allies closed in. The argument that the Nazis needed the slave labor in the Reich itself and were therefore willing to divert much-needed transport to move them there is destroyed by cold-blooded fact. The contrary seems to be the case. The few who had managed to survive the beatings, the starvation, and the disease in the camps were now systematically slaughtered as they were transported, often on foot, on their hopeless journeys.

While the inmates of the camps in Upper Silesia were being evacuated, time had also run out for the hundreds of German Jews who had escaped deportation and certain death because they had Aryan husbands or wives. Hence the deportation orders being delivered by Victor Klemperer on 13 February.

• • •

Dresden did its best to cope with the influx of refugees from the east, but the city had become so overtaxed that police checkpoints were set up at the eastern approaches to encourage the refugees to bypass Dresden and proceed directly to the west. There was no room for any more of them in the already dangerously overcrowded city. As these legions of the dispossessed made their way across the bridges of the Elbe, the view south made them forget, temporarily, their own sorry plight and that of their country, which was in its death throes. Dresden had survived. Perhaps, they dared to hope, other cities had as well.

The refugees' respite was brief. They could not tarry. Not even the most fervid and ardent supporters of Adolf Hitler and National Socialism could pretend that the war was just going badly. It was lost. The Saxon capital might be intact, but they must move on. The police at the barricades politely but firmly showed them the way west.

As Victor Klemperer made his rounds of the Jews' houses, Sybil Schneider, a Silesian farm girl, and her family were approaching the city in a horse-drawn wagon. The Schneiders' wagon was piled high with the few possessions that they had hurriedly packed when they'd fled their farm home before the advancing Soviet army.

The girl was excited about seeing the Saxon capital and perhaps resting there. Also, the weather had cleared, as the meteorologists with the RAF had predicted. It was now a sunny, perfect spring day in Saxony.

But Sybil's father had other ideas. He was only too glad to move on when directed by the police. While Dresden had not been bombed, he said, no city was safe. They would camp on the other side of the city, out in the open countryside.

Even had Herr Schneider chosen to remain in the city, he would have found it difficult to find a place to spend the night. Nearly every apartment and house was crammed with relatives or friends from the east; many other residents had been ordered to take in strangers. There were makeshift campsites everywhere. Some 200,000 Silesians and East Prussians were living in tents or shacks in the Grosser Garten. The city's population was more than double its prewar size. Some estimates have put the number as high as 1.4 million.

Unlike other major German cities, Dresden had an exceptionally low population density, due to the large proportion of single houses surrounded by gardens. Even the built-up areas did not have the congestion of Berlin and Munich. However, in February 1945, the open spaces, gardens, and parks were filled with people.

The Reich provided rail transport from the east for hundreds of thousands of the fleeing easterners, but the last train out of the city had run on 12 February. Transport farther west was scheduled to resume in a few days; until then, the refugees were stranded in the Saxon capital.

Herr Schneider had no intention of waiting for a train. His horse and wagon would do. He proceeded with his family slowly around the darkening city and on to the low hills to the west.

● ● ●

Eight days earlier a rather more distinguished refugee had arrived from the east. On the morning of 5 February, the very day that Spaatz cabled Kuter in Yalta that Dresden and other targets in the east would be bombed as weather permitted, an unusual car—a steam car fueled by wood—arrived at Villa Wiesenstein in the mountain village of Agnetendorf, in Upper Silesia. For four decades, the villa had been the retreat of novelist, poet, playwright, and Nobel laureate Gerhart Hauptmann, now eighty-three years old.

No bombs had fallen and no invading armies had appeared in the Riesengebirge, the mountain range between Silesia and Bohemia, and the birthplace of the Elbe. But the war was coming ever closer each day as the Red Army continued its advance to the west.

For the past two years, so many thousands of Germans fleeing the Soviet troops in the east and the air raids in the west had flocked to the area that it had become known as Germany's air-raid shelter. No one, no matter how privileged, was exempt from housing refugees, who numbered in the thousands, and the Hauptmanns had had to take in two women and seven children.

His solitude shattered, Hauptmann, after much reflection and anguish, decided to remove himself to Dresden, where so often in the past he had gone to refresh his spirits. Then, too, Margarete Hauptmann was ailing. The car had been dispatched by Weidner's Sanatorium, in the Dresden suburb of Oberloschwitz, to fetch the couple and Anni, their servant and secretary. Weidner's had agreed to admit Frau Hauptmann for treatment, and her husband, in the solitude of a cottage on the grounds of the famous hospital, might also find a degree of serenity.

After the Hauptmann's arrival, the physicians at Weidner's determined that Margarete Hauptmann needed more intensive care than could be provided by a sanatorium, and she was transferred to a hospital in Dresden proper. The old man stayed up on the heights and on his walks in the garden reflected on his ties to this magical city. He could see the tower of the Johanneskirche, where he had married his first wife, and the Royal Academy on the Brühl Terrace, where he had studied art. Down there were the theaters where his plays had been produced, and spread out along the Elbe was the Hotel Bellevue and its gardens. For years the hotel had, in the German style, treated the visiting writer like royalty. "Really, one is compelled to love it, my jewel, my Dresden," Hauptmann remarked to a companion on one of his strolls. "May it never share the fate of other cities!"

Soon Margarete Hauptmann returned to the cottage at Weidner's. The hospital in Dresden had determined that she was not as ill as first diagnosed, but there was another, darker reason for her quick return. Anni had brought her the disturbing news that Hauptmann was drinking heavily and quickly declining.

After her return to the sanatorium, Frau Hauptmann soon had the situation in hand, and under her ministrations or, more probably, her proscriptions, Gerhart Hauptmann sobered up. On 13 February he was so much improved in body and spirit that he was able to write a new poem, "Zauberblume" ("Magic Flower").

The rest of the day was whiled away with friends at a luncheon, followed by a nap, then afternoon tea, during which the faithful Anni read aloud. Later, Hauptmann shared a quiet dinner with his wife. There was talk of leaving the cottage at Weidner's for the more congenial atmosphere of the Hotel Bellevue, and then Hauptmann went to bed.

CHAPTER NINE

A PILLAR OF FIRE

BY NIGHT

Bomber Command
Takes the Lead

The sun had long since set when the first of the Lancasters of
5 Group, the Pathfinders, or flare force, of 83 and 97 Squadrons, lifted
off and headed for Germany. It was approximately 1720 hours on 13 February 1945.

In an age of satellites and global positioning systems, navigation in
February 1945 seems primitive indeed. Often the finding of a target was
little more than sophisticated guesswork, although the newest system,
called loran, which was used on this raid for the first time, was far ahead
of any previous device. But mistakes were still not uncommon. As has
been observed, bombing a city was the least of it. Finding the city was
the problem.

Flying just minutes ahead of the main bomber fleet, the Pathfinders
had a single objective: to find Dresden and drop parachute flares, which
would illuminate an area one to two miles square.

When the ground below was lit up as if by daylight, the second phase
of the raid would begin. The faster and more agile Mosquito marker
planes, which would not take off for almost two and a half hours after
the Lancasters were airborne, would now have to identify the central
aiming point and then drop their 1,000-pound TIs, the target indicators.

The bombardiers in the main bomber fleet, which was to approach from the northwest, were then to center their bomb patterns on the brilliant red glow from the target indicator bombs. These intricate maneuvers were, at least in theory, guided by a master bomber who circled the city in another Mosquito and conducted the raid as if he were the leader of a great orchestra.

The metaphor is an apt one. As in a symphony, everything must come together in a well-defined sequence and time frame—twenty to twenty-five minutes—from the illuminator flares from the Pathfinders, to the target indicators from the Mosquito marker bombers, to the rain of high explosives and incendiaries from the main bomber force.

Some ten minutes after the Pathfinders were airborne and en route to Saxony, the main bomber force, code-named "Plate-Rack," began taxiing into position for takeoff. Within a half hour, 254 Lancasters, all from 5 Group, Harris's old command at Grantham, with their cargo of almost 900 tons of high explosives and incendiaries, were en route to the assembly point at Reading and thence to the Channel and on to the Continent.

This night every crewman on any plane that was to come anywhere close to the Eastern Front carried something new: a Union Jack embossed with the words, in Russian, "I am an Englishman." It was hoped that this might save the life of anyone who had to parachute behind the Russian lines, but no one much counted on it.

The weather that had caused the scrubbing of the daylight American raid was even more dangerous for the night operations of the British. Navigation was more complicated, and the return in the dark and the fog to the home bases was often a nightmarish experience. However, unlike the Eighth Air Force, which had been called on to bomb the rail centers and marshaling yards, "precision targets," the RAF had a more broadly defined assignment. Their target was simply the "town area." Visibility was less important.

Tonight's raid would become the prime example of the Bomber Command theory of the double blow, an air attack in which a second wave of bombers would arrive just as the firefighters and rescue teams below were fully occupied in battling the fires caused by the earlier raid and attempting to bring out survivors.

Only a handful of raids ever actually conformed to this double-strike model, which was a supposed cornerstone of Bomber Command policy. Those that did were cataclysmic, and thus the question is why the method was not used more than it was. The reason or reasons are rather simple: bad weather and the lack of men and machines for a double or triple blow.

The Dresden raid now began to unfold. In its execution, it was theory put into flawless practice: two waves of bombers, three hours apart, followed the next day by a massive daylight raid by more bombers and escort fighters with the additional task of strafing rail and road traffic.

Other raids planned for that night were designed to keep the German defenses in the dark as to the RAF's true intentions toward Dresden. Mosquitoes attacked Magdeburg, Bonn, Misburg, and Nuremberg, and another 360 Lancasters and Halifaxes—a larger force than that headed for Dresden—were dispatched to bomb the synthetic oil plant at Böhlen, just south of Leipzig and less than sixty miles from Dresden.

· · ·

The two bomber streams followed more or less parallel courses for the journey out. They crossed the Channel and entered French airspace near the Somme. Their route was thus far a relatively safe one, since the Allied lines lay far to the east at this stage of the war. Window, aluminum foil strips that jammed German radar, was liberally scattered along a broad north-south front west of Duisburg, to west of Mannheim, a 120-mile screen behind which the bombers advanced into the Reich.

When they emerged from behind the screen of Window, the German trackers could see that there were clearly two distinct bomber streams. The Plate-Rack bomber fleet crossed the Rhine just north of Cologne. The force bound for Böhlen crossed farther south, just north of Koblenz.

But any number of possible targets lay in their paths as they pressed on, and the German radar operators and air defense teams now had to make agonizing projections as to where they might actually be heading.

The standard operating procedure was for the tracking data to be refined and a series of preliminary warnings issued.

On the night of 13 February 1945, the system seems to have failed. There was no preliminary warning even when it was obvious that the planes were heading for Saxony, and it was not until the bombers were almost over the city that the air observers realized that Dresden was the intended target. Thus when the *Fliegeralarm*, the actual air-raid alarm, did sound, Dresdeners had just a few minutes to find cover.

Meanwhile, the two bomber forces maintained their parallel course until just before 2200 hours, when the planes on the more southerly route peeled off toward Böhlen. At about the same time the northern wave of planes, all Lancasters, made a turn to the southeast, a heading that would bring them to the Elbe and then, just a few minutes later, to Dresden.

Of the original 254 Lancasters designated for Dresden, ten were now out of action for one reason or another, a not unusual number. The attacking force thus comprised 244 Lancasters, carrying over 500 tons of high-explosive bombs and more than 375 tons of incendiaries.

• • •

As the British air fleet lumbered toward Saxony, Winston Churchill and the British delegation were comfortably ensconced aboard SS *Franconia* in the harbor at Sevastopol. The Yalta Conference had ended two days earlier, but the British united front that had been so evident when important issues were at stake had disappeared.

To the dismay of their aides, Eden and Churchill were arguing over the next stop, Athens. Churchill kept everyone on edge with his to-ing and fro-ing. He would go to Athens. He would not go to Athens. Each time he decided in favor of the trip Eden became more annoyed. The foreign secretary did not want to be upstaged in the Greek capital by the prime minister. An exasperated Alexander Cadogan said to Lord Moran, "I never bargained to take Tetrazzini and Melba round the world together in one party."

By the next morning the little contretemps was settled—everyone would go to Athens—and the British party was driven from Sevastopol to the airfield at Saki for the flight to the Greek capital. En route, Churchill, again displaying that touch that distinguished him from lesser beings, had the pilot circle the island of Skyros and the tomb of Rupert Brooke.

. . .

Just before 2000 hours, the eight Mosquitoes that were to drop the target indicators on the central aiming point and thus lay out the bombing path for the heavies took off from their base at Woodhall Spa.

A few minutes later, the master bomber, Wing Commander Maurice Smith, and his navigator, Pilot Officer Leslie Page, climbed into their Mosquito at Coningsby. The fast Mosquitoes would reach Dresden, if all went according to plan, just behind the Pathfinders and just ahead of the Plate-Rack force.

The Mosquito was designed to fly at high altitudes to avoid flak and at great speed to elude interceptors, but the nine planes on this mission would be operating at the outer limits of their capabilities. They were thus obliged to take an almost direct route from their bases to the Saxon capital.

Their route took them out across the North Sea to Holland and then directly southeast. They would approach the target from the southwest, swooping down from 20,000 feet at Chemnitz to well below 1,000 feet at Dresden.

. . .

While Gerhart Hauptmann, his wife, and his secretary were making do in reduced but still comfortable circumstances in Oberloschwitz, overlooking Dresden, the Silesian farmer Herr Schneider was settling his family for the night at their camp in the hills on the western side of the city. A few minutes before ten o'clock, they heard the sound of airplane engines. As they looked apprehensively for the source of the noise, the night sky over the city to the east was turned to day by white and green flares.

The flares were eerily beautiful on this winter evening, reminiscent of prewar *Feuerwerk* along the Elbe. But these were not civic fireworks to celebrate Shrove Tuesday. Lancaster Pathfinders from 83 Squadron, 5 Group, of the RAF had released green primaries and white illuminator magnesium flares to light the way for the target indicator Mosquitoes that were racing toward Dresden.

The Pathfinders had picked out the unmistakable S-curve of the Elbe that identified the target as Dresden. The first flares, the primary greens, fell directly in the bend of the river. Using the primary greens as a marker, the other Pathfinder aircraft began to unload their brilliant whites. The distant spires of the city stood out in sharp relief in the glow.

As the flares floated slowly to earth, almost at once there was another roar of planes. The nine Mosquito bombers, eight marker planes and the master bomber, had begun their run. As they made their vertiginous descent toward the city, they passed over the refugee camps. The Schneider family had good reason to be grateful that the father had insisted that they move on rather than rest in the city. The attack he feared had begun.

The timing of the Mosquitoes was perfect, and from the refugee camp there could be seen the reddish glow that had begun to replace the brilliant whites and greens. The Mosquitoes had begun to drop the target indicators.

. . .

The nine Mosquitoes had descended from almost 20,000 feet in just five minutes in order to fulfill their mission. In just a few more minutes the main bomber fleet would arrive, and they needed the target indicators to be afire to guide them to the bombing zones. The master bomber now broke radio silence. He called out, "Controller to Marker Leader. How do you hear me? Over." The marker leader, Flight Lieutenant William Topper, who would drop the first target-indicator bomb, replied that Wing Commander Smith was coming in loud and clear.

Topper was now just 2,000 feet above the city, which was brilliantly illuminated by the marker flares. He could make out many of the landmarks, which he had seen on the briefing photographs and target maps.

The Hauptbahnhof, the main railway station, with its glass roof, was easily identified, as were the tracks snaking out from it, which would lead him to the central aiming point, a sports stadium close by the railroad bridge that crossed the Elbe beside it. The stadium had been chosen because of its unmistakable oval shape and its proximity to the river.

Shouting, "Marker Leader: Tally-ho!" to signal that he was going in and that all other marker Mosquitoes should hold back, Topper roared down to 800 feet and released his 1,000-pound target-indicator bomb. Below him the stadium was lit up by a burst of red fire. The TI had landed within a hundred yards of it, an almost perfect drop. In quick succession, more Mosquitoes began to drop their red TIs into the stadium, but since the preliminary marking had been so accurate the master bomber decided to hold a few in reserve, in case they were needed for further marking.

High above the Mosquitoes, a Lancaster bomber circled the city to act as radio relay for the marker bombers, the master bomber, and the home base if necessary. The pilot reported that he could see the red TIs burning 18,000 feet below, through the thin cloud cover. All was in readiness for the fast-approaching Plate-Rack force, which would clearly have no trouble finding the target.

The plan of attack called for the first wave of Lancasters to cross the city from the northwest to the southeast. The central aiming point, the stadium, was approximately a mile from the Friedrichstadt marshaling yards, but this important target was on the approach path. Unless the bombing backed up on the aiming point it would be passed over.

But the elements that were to enable the RAF to raise a firestorm lay directly ahead of the central aiming point: the Altstadt. Congested old Dresden, with its medieval street plan, highly combustible ancient buildings, and several hundred thousand people, lay entirely within the bombing path of the first wave of planes.

With frightening precision, the first raid in the Bomber Command and Eighth Air Force plan to completely destroy a large city with a triple blow of air strikes began to unfold. The 244 Lancasters of 5 Group fanned out from the aiming point, the sports stadium by the Elbe, and prepared to release their cargo, 875 tons of high-explosive bombs and incendiaries. At 2210 the first bombs began to fall.

The heavy bombs and thousands of smaller incendiaries that rained down on the city in the first wave would, Arthur Harris had long theorized, set so many hundreds of small fires that no matter how well organized or well equipped a firefighting service might be it could not hope to cope with all of them. Further, the firefighting efforts would be hampered, if not halted, by the huge blasts caused by 2,000-pound, 4,000-pound, or even more powerful high-explosive bombs. As Harris said in his memoirs, if "a rain of incendiaries is mixed with high explosive bombs there is an irresistible temptation for the fireman to keep his head down."

The first wave of planes from Bomber Command had, as it turned out, the relatively simple task of raising a fire by igniting the combustible Altstadt of Dresden. The resulting beacon would light the way for the larger second wave, scheduled to arrive three hours later.

The second wave would appear over Dresden at the very time that the optimum number of fire brigades and rescue teams were in the streets of the burning city. The high explosives of the first wave would have destroyed most of the water mains, and the collapsed buildings would have rendered the streets impassable. The second wave would compound the earlier destruction many times and, by design, kill the firemen and rescue workers so the destruction could rage on unchecked.

It was soon apparent to the master bomber that there was no high-altitude flak and he could bring the Plate-Rack force down to just 8,000 feet, the upper limit of the range of the few 20-millimeter guns that were throwing up flak. At that altitude, the entire city was visible to the bombardiers.

In his Mosquito, master bomber Maurice Smith, like the maestro he was, exhorted the bombardiers, praising their accuracy and correcting the tempo as necessary. "Good shot!" "Back up!" "Back up!" Everywhere below him fires were breaking out as over 200,000 incendiaries crashed through the roofs of apartment houses, museums, churches, palaces, theaters, and government buildings.

The high-explosive ordnance, bombs ranging in weight from 500 pounds to over 4,000 pounds—two-ton "cookies"—did their assigned tasks well, rupturing water mains and interdicting emergency workers' access. They also carried out an even more deadly mission. The enormous pressure waves created by the cookies blew out doors and windows, thereby increasing the effectiveness of the incendiary bombs, the weapon that was designed to do the most damage. Buildings were turned into vast flues as air was drawn through blasted-out doors and windows to feed the already fiercely burning incendiaries. Firefighters, both professional and amateur, would soon be overwhelmed.

In just twenty minutes the mission of the aircrews of 5 Group had been completed and they had turned back toward England. Wing Commander Smith turned his Mosquito as well. He had been over the city for less than half an hour. As the Plate-Rack force began the long return flight, behind them the plane crews could see thousands of small fires burning.

■ ■ ■

By the time Victor Klemperer had finished his mournful errands late on 13 February and returned to his crowded quarters at the Jews' house at 1 Zeughausstrasse, the wintry day had become "perfect spring weather," as he recorded later in his diary.

Around 2130 that evening he sat down to have coffee with his wife. A few minutes before 2200 the *Fliegeralarm*, a full-scale air-raid alarm, sounded. The Klemperers and the other residents of the Jews' house rushed down to the air-raid shelter that had been set aside for Jews in the building next door, 3 Zeughausstrasse. Upstairs was the headquarters for the now tiny Dresden Jewish community, as well as the assembly point for the work details and deportations.

In the darkened shelter, the Klemperers trembled at the sound of airplanes and the crash of bombs. There was fear, he said, but no panic, and when the all clear sounded at 2330 they left the cellar and returned to their rooms.

They could see from the smoke and the flames that a major raid had occurred, but their building was intact and Klemperer, who was exhausted from his day walking the streets of Dresden, thought only of sleep. He and Eva went back to bed.

. . .

While the Klemperers slept, the small fires set by the thousands of incendiaries from the first wave of British planes began to spread and intensify. One of the few civil defense measures made available to the citizens of Dresden—buckets of sand—proved useless in fighting the fires that suddenly seemed to be everywhere.

The flames raced from room to room, from floor to floor, and from building to building, joining forces and growing ever larger and stronger, leaping across courtyards, alleys, and the narrow streets of the Altstadt.

The process was repeated on an ever-increasing scale as houses ignited and burned, then entire blocks went up, until whole sections of the city were afire. Streets and alleys became rivulets of fire that coalesced into rivers of fire that converged until they formed an ocean of fire that covered Dresden.

As the storm grew, air from outlying areas was sucked into the center to feed the flames, creating huge backdrafts, then gales, and finally winds of hurricane force, which swept everything into the fiery maelstrom that was consuming the city center. Trees were uprooted. Trams, trucks, even railroad engines were overturned and thrown about.

Temperatures soared to a thousand, fifteen hundred, two thousand degrees. Lampposts, street signs, and even the bricks themselves disintegrated. The open streets became death traps as the asphalt melted in the terrible heat and the fleeing refugees found themselves unable to move. After terrible struggles to free themselves, they collapsed and died, falling into the burning tar, where they were incinerated.

People who were blocks from the flames and thought themselves safe were suddenly picked up by the hurricane-force winds and pulled into the inferno, where their bodies ignited and their corpses were reduced to ash. In the makeshift air-raid shelters, thousands suffocated as the superheated air pulled cooler, breathable air from the basements where they had sought shelter. Instead, these havens from the death and destruction above became death traps filled with overheated and poisonous gases. Thousands of others died when their internal organs were ripped apart by the tremendous concussions caused by the high-explosive bombs.

As the wooden beams and trusses and supports gave way, floors and roofs collapsed, burying the thousands huddled in the cellars below. Entire blocks of buildings with nothing to support them buckled and fell into the streets. Firefighters, ambulance drivers, and rescue teams found their way blocked by giant mounds of burning rubble in every avenue and street. Instead of fighting the fires and extricating the injured, they soon would be looking for ways out of the conflagration themselves.

· · ·

At 0105 air-raid alarms again sounded, but since the electrical system had been largely destroyed in the earlier raid, these were hand-cranked devices limited to small areas of perhaps a block or so. Bomber Harris's second wave—529 Lancasters from 1, 3, 6, and 8 Groups—had arrived punctually at the appointed hour.

Their route into the Reich had been somewhat farther to the south than that of 5 Group, and they approached the city from almost due west. Pathfinders from 8 Group were the designated markers. They had no trouble finding the target. The red glow from the burning city was visible on the horizon from more than sixty miles out.

The weather had cleared further, as predicted, and as they neared Dresden, the Pathfinders in the second wave could see that the only visual impediment was the thick smoke from the fires. Although they were superfluous, at 0123 hours away went the marker flares, which had been designed to light up a target that now needed no illumination. The city below was completely in flames, engulfed in a firestorm.

When the master bomber, Squadron Leader C. P. C. de Wesslow, and his deputy, Wing Commander H. J. F. Le Good, arrived just minutes later they were faced with a quandary. The first wave was such a success, with the entire city on fire, that to proceed with the prearranged bombing plan was no longer the most effective use of their own high explosives and incendiaries. Dresden was, in actuality, already one giant target indicator.

The decision was quickly made to mark areas outside the firestorm and drop the bombs accordingly, thus expanding the area of destruction. Le Good, who went in first, dropped his target indicators to one side of the fires, and the other markers followed suit, first to one side of the firestorm and then to the other, to lay out the path for the bombing fleet.

Bombs now began to rain down on the Hauptbahnhof, the Central Station, which had escaped relatively untouched in the first raid since it lay outside the direct bombing path. Hundreds of refugees had taken shelter in the tunnels underneath the station, and the trains had been shunted out of the station three hours earlier. But in the belief that it was now safe to do so, the trains had been brought back into the station to reload their passengers.

As the high explosives and incendiaries tore through the immense glass cover over the train shed, thousands of shards rained down on the people crowded onto the platforms below. Those who were not killed or critically injured by the falling glass were blown apart by the explosions or burned to death by the incendiaries. The hundreds of refugees who were huddled in the darkness of the tunnels met a similar fate as the bombs ripped through the ceilings and created an underground inferno.

The master bomber was somewhat baffled by a large black area abutting the city center, which strangely showed no sign of fire. He ordered it bombed. This last place was the Grosser Garten, and now the great public park also became a scene of fire and devastation as incendiaries and high explosives ripped up the earth, flattened the trees, and tore into the vast refugee camp set up there, to which many other thousands had fled to escape the firestorm in the nearby neighborhoods.

Victor and Eva Klemperer, asleep and unaware that the city outside the Jews' house was completely on fire, were roused by the handheld air-raid sirens being sounded in the street outside. As they raced back to the Jews' house cellar bombs were already falling everywhere around them.

They remained in the cellar until the all clear was sounded at 0215, but when they emerged, Eva Klemperer realized that their world had changed forever. The air raids might have destroyed her city and killed thousands of people, but they had also provided a long-hoped-for but unexpected lifeline for her husband and herself. She immediately determined to take advantage of the ensuing confusion.

She removed the yellow star from Victor Klemperer's coat, and with little more than the clothes on their backs they joined the great stream of refugees beginning the trek south toward Bavaria. For the few weeks remaining until the fall of the Reich, they managed to blend in with the thousands of other displaced persons moving about the countryside, and thus they survived the Holocaust.

. . .

By 0155 on the morning of 14 February, the last British bomber was en route home to England. The double blow had turned out to be one of the most successful operations in Bomber Command history and one of the safest. Only six aircraft had been lost, just one to enemy fire, the victim of one of the two German fighters that had come up to defend the city.

Altogether, in a total of about forty-five minutes, more than 650,000 small incendiaries and hundreds of high explosive bombs ranging in weight from 500 to 8,000 pounds had rained down on Dresden.

The British bombers had turned the city into a vast sea of flame, a firestorm that would not burn itself out for days. But it was left to the Americans, who had been slated to strike the first blow, to deliver the coup de grâce to the mortally wounded Florence of the Elbe.

CHAPTER 10

A COLUMN OF SMOKE

BY DAY

The American
Third Wave

At 0300 on 14 February, thousands of airmen were roused from sleep at the American bomber and fighter bases scattered across England. With less than ten hours of daylight at this time of year, every minute was precious. Daylight helped to ensure not just the success of the bombing run but also the return trip home. The Allied advance had made available many emergency landing fields in France and hundreds of aircraft had made use of them, but there was still the risk of bringing a badly shot-up bomber home in the dark or, worse, ditching in the English Channel.

Carl Spaatz and his deputies in the Eighth Air Force were determined to take advantage of the promised break in the weather, and on this day they would launch almost 1,400 heavy bombers and nearly 1,000 fighter escorts against targets in Germany.

The reversal of the bombing order of the original Thunderclap plan had also resulted in a change in Spaatz's promise of sending a 1,400-bomber armada against one target. The American force was now to be split into three main components. Some 461 bombers were assigned to Dresden, 157 to Chemnitz, and 375 to Magdeburg. A smaller force of 84 planes would bomb Wesel.

The airmen slated for a mission were served a serious breakfast, which featured real eggs with Spam, and at about 0440 they crowded into the briefing huts for the general briefing. The men of the First Air Division learned that their mission was a deep penetration into eastern Germany, to the Saxon capital of Dresden, a round-trip of some fifteen hundred miles.

The 461 B-17s assigned to Dresden would first head across the North Sea to the Dutch coast, where they would be joined by their escort of 316 P-51s, many of them from newly established fighter bases on the Continent. The bomber crews would thus have no worries about adequate fighter protection as they made their way deep into Germany.

After the rendezvous with their "little friends," the fighters, the B-17s of the First Air Division would proceed to Quakenbrück, fifty-five miles southwest of Bremen, and from there they would head directly across Germany to the initial point, Torgau, sixty miles northwest of Dresden, on the Elbe.

Flying up the river from Torgau, it should have been a simple matter to find the target, either visually or using H2X radar. Dresden should have been unmistakable, lying as it did in the bend of the Elbe. But for some of the navigators it turned out not to be so.

In the event of a sudden change in the weather, the alternate target for the First Air Division was Kassel. Some ninety miles west of Dresden, Kassel had been bombed by the Eighth Air Force many times since mid-1943, most recently just two weeks before. Many of these crews thus had some experience with flying deep into Germany.

After the general briefing, there was a specialized briefing for each crew position, and then the men went to the personal-effects hut to turn in any items or papers that in the event of capture might be of use to the Germans in determining where an air crewman was stationed and where the planes were based. The only identifying documents allowed were military-issue dog tags.

Hidden on their persons, however, were religious artifacts, pictures of sweethearts, wives, or mothers, and good-luck charms of every description—a rabbit's foot, a battered cap, a lucky scarf. Many airmen purposely left their beds unmade, a superstition that supposedly guaranteed a safe return. The combinations to guard against harm were countless.

· · ·

The next stop was to pick up their flight equipment, and then the crews boarded trucks to be driven out to the waiting planes to begin the preparation for takeoff. It took nearly an hour to go through the long checklist. Each item was called out and verified by the pilot and copilot. Every switch, gauge, and valve had to be double-checked. The procedure was replicated aboard each Flying Fortress and Liberator before the great planes with their combined crews of over 10,000 American airmen took to the skies and headed for the Continent and the day's work.

The powerful engines came to life and the planes began to move. Between 0700 and 0800, the aircraft began to lift off and make for the assembly areas. The predawn warm-up of over 6,000 engines and the takeoff of nearly 2,500 bombers and fighters shattered the quiet of the English countryside. Thus, almost every day, did the Eighth Air Force test the patience and patriotism of the residents of the towns and villages that very often lay directly in the flight paths or just outside the sprawling bases.

Hundreds of planes roared overhead on their way to the assembly points where the bomber streams formed up and headed for Saxony and, unknown to them, its already destroyed capital.

In a much-disputed and much-denied directive, even though it was by no means a deviation from standard operating procedure, the P-51 fighter pilots were also instructed after the bomb run to range afield and strafe "targets of opportunity"—columns of troops, convoys of trucks, and railroad trains. In short, anything that moved was an acceptable target, even people in the streets, as eyewitnesses alleged for many years afterward. This further "atrocity" has become part of the Dresden legend.

The strafing policy had begun early in 1944 in order to maximize the use of the fighter squadrons. When there were no large missions scheduled, fighter groups were often sent out independently on strafing and bombing missions.

Indeed, it was on one such mission over Normandy, on 17 July 1944, that a British fighter pilot strafed the staff car of Erwin Rommel near Livarot. The field marshal was injured so seriously that he was taken to Germany for treatment and convalescence. He never returned to the front. When it was discovered that he was deeply implicated in the 20 July plot against the Führer, he was forced to commit suicide.

• • •

At Podington Air Base, some fifteen miles east of Northampton, Second Lieutenant Walter S. Kelly; his copilot, Second Lieutenant Alexander M. Ellett Jr.; the navigator, Flight Officer Walter S. Sierzant Jr.; and the bombardier, Staff Sergeant Roman Pasinski entered the briefing room.

Comic strips were a favorite source for names of aircraft in World War II, and their B-17, the *Flat Top,* carried on its nose a picture of the eponymous character from the comic strip *Dick Tracy.*

A native of Repton, Alabama, Kelly was a senior at Auburn University when he enlisted in the army in February 1943. After twelve days of basic training he was sent for what he called "pre-pre-flight training" at Centre College in Danville, Kentucky, where he sang in the choir of the Methodist church and where he met and fell in love with a high school senior named Margaret Armstrong. Kelly went on to train at various bases around the country and finally, in May 1944, he was commissioned as a second lieutenant and earned his pilot's wings.

Margaret Armstrong, who had completed her freshman year at Randolph-Macon College, in Virginia, traveled to the base where he was stationed in Stuttgart, Arkansas. They were together on D-day and read about the invasion in the newspaper. Later, they walked the streets of the small town, looking in shopwindows, and then sat on the fire escape of Margaret's hotel, "feeling a little unsettled," as she recalled many years later.

In December 1944, Kelly was ordered overseas to England, and Margaret, now wearing his pilot's wings, was in her sophomore year at Randolph-Macon. In one of those coincidences that often define a life, on the campus one day she struck up a conversation with another girl who was wearing gunner's wings. It turned out that the wings had been given to her by William Balentine, of Greenville, South Carolina, a member of Walter Kelly's flight crew.

Meanwhile, Second Lieutenant Kelly and the crew of the *Flat Top* were getting their first taste of aerial warfare over Germany. On 15 January 1945, they were dispatched to Freiburg. Two days later they bombed the rail yards at Paderborn. On 28 January the target was Cologne and on 1 February the *Flat Top* bombed Ludwigshafen.

Kelly's next flight was in many ways the supreme test for all bomber pilots: Berlin. An amalgam of the military, the psychological, and the political, Berlin was the heart of the Reich, and as such it carried a symbolism like that of no other German city. It was both hated as an enemy and desired as a target by all bomber crews. Its formidable antiaircraft defenses also instilled much fear in them, especially the more experienced airmen.

On 3 February 1945, the *Flat Top* was part of the massive American thousand-bomber raid on Berlin. Although the Luftwaffe fighter forces were much weakened by early 1945, they still presented a threat, and the antiaircraft defenses were more powerful than ever. The retreat of the Wehrmacht back into the Reich had made more of the 88-millimeter guns available for air defense around key targets, and the flak, always a serious problem over the capital, was particularly heavy on this day. Twenty-three planes were lost, 339 damaged, and the casualties (dead, wounded, and missing) totaled 218.

Kelly and the crew of the *Flat Top* fared reasonably well. They returned to Podington with just two holes in the aircraft. All were aware, however, that a few more inches in either direction could have brought them the fate of their colleagues who had gone down over Germany.

So by 14 February 1945, Walter Kelly and all his crew—save one, the radioman, for whom this was the first combat mission—were seasoned veterans of the air war over Germany. They had five successful missions under their belt, including the Big B itself.

· · ·

Ten miles to the east of Podington, at Kimbolton, the crew of another B-17, the *Miss Conduct*, were performing an identical ritual. The crew, under the pilot, Second Lieutenant Stanley W. Cebuhar of Albia, Iowa, was part of the 527th Bomb Squadron of the 379th Bombardment Group. They had been together for most of the plane's missions, but there was a relative newcomer, the navigator, a twenty-year-old from Minnesota, Second Lieutenant Raymond G. Engstrand.

In June 1943, Engstrand had enlisted in the army and begun five weeks of basic training as his first step toward duty in the army air forces. Since he had entered the military directly from high school, Engstrand was first sent to a small college in Nashville, Tennessee, as preparation for further training and an officer's commission.

Six months later, in early 1944, Engstrand began preflight training, which led, however, not to flight school but to training as a bombardier, which included a stretch at gunnery school. Engstrand and several of his fellow trainees at the base in Kingman, Arizona, were quarantined by an outbreak of scarlet fever, but the delay was temporary and by August 1944 Engstrand was training with a full crew—flying B-24 Liberators in the sunny skies over the Southwest.

On 11 December, his training completed, Second Lieutenant Engstrand shipped out aboard the converted cruise liner *Manhattan* from Boston, bound for Liverpool. Nine days later, with some relief, he arrived in England. There had been widespread speculation aboard the ship that they were going to proceed directly to the Continent as reinforcement ground troops in the Battle of the Bulge. Like most shipboard scuttlebutt, the rumor was false, and in a few days Engstrand was checking into the American base at Kimbolton, in Cambridgeshire.

A few days later, on Christmas Eve, a sickening event in the English Channel underscored the still deadly might of the Nazi war machine. A German submarine torpedoed a Belgian troopship, the SS *Leopoldville*, carrying 2,235 American troops; 763 infantrymen drowned.

The English weather was as predicted, with a fog so thick that the men had to be led to their billets. And when the fog burned off there was a surprise: there was not a B-24 in sight. Engstrand and his Liberator-trained colleagues were going to fly in B-17s with the 527th Bomb Squadron of the 379th Bombardment Group.

The transition was a relatively easy one, and although the die-hard

B-24 men loyally entered into their shotgun marriage with the B-17, the Liberator remained their true love. This flexibility was characteristic of the Allied war effort. Men were assigned where they were needed and they did their duty.

However, the new arrivals in England faced a different air campaign than that of their predecessors. The raids in late 1944 bore little resemblance to those staged by the first American pilots deployed to England. Greater range, fighter protection, and a large swath of friendly territory on the Continent increased the chances of survival.

Pilots struggled to get a damaged plane back over friendly territory, where they could bail out. At least one pilot turned his B-17 back toward enemy territory and put it on automatic pilot before bailing out, turning the plane into an improvised flying bomb.

Another very large difference was that crews no longer functioned as a complete unit, one that was assigned to a single aircraft. Rotation, death, and injury ensured that no group of men stayed together for any length of time. It was not unusual for an airman's first mission to be with men he hardly knew. The same was true of the planes. Bombers were designed to be interchangeable, and crews quickly adjusted. They flew what was available.

In addition, in August 1944 a new rotation policy had been instituted. Formerly, Eighth Air Force combat personnel were sent home for a thirty-day leave, but then they had to return to active duty in Europe. Knowing that they would return to the cause of their anxieties effectively canceled the benefits of rest and relaxation in the States.

From now on, when a man's tour was over, he was sent back to the States for reassignment elsewhere. The effects of the new policy were dramatic. Cases of chronic and acute combat fatigue dropped by more than 50 percent. The less severe anxiety reactions dropped by 90 percent.

By late 1944, flak, not enemy fighters, posed the greatest danger. Consequently, two waist gunners were seen as superfluous, and thus many B-17s now flew with a nine-man crew instead of the original complement of ten. But the *Flat Top* had a full crew: pilot, copilot, bombardier, navigator, top turret gunner/flight engineer, radioman, right waist gunner, left waist gunner, ball turret gunner, and tail gunner.

There were other operational changes as well. Early on, the bombardier in effect flew the plane while on the bomb run. This approach was both inaccurate and wasteful. Greater concentration could be attained if the bombardier in the lead aircraft targeted the central aiming point and the other planes in the bomber stream coordinated their bomb release with him.

Thus came into being the "togalier"—a combination of bombardier and nose gunner—whose job was to "toggle," or release the bombs by hitting a toggle switch on the signal of the bombardier in the lead plane. During the few minutes of the bomb run the togalier sat in the Plexiglas nose of the B-17. Otherwise he manned a machine gun in the chin turret of the plane.

A further refinement in bombing tactics was the placement of a flight officer in the tail gunner position of the lead aircraft. From that vantage point he had a clear view of the bomber stream to the rear and was better able to keep the lead pilot apprised of the action.

The four ranking officers on the *Miss Conduct* crowded into the smoky briefing room to receive their orders for the day. The other six crew members—Technical Sergeant Lester F. Higginbotham of Frankfurt, Indiana; Staff Sergeant Waldon R. Hardy of Seattle, Washington; Staff Sergeant George R. Byers of Stockton, California; Sergeant Francis E. Beam of Galion, Ohio; Sergeant John P. Dillon of Asheville, North Carolina; and Staff Sergeant Lloyd H. Gates Jr. of Jackson, Mississippi—would have to wait until they were briefed by the senior men before learning when and where they were going that day.

Behind the briefing officer was the familiar map of northern Europe. However, the mention of the Saxon capital signaled even to the veterans, many of whom were near the twenty-five-mission limit, that something different was in the offing. Such a raid called for a deep penetration into Germany, almost seven hundred miles, and might run as long as eleven hours, with six hours on oxygen. Everyone would be taxed to the limit.

The intense cold, the constant vibration and noise, and the ever-present threat of a violent and horrible death tested even the strongest men. Ironically, only one of the four men who were directly briefed played an offensive role in the mission: the bombardier. The pilot, copilot, and navigator were concerned only with keeping the plane on course and in formation—no small task.

The other crewmen who were directly engaged with the enemy were the gunners. For them the long flights were particularly arduous. In the early bombing campaign, waist gunners spent almost the entire flight directly exposed to the elements. Unlike the positions in the top turret, the ball turret, the tail, or the nose, there was no Plexiglas surrounding their guns. Freezing wind, rain, sleet, and snow swept into the fuselage. The temperature was often as low as minus sixty degrees. In 1943, 38 percent of Eighth Air Force casualties were caused by frostbite. The waist gun positions remained exposed until the end of 1943, when Plexiglas windows were installed. Fleece-lined flight suits and electrically heated boots also helped lower the rate to .5 percent in 1944, but the danger of frostbite was ever present.

In his isolation in the extreme rear of the aircraft, the tail gunner lay in a prone position and constantly scanned the sky to the rear for enemy fighters. The ball turret gunner flew doubled up in a Plexiglas bubble that was suspended below the B-17 and could be rotated a full 360 degrees. Except for takeoff and landing, he passed the entire flight alone in his cocoon.

For the *Flat Top*'s radioman, Sergeant Ernest Robertson, a young airman from Acworth, Georgia, this was to be his first taste of combat. The long mission to Dresden would be a baptismal rite. His many months of training were over. In a few hours, he would be a combat veteran. Duty such as this demanded courage, skill, physical strength, and quick reflexes—and not a little bravado and optimism. It is little wonder then that the bomber crews were composed of exceptionally young men, many of them barely out of their teens.

"I was the old man in the crew," recalled Colonel Robert Morgan, the captain of the legendary *Memphis Belle*. Morgan was all of twenty-three years old when he became the first B-17 pilot to complete twenty-five missions—with a raid on the submarine pens at Lorient on 17 May 1943.

The swagger of young World War II airmen was not the usual teenage or post-teenage machismo. It was, considering the statistical certainty that on any given day some would die, be wounded, or end their war staring through the barbed wire of a German prisoner of war camp, a necessity.

As predicted, the weather high over Europe was clear, with a brilliant blue sky, but 27,000 feet below the bombers the ground was obscured by 10/10 cloud cover. However, as the planes went deeper into Germany, some of the cloud cover broke and, as Engstrand recalled years later, Chemnitz could be glimpsed through broken clouds far off to the starboard side of the plane.

The break in the clouds was brief, however, and it was obvious that the ground would not be visible until the planes were near Dresden, if at all. The bombing would be by H2X. As the bomber fleet roared up the Elbe, it soon became apparent that finding Dresden was not to be a problem. Dead ahead was an unmistakable target marker. A column of smoke rose to at least 15,000 feet through the cloud cover. It was the burning city.

As the American B-17s began the bomb run a few minutes past noon, there were occasional glimpses of the ground below, although the mixture of clouds and smoke had created 7/10 cloud cover. Some crew members recalled that they had even seen patches of snow.

The aiming point was the Friedrichstadt marshaling yards, but because of the cloud cover bombing was basically blind and the bombing pattern was spread out. Other parts of the city were hit as well, in particular parts of the Neustadt, north of the river and directly ahead of the aiming point.

• • •

Just as earthquakes are remembered long after as having lasted an eternity, so it was with the air raids of World War II. For the victims of a raid the aftermath was, of course, a long-term, often harrowing experience. For the bomber crews, the raids were brief affairs, and this third, American, raid on Dresden was brief indeed. Between the moment the first bombs fell and the order for the withdrawal of the B-17s, the elapsed time was just a little more than ten minutes.

But in this fraction of an hour, another 771 tons of bombs fell on the burning and wrecked Saxon capital—475 of the 500-pound high-explosive bombs and over 136,000 of the small but deadly incendiaries.

The American raid was judged as having produced only "fair results," but the psychological damage to the people who had survived the first two waves of bombers was incalculable. The daylight raid came as thousands of rescue workers were pouring into the city, trying to extinguish the fires and to extricate the injured and dying from the air-raid shelters, cellars, and wreckage.

The U.S. raid also gave rise to charges of a further atrocity against the civilian population of Dresden. Reports, neither substantiated nor refuted in the sixty years since the raid, immediately began to circulate about the American fighter escorts. It was charged that while looking for so-called targets of opportunity, which was part of their orders, the P-51 fighter escorts indiscriminately strafed survivors in the streets and the refugees who had fled to the parks and to the meadows along the banks of the Elbe.

• • •

Of the 461 American First Air Division B-17s scheduled to bomb Dresden, just 311 were effective. They were protected by 281 of the originally assigned 316 P-51 fighter escorts. But where were the other 150 American bombers that had been dispatched to bomb Dresden on 14 February with their load of over 300 tons of high explosives and incendiaries?

Bad weather combined with poor navigation had begun to dog the planes as soon as they entered European airspace. Eighty-eight of the bombers were forced to drop their bomb loads, some 150 tons, on Brüx, Pilsen, and assorted other targets of opportunity. The remaining sixty-two B-17s, in a celebrated miscalculation, underscored how problematical the so-called precision bombing actually was, even this late in the war.

The bombardiers on these planes saw on their screens the perfect image of a large city in the bend of a river, which dovetailed perfectly with the pictures and maps of Dresden. It was not Dresden. That city was half an hour behind them. The B-17s had strayed into Czechoslovakia, and the city below was Prague. More than 150 tons of bombs were dropped on the Czech capital.

. . .

After the bomb run over Dresden, the American fleet turned to the west and began the arduous and dangerous journey back to England—six hours and almost seven hundred miles away. Once again there was 10/10 cloud cover until they reached Frankfurt. They crossed the Rhine south of Koblenz. The Mosel was visible off to the left of the aircraft.

There was light flak, but the Allied lines lay just a few miles away. All seemed to be going well when, in the tail of the *Miss Conduct,* Sergeant Dillon felt a bump above him. He looked up to see that a large chunk was missing from the stabilizer above his head. His frantic message to the pilot that they had been hit was immediately echoed by Sergeant Beam. Another shell had hit the waist of the plane. Almost immediately copilot Reopelle shouted that another burst had hit the right wing and they were on fire. Lieutenant Cebuhar ordered everyone out of the plane.

In the tail, Dillon prematurely opened the escape hatch before attaching his parachute, and it was swept away in the slipstream of the plane. He desperately began the long crawl forward to find another chute.

Engstrand opened the forward escape hatch, glanced apprehensively at the propellers, and dropped out of the plane. He could see that the ball turret guns were pointing straight down, and he hoped that this was a sign that Sergeant Byers had managed to extricate himself. Then the plane blew up. "It was like metal confetti all around me," recalled Engstrand.

He landed on a hill to the east of the Our River, the border between Germany and Luxembourg, and he soon realized that he was between the two battle lines. Artillery shells were roaring overhead. He also could see another member of the crew floating to earth; the man landed about a half mile away. Suddenly the deafening roar of airplane engines shook the ground. Two American P-51s were buzzing him and the other downed flier. It was an encouraging but futile show of support.

Engstrand ducked inside a small farm shack and took stock of his situation. Clearly he was at least within artillery range of the Allied lines, but how to get there? The sound of someone shouting in German put an end to his speculation. Cautiously he opened the door and stepped outside. After no more than five steps rifle fire froze him in his tracks. When he attempted to raise his hands he found that his shoulders had been dislocated in his escape from the plane. He made no further moves but stood silently as the German patrol advanced with their rifles pointed at him. Engstrand then heard the most chilling greeting of his life: "For you the war is over."

He was marched away to a building where the crewman he had seen earlier was being held. "Hi! My name is Ray Engstrand," he said to the other airman. "What's yours?" The Germans, of course, knew that they were from the same crew. As Engstrand later said, "We were all the same age, and I think they were as nervous as we were."

The two young Americans were taken to a nearby interrogation center; on the way they passed the wreckage of the tail of the *Miss Conduct*. Engstrand later speculated that the other part of the plane had landed behind the Allied lines, with the bodies of the radioman and the ball turret gunner.

The interrogations were the beginning of a six-week ordeal as a prisoner of war. Engstrand was beaten and threatened with execution when he would not talk. He was able to make it because, as he said, "I was young and strong and knew I could take whatever they dished out."

The prisoners, among whom were three other crew members, Cebuhar, Beam, and Dillon, who had managed to find another parachute on the crippled plane, were taken to Bonn, mainly on foot. At one point they traveled briefly on a truck captured from the U.S. 106th Infantry Division. There was no water and only a small piece of bread.

From Bonn they were transferred to a camp near Cologne, where they were loaded into a boxcar. Five days later they were in Stalag 11-B at Fallingbostel, about forty miles north of Hannover. On a phonograph, one of the guards played a song Engstrand had never heard before, "September Song."

On 21 March the prisoners were taken to Hannover and loaded on a train to Frankfurt. The Americans were already across the Rhine, and as the Germans retreated back into the Fatherland they marched the prisoners ahead of them. On 28 March, as the exhausted men struggled along a road, a group of P-47s swept low and wagged their wings. The Americans were at hand. The prisoners must hold on.

The next day, the prisoners were halted by an SS tank unit. Only the intervention of a Luftwaffe major prevented a massacre. On 30 March at about 1600 an American tank unit began to fire on the town where they had taken shelter, and when the Germans threw away their weapons and ran off, Engstrand came out of the cellar where he was hiding and grabbed a German pistol as a souvenir of the war. His fellow prisoners were certain he would be shot, but the commander of the American unit blithely said they were never in real danger because he had known all along who they were.

Their German guards who had stayed behind now found themselves in the same predicament that the Allied prisoners had been in just a day or two before. Only the intervention of one of the British prisoners, a major, prevented their being gunned down by the Americans. These are good Germans, he told the tank commander, noting in particular the Luftwaffe officer who had saved them from the SS.

• • •

Like the crews of the other American planes, the men aboard the *Flat Top* had also been surprised but relieved by the ease of the mission. There was neither flak nor fighter interception over Dresden.

Visibility was another issue altogether. Cloud cover ranged from 7/10 to 10/10, much of it caused by the dense smoke from the fires that were still burning throughout the city. At an altitude of between 27,000 and 28,000 feet, the city was well nigh invisible therefore, and the bombing was done by H2S.

The *Flat Top*'s bomb run had gone without incident, and Kelly turned the plane from its north-northeast heading and began the return flight to England and their home base. He and his crew remained wary and on the alert. There were many well-defended cities beneath them on the return flight path before they crossed into friendly territory. But the Western Front now reached almost to the Rhine, and once they were over the Allied lines, they could relax somewhat and settle in for the long flight to Podington.

· · ·

A few days later, Margaret Armstrong looked up to see the fiancée of Sergeant Balentine standing in the door of her room in the dormitory at Randolph-Macon College. The young woman was crying. Her mother had just telephoned with the news that the *Flat Top* was missing in action.

Margaret Armstrong, the young girl from South Carolina, and the families of the crew of the *Flat Top* spent the next eight months in a state of uncertainty and dread. At last, in the autumn, their vigil of hope ended. On 15 October, Hap Arnold wrote to the families of the crew that the men "previously reported missing on February 14, 1945, died in action on that date over France." Like many deaths in wartime, their end had come suddenly and from an unexpected quarter.

After capturing Dunkirk in June 1940, Germany quickly moved to reinforce that important port city, which had become such a galling symbol of defeat to both the British and the French. To the Germans, of course, it was a symbol of the superiority of German arms and the strategy known as *Blitzkrieg* and would remain so to the very end of the war.

The Germans constructed a vast underground garrison, protected from bombardment from the sea and air by yards of concrete and earth and camouflage. The city was circled by gun emplacements, which held massive coastal and land artillery batteries designed to repel attack from every direction. Central to the defense as well was a string of antiaircraft batteries and a force of 12,000 men. The overall commander of the garrison, port, and submarine pens was Vice Admiral Friedrich Frisius.

Just outside the fortress city, its German occupiers maintained four large farms to supply the garrison with beef, dairy products, vegetables, and fodder for the nearly one thousand horses used for transport. The bulk of the foodstuffs was produced by slave labor or commandeered from the local populace. Admiral Frisius kept a six-month reserve of supplies inside Dunkirk in case it was cut off completely.

At about 1500 hours on 14 February 1945, the crew of an antiaircraft battery at Couderkerque, on the outskirts of Dunkirk, heard the now familiar droning of an approaching American four-engine bomber. They watched in disbelief as the plane came in low from the east. The identifying markings of the B-17, which had to be returning from a raid on the Fatherland, were easily discerned by the gunners. In a matter of minutes, the plane would be over the English Channel and safely out of the range of their 88-millimeter antiaircraft guns.

At that moment aboard the plane, there was no thought of danger from the ground. Every effort was being directed to keep the plane in the air for the remaining minutes until it reached the safety of the coast of England. The *Flat Top* was dangerously low on fuel, and Kelly was struggling to reach one of the emergency landing fields just across the Channel.

The antiaircraft gunners opened up on the bomber. The first two bursts were wide of the target, but the third caught the plane squarely in the port wing. The great plane shuddered as it was hit, and a shout went up from the gun crew.

Sergeant Robertson, seated at his radio, heard a loud crunch as the shell exploded and he felt the plane lurch. He looked out the window and saw the port wing of the bomber beginning to buckle. Unstrapping himself from his seat, he ran back to the midsection of the plane, shouting to the two waist gunners that they had to get out. The plane was going down. Neither of them moved or responded. "They just sat there," he recalled later. "They just froze."

Almost immediately, a large crack opened in the fuselage beside him. Robertson did not hesitate. He dived through the opening. He was outside the plane and hurtling toward the earth. He jerked the rip cord on the parachute and in an instant felt a violent tug as his parachute opened. Robertson began the floating descent down toward what just minutes before he and his fellow airmen had thought was friendly territory.

He was completely alone. There were no other parachutes. The Fortress had disappeared. Below him lay what seemed to be a large lake—the Germans had flooded the fields near Dunkirk—and, as the sergeant hit the cold but shallow water, the parachute acted as a sail and began to drag him along toward dry land. Robertson disentangled himself from the shrouds and limped out onto a dirt road.

He had landed on one of the German farms. There was no one in sight. He soon realized, however, that he was not going to get very far. His ankle was broken, and he was wearing only the electrically heated inner boots. The sturdier outer flight boots had been ripped from his feet by the force of the parachute opening.

A German patrol soon found Robertson hobbling down the road. He was taken to the Dunkirk city jail, where he joined other prisoners from Canada and the United States.

There then occurred one of those coincidences that sometimes create a bond between even the bitterest enemies. When the German officer in charge learned during the interrogation that Robertson was from Georgia, his demeanor softened somewhat. He had run the high hurdles on the German team at the 1936 Olympics in Berlin, and he had become friendly with an American hurdler from Robertson's home state.

The Wehrmacht officer ensured that the sergeant's ankle was cared for and that he was well treated during the sixty-three days he was a prisoner of war. In April, Robertson was repatriated in an exchange of prisoners of war negotiated by the International Red Cross.

The *Flat Top* had crashed on land just a few miles short of the Channel. The bodies of Kelly and the seven other men who had gone down with the plane were recovered from the wreckage and buried by the Germans outside Dunkirk. They were not officially declared dead until the following October, when the graves were examined by the Americans. Kelly's body was shipped home on an army transport and buried in his hometown. He was awarded the Purple Heart and the Air Medal.

Dunkirk, like several other isolated German-occupied garrisons scattered along the French coast, held out until the very end of the war. This small French coastal town, which had become so famous at the beginning of the war as a symbol of military folly, British resolve, or both, was among the very last Nazi strongholds to fall to the Allies. Dunkirk did not surrender until 9 May 1945.

Sergeant Robertson's war injury continued to vex him more than fifty years later. From a veteran's nursing home in Decatur, Georgia, he castigated Montgomery for the loss of the *Flat Top* and the deaths of his companions. The victor of El Alamein, said Robertson, bore responsibility because he had failed in his assignment to clear the remaining Nazis out of the French coastal areas and adjoining Belgium and Holland.

Margaret Armstrong traveled to Alabama for her fiancé's funeral. Eventually she married and had children and grandchildren. But she retained her memories of Walter Kelly. "I can still remember his accent," she recalled a half century later.

CHAPTER ELEVEN

ASH WEDNESDAY,

1945

A City Laid Waste

When he emerged from the air-raid shelter at Weidner's Sanatorium at dawn on Ash Wednesday, Gerhart Hauptmann caught his
breath. The evening before he had beheld from the heights of Oberloschwitz a city still celebrated for its grace and beauty. This morning
the fabled spires and towers rose from a sea of flame and smoke. Sections
of Dresden would become visible as the firestorm swept away the
smoke, like a curtain being pulled back, revealing a city in its death
throes. Almost at once the curtain would fall again, but the fiery hurricane would sweep away the pall covering another part of the city and the
poet would be given a glimpse of yet more horror. Hauptmann at once
began an elegy to the city he called "my jewel."

"A person who has forgotten how to weep," he wrote, "learns how
once more at the sight of the destruction of Dresden. Till now, this clear
morning star of my youth has illumined the world. I know that there are
quite a few good people in England and America, to whom the divine
light of the Sistine Madonna was not unknown, and who now weep, profoundly and grievously affected by the extinguishing of this star. . . .

"From Dresden, from its wonderfully sustained nurturing of the fine
arts, literature, and music, glorious streams have flowed throughout all

the world, and England and America have also drunk from them thirstily. Have they forgotten that?

"I am nearly eighty-three years old and stand before God with a last request, which is unfortunately without force and comes only from the heart: it is the prayer that God should love and purify and refine mankind more than heretofore—for their own salvation."

. . .

A young Dresden historian, Matthias Neutzner, began a systematic study of the Dresden raids in the 1980s. His landmark work, collected in two books—*Angriff: Martha Heinrich Acht—Leben im Bombenkrieg, Dresden, 1944/45* and *Lebenszeichen: Dresden im Luftkrieg, 1944/1945*—provides invaluable first-person accounts by survivors of the firestorm.

A woman identified as Nora L., the daughter of a laborer, recalled her own family's ordeal the night of 13–14 February. She was then thirteen years old and lived with her family at 50 Holbeinstrasse, in Johannstadt, which lay in the direct line of attack of the first wave of bombers.

During this raid, Nora, her parents, and her two brothers, aged fifteen and five, huddled in the basement, listening to the roar of the British aircraft and the crash of bombs. They had brought with them the always-packed emergency suitcase and their identity papers.

Nora said she was trembling so badly that people sitting with them became alarmed and entreated her mother, who was holding the youngest child on her lap, to attend to her. But, said Nora, "She could not, she was like a piece of stone."

As terrible as the ordeal in the cellar was, the girl was relatively safe there. It was when they emerged from the shelter that their nightmare began. The parents were determined to save what they could from their burning apartment building, and they left the girl and her little brother in the nearby Dürerplatz. It was a large square with grass and trees, and the parents felt that the children would be safe there from the burning debris, which had begun to fly through the air as the flames grew.

When her parents did not return and the flames became more threatening, a young neighbor from their apartment building, who had also taken refuge in the comparative safety of the Dürerplatz with her baby, took charge of Nora and her little brother. They set off for the open spaces along the Elbe, just a few blocks away, as Nora recalled.

"I took my brother by the hand and we left. We tried to get through in the direction of the Elbe. The woman carried her baby. I had the suitcase and two blankets. It was a lot to carry. Some items I carried on my back, some stuff under my arm and I dragged my little brother behind me.

"We tried Dürerstrasse, but that was no longer possible because the burning houses collapsed. We kept in the middle of the street to avoid the stuff that came flying—bricks, window frames, and whatever. It was a firestorm like a tornado. We imagined it to be simple. And it was not really far, only twenty-two meters to Fürstenstrasse. But we could not get through. The woman with the baby kept urging me on and I tried to hide my fear. But there was no alternative and then we decided to enter a house and wait in the cellar till morning. And there we witnessed the second raid and that was even worse. The first time my parents had been around me and now I was alone with the little one."

The girl and her brother and their unnamed but heroic guardian had fortunately sheltered in a large house in a row of houses with connecting basements. One of the few air-raid precautions taken in the city was to replace the thick cellar walls between adjoining houses with thin partitions. As one basement filled with smoke or the house above collapsed, the inhabitants would then be able to knock out the thin brick or plaster partition and flee into the next house. And thus, by fleeing from house to house the people would, theoretically, be able to reach safe ground.

In actuality the system often doomed more people than it saved. In a firestorm, the fire was all around. A group fleeing one burning building might very well run directly into a group fleeing from the opposite direction. And when the fires had died down, thousands of bodies were found in the end houses of city blocks, where the people fleeing the flames and smoke had found themselves with no more walls to tear down. The system had created hundreds of fatal cul-de-sacs.

Other precautions also turned out to be a cause of death rather than a preventive. Gigantic open rectangular water tanks were erected in several of the squares, the one in the Altmarkt being particularly large. Ostensibly for use by the fire brigades after the water mains were destroyed, these uncovered reservoirs turned into death traps.

In a desperate attempt to escape the flames, hundreds of people scaled the walls of the tanks and jumped into the water. Inside, they soon realized their mistake. Unable to scale the walls and get out of the tanks, they either drowned or were boiled alive in the superheated water.

When the second raid collapsed the house above them, Nora and her brother began the trek through the subterranean passages from house to house in the block where they had sought refuge. "We passed from one cellar to the next. First I passed through our bags, my brother and so on. . . . But we finally got out and I don't remember how. I could do it only because the woman with the baby kept urging me on."

She was fortunate. They were able to exit onto the wide Fürstenstrasse, where it was possible to breathe, and with breath came some hope, even though most of the neighborhood of Johannstadt was a burning wreck. The hospital at the end of the Fürstenstrasse, near the Elbe, had survived the raid, and there the children stayed until dawn, when they headed for the safety of the river.

"Then we went to the Elbe," she said. "It was a gruesome picture. Corpses lying about, sometimes only a head or leg. And I trudged along with little brother. I had lost the woman in the crowds. Large numbers of people were at the Elbe. Those who had lived nearby had things they saved from the houses and put them down at the bank. Many had fled to the Elbe after the first raid and had died there."

Nora led her brother around the pitiful piles of shattered possessions and the mutilated corpses and crossed the river via the Albertbrücke, which had a large hole from a high-explosive bomb.

"My parents had told us that when something goes wrong—and one had to expect that it would, there were rumors—we will meet in Wilschdorf, where the family had a garden. So we made for Wilschdorf and it took a long time. Progress was slow, we had not slept and were exhausted. But we were in the Neustadt. There were houses standing and we felt a little safer."

The safety, however, was illusory. At midday, the third raid, this time by the U.S. Eighth Air Force, began. Nora and her brother had taken shelter at a hospital at the intersection of Liststrasse and Grossenhain-erstrasse, and she vividly remembered hearing the detonations of the bombs from the American B-17s.

At this hospital shelter, three other children, also refugees from 50 Holbeinstrasse, were overjoyed to see Nora and her brother. "So now we were five on the way to Wilschdorf," she related.

The other children, who were even younger, soon tired and said they could not go on, but Nora managed to get them to the next reception center, where they were able to spend the night. The next morning, since the children were still too exhausted to resume the trek, she decided to go on to Wilschdorf alone, get a cart, and return for them.

"My brother of course did not want to be separated from me, so we followed Moritzburger Chaussee toward Wilschdorf. Trucks loaded high with corpses passed us going to the Heidefriedhof [the central cemetery]. That was on 15 February."

After almost two days on foot, the heroic thirteen-year-old girl and her little brother covered the twelve miles from their home on the Holbeinstrasse to the family garden plot in the suburb of Wilschdorf. Her parents' joy was matched only by that of a neighbor who also had found her way to Wilschdorf but was grieving for her lost children.

"I could tell her that they had also been saved," said Nora. "So we went and got them right away."

. . .

The great decision facing every survivor after the initial bombardments was whether to remain in the relative safety of the shelters or leave them for the dangers in the streets. Typical was the woman who stayed in a shelter throughout the two raids but then decided to take her chances aboveground. She emerged from the basement into the heart of the firestorm. She later recalled the experience:

"In the street all hell had broken loose and I became suddenly aware of the violent storm from which we had been protected in the basement. It blew like a hurricane from the direction of Borsbergstrasse. Of some houses, only the roofs were in flames, others spewed flames from the first floor apartments. The heat was so great that I was not conscious at that time of my burns. . . .

"Parts of roofs fell from some houses into the street or the burned floors within the buildings came down making an enormous noise and released giant clouds of sparks moving through the street. When the stones gave way, they and the roof tiles crashed on the granite tiles of the sidewalk and broke apart. The air was filled with the stench of burning material and biting smoke and clouds of sparks came at us from all sides. These obstacles delayed our flight. We did not see any others, who should have also been fleeing at this time. Our residential area appeared to have turned into a fiery hell devoid of people."

• • •

A Dresdener who directed a Red Cross camp in Meissen mourned for her bombed city, and her cries might have been those of millions of other Germans: "I don't understand anything anymore. It always sounded different when they spoke of other cities. But perhaps it was never the same as here." In the same mournful letter written to her daughters on 15 February 1945, she mentions that while the raid was in progress she "stood in our small yard and guarded my Polish women, because they keep running from the shelter and out in the street."

The Polish women at the Red Cross camp were part of the more than eight million "foreign workers" in the Third Reich. Whether these women were there willingly is not clear. One recoils at the thought of the German Red Cross using slave labor. Then again, many military prisoners of war wound up in slave-labor camps.

Determined to find her children, whom she had left at their home in Dresden, the Red Cross worker started out on the morning of 14 February to look for them. Her moving account of the search for her children could be that of any desperate mother, whether a citizen of London, Coventry, Rotterdam, or Hamburg. Ideology and politics become distant concerns when one's children are in danger.

At the Meissen station, she was told that trains were running as far as Radebeul, about halfway to Dresden, but at Kötzschenbroda everyone was obliged to leave the train since the tracks ahead were destroyed. The trams, however, were operating as far as the terminal at Radebeul, after which the woman had no choice but to proceed on foot.

It was by then noon and the third wave of planes, the American Eighth Air Force, appeared over the city. "The bombs fell, they were shooting from the planes and everyone ran to the next bomb shelter," she said.

After the all clear, the woman was able to flag down a car bearing a red cross. Since she was in uniform the driver agreed to let her ride as far as the Neustadt, but after just a short distance the car could go no farther. The road was impassable.

"The car stopped below an underpass and we saw the first corpses," she related. "So I got out and planned to walk to the Marienbrücke, because the Augustusbrücke was said to be destroyed. People coming from there told me it was impossible because of the thick smoke and I knew they were right. The whole city was behind a thick black layer of smoke. So I went through the park toward the Neustädter Markt. There I met fire brigades from Meissen and other places, but they did nothing, although houses were burning all along the Elbe, although there should have been enough water. They told me that it was impossible to enter into the city without a gas mask or goggles and all of them had red, inflamed eyes, same as I today.

"Twenty paces away from me fell the burning roof of the Japanese Palace on the street. I ran to Meissener Gasse, which burned bright. Detoured through another street that was not so totally bad and reached the Neustädter Markt, where many houses were burning or had collapsed. The base of the memorial [the equestrian statue of Augustus the Strong] stood and the steeple of the Martin Luther Church could be seen.

"But fear for my children drove me on and I chanced along onto the [Augustus] bridge, while the men stayed back. The driving surface had large holes, handrails torn off, stones broken, but I did not care, all I wanted was to get across and I made it. On the Schloss-platz were two units with shovels but they just stood there. I did not see anybody moving a hand or dig as long as I was in Dresden. Could not pass through the Schloss-strasse, which was blocked by mountains of debris. So also the Augustus-strasse. The Ständehaus was aflame. The [Brühl] Terrace, I think, was still there and of the Schloss, the lower part. I could not see and remember everything. And the thick smoke and rain of sparks from the burning houses, because on top of everything, a strong wind came up.

"At where the Neumarkt starts, I passed burning streetcars and debris several meters high. But it was not possible to cross. Debris covered all to a height of several meters."

She returned the way she had come, and at the Georgentor, the great neo-Renaissance gate leading into the Royal Palace, a rider on a motorcycle stopped her and asked if he could get through to the police headquarters on the Schiessgasse. Learning that the way was blocked, he decided that he would detour around the ruins by way of the Elbe and the Carolabrücke.

"I said I wanted to go with him," she recalled, "climbed on the passenger seat and we proceeded over burning stuff, wood, etc., to where the Ringstrasse begins and where I got off. The police station was gone."

By this time she had crossed most of Dresden, from the outskirts of the Neustadt, across the river, and through the Altstadt. The piles of rubble that she was forced to negotiate or detour around had been, just a few hours before, some of the most beautiful buildings in the world.

She had passed the ruins of the cathedral, the broken and burned-out Zwinger, the wreckage of the *Schloss*, the collapsed and burning opera house, the ruins of the Albertinum, and the blackened but miraculously still-standing Frauenkirche.

In an ordinary time, she would have been able to reach her neighborhood—the area around Sidonienstrasse, Lüttichaustrasse, and Beuststrasse, not far from the central train station, the Hauptbahnhof—in fairly short order. The walk from the Neustadt is not a long one. But this day she had already been en route for hours.

Now she began to see the human toll from the carnage. There were, she said, "corpses everywhere . . . a gruesome picture, one next to the other, one on top of the other, naked, burned and totally carbonized . . . shrunken clumps that used to be humans. . . . Lüttichaustrasse was totally blocked by ruins. I tried to walk hand in hand with a man since by oneself it was not possible anywhere because of the constant sliding. I had to give up before I got to Moltkeplatz.

"I thought that along a residential street with detached houses that were not built so close to the street I might be able to pass and so went to Beuststrasse. Here again, every house was destroyed, no tree left, debris in the street. But crawling under or over downed trees and the wreckage of houses I made it. Then Sidonienstrasse. Mountains of debris and not one house that was not burning as everywhere else in the inner city. I met a gentleman and hand in hand we climbed over the ruins.

"With great effort, scraped shoes and burning eyes we arrived among burning houses, chunks of which fell into the street without pause, over stones, debris, and burning wood to our corner."

She soon discovered that it was impossible to get near her house because of the debris and the flames, but she did not despair, holding out hope that the children had somehow managed to reach a shelter and perhaps were now already out of the city.

If she had truly believed that they were buried, she said, "I would, in that case, have had to try all by myself to dig a way to the air-raid shelter and to remove every single stone."

Unlike thousands of survivors, this desperate mother found her perseverance rewarded. Her children and an aunt had managed to reach the air-raid shelters and then afterward make their way to the refugee center at Possendorf.

Others would never know what had happened to their friends and relatives. Were they entombed beneath mountains of rubble? Had they been burned alive or suffocated in the cellars as the firestorm swept over them? Had their bodies been put to the torch in the great funeral pyres in the pubic squares? Or did they lie with thousands of others, unidentified, in the huge communal graves dug outside the city? For many months the ruins of Dresden were covered with notices, often containing photographs, tacked up by survivors desperately looking for the missing.

· · ·

In spite of the raids, the German postal system continued to function, albeit sporadically, and many of the letters and cards from the bombed-out Dresdeners have survived. In addition to longer letters, there were brief notes—senders were limited to just ten words—on red-bordered postcards, which had been issued by the authorities for use in emergencies.

Typical of the letters describing the raid was one from a woman who had found refuge in a school at Reichstadt. She and two other women and an infant had escaped with just a few clothes from Dresden's Altstadt.

"After the first raid, we had to get out of the cellar without knowing how and when. Everything thickly covered with smoke. No passage open. We sat there for a long time. Then passed through Viktoriastrasse into a sea of flames. By myself I would probably not have found the courage and strength to pass through fire and tons of debris. We just wanted to find an open area. Everything in flames. Turned the corner toward main station. Train station still stood and we went upstairs to the guard room. Fearful masses of debris. We thought ourselves saved. After a few minutes of silence the 2nd air raid alert sounded. 1½ hours at train station in basement. . . . The basement ceiling held, but we did not believe we could get out and lay down to die. At about 0500 came word that a passage was open. So we took backpack and suitcase and all and clambered out with great effort. Again a gigantic fire. So we sat in the street for a few hours.

"Now we are in a school in Reichstadt. It is more than primitive. Toelschen, see if you can send us something. I own what I am wearing, nightgown, panties, sweat pants, pullover, jacket, coat, torn shoes and stockings. Not even a belt. It is awful, I cannot yet comprehend fully and could weep all the time."

This woman and her companions were fortunate to escape from the Hauptbahnhof. Hundreds of other refugees and Dresdeners who had fled to the Central Station perished when the superheated air and poisonous gases swept through the maze of underground tunnels and passages where they had sought refuge.

· · ·

Hans-Joachim D. was fifteen years old in February 1945. He lived with his widowed mother, two-year-old-brother, and some relatives who had fled Silesia in an apartment on the Wiener Platz at the Pragerstrasse, directly across from the Central Station.

The family realized that something was amiss when they turned on their radio shortly before 2200 hours and there was no music. Suddenly, they heard an announcement that large bomber formations were approaching the city and there was a "Maximum Threat for Dresden."

The announcement, he recalled, was almost immediately followed by the roar of airplane engines. From the garden, the boy watched as the "Christmas trees" and marker flares lit up the night sky, but he quickly retreated into the cellar, a public air-raid shelter designed for sixty that was soon packed with over a hundred people.

"The first night raid seemed endless. It was horrible in the tightly packed cellar. The many people, the unending thunder of falling bombs, nearby explosions and pressure waves, which tore even the strong metal doors off their hinges. At the door a wave of fire rolled into the shelter and the whole stairwell was in flames. A glance through the cellar window showed that the path through the garden was also blocked.

"Finally we found a passage through a first floor apartment and through a wall of flames to Wiener Platz. . . . Around us screaming, despairing people. Refugees with their last belongings. We looked along Pragerstrasse, formerly so splendid and elegant, where the 19th-century building of the Kaiser Wilhelm Café was hidden by flames. Flames shot everywhere from shop windows. It looked like a painting of hell. Further away, resembling a torch, the tower of City Hall. Flames came out of its roof below the Golden Man."

This last is a reference to the gigantic gilded statue of Hercules that stood atop the tower of the Rathaus, or City Hall. The tower with its golden statue miraculously survived and once again crowns the rebuilt Dresden City Hall.

Like many of his fellow citizens, the young man attempted to return to the family apartment to salvage something before the building was totally consumed. He left his mother and brother in a house behind the Hauptbahnhof and returned to Wiener Platz, where with the aid of fellow tenants, some French workers, he carried suitcases, dishes, and food into the square. He hoped the pitiful pile of belongings would be safe there until they could be gathered up the next day. But now the second wave of bombers appeared.

"Suddenly we heard the whine of a siren again, very weak. It was not the large ones on the rooftops, which had all been destroyed. This thin whine came from a portable hand-operated siren. They come again! Passed on from mouth to mouth. Again the bombs crashed down and the bombers roared through the sky. We ran for our lives and reached the house where I knew my mother and brother would be. It was a miracle I found them again in the crowd that ran to the shelters. This was also a public shelter. So many came in that the stairway was full of people and the steel door could hardly be closed. Several steel lockers stood in the shelter corridor in a row. We found space between two of them and this turned out later to be what saved us.

"We lay on the floor, mouths open—as we had learned to do because of the explosion pressure—when the terror began again. We felt that the bombs were concentrated on the rail station and buildings near it. A full hit during the first few minutes destroyed the adjoining house down to the cellar. A cellar wall broke open and a flood of fire reached the people standing and sitting in our cellar. Women, children, and men fell over each other in a panic. The screams of the wounded mixed with the roaring of the explosions above us.

"Then followed a tremendous boom that lifted us off the floor. A pressure wave raced along the cellar corridor. Then it was still. This pressure wave had torn the lungs of almost everyone in the cellar corridor. Only the few of us who had lain between the steel lockers survived."

The boy, his mother, and his little brother did survive, and after several hours in the pitch-blackness of the cellar, among the piles of corpses, they were rescued when a hole was opened through a wall into Winckelmannstrasse by a rescue team that had heard them knocking on the wall.

"Outside we encountered the indescribable firestorm," he said. "In front and behind us, the roofs of two houses fell down. For some minutes, my mother and brother had disappeared in a cloud of sparks. Then I heard a voice from the other side of the street, 'Over here!' Holding onto each other, our clothes on fire, we jumped across the already burning asphalt and reached a house that had little damage.

"This single villa on Winckelmannstrasse survived all air raids and is now the Hotel Classic. There, our saviors threw wet blankets over us, took us into the cellar and so let us survive the night a second time."

The boy, his mother, and his little brother set out in the morning for his grandparents' house in the suburb of Kemnitz. Their circuitous route led them over piles of smoking rubble many meters high, and everywhere were corpses, many of them carbonized. A few days later, he and his grandfather, pulling a wooden handcart, returned to the Wiener Platz to look for the household goods.

"How I wish we had not done so," he recalled. "Everything was actually there on Wiener Platz, where we had dumped the things after the first raid. But everything had melted: glass, flatware, porcelain. Behind the train station, under the track overpass, were stacked hundreds of dead and more were being added all the time from the station and nearby cellars. A wave of bad-smelling heat from the cellar where we had barely escaped hit us in the face. Of our house, only a piece of wall and a mountain of debris lay on Wiener Platz.

"As was the routine, we wrote our address on a wall: 'We are alive, live in Kemnitz, Flensburgerstrasse 16.'

"This scrawl remained there for a long time. Today, the tunnel on the train station side passes through what was our cellar."

· · ·

In the early evening of 13 February, fourteen-year-old Renate Heilfort was standing in the ticket line at the cinema on the Postplatz. The line was long, and when it was announced that there would be no more tickets available until the nine o'clock showing the young girl decided not to wait but to take the tram home to the suburb of Zschachwitz, a distance of about five kilometers. This decision would save her life. Not long after she reached home the first bombs began to fall on the Postplatz, which was at the center of the firestorm. The theater and all the surrounding buildings were obliterated.

. . .

Gerhart Sommer, who was eight years old in 1945, lived with his mother, his little sister, and his thirteen-year-old brother, who was an assistant on an ambulance, in the suburb of Reick, just southeast of the Grosser Garten. His father was with the Wehrmacht in Hungary.

One is struck time and again, in the wrenching stories of the survivors, by the central role played by women and children, who were, of course, the main component of the civilian urban population.

Gerhart's mother herded the two smaller children into the basement of the house when the alarm sounded. His brother was on duty in the town center. First, however, she checked to make sure that each had a handkerchief. This was not just a typical mother's admonition. A handkerchief soaked in one's own urine could serve as a makeshift gas mask and save one's life in the dense smoke in the streets or in a cellar suddenly filled with smoke and carbon monoxide.

As they fled into the basement shelter, the "Christmas trees" had started to fall and the city was lit up like daylight. It was eerily beautiful, recalled Gerhart, but the mother did not allow them to tarry.

Within minutes the bombs began to fall, and although Reick was well out of the central targeting area, several high-explosive bombs fell within a hundred meters of the house. The concussion was so great that even at that distance the family was lifted into the air and flung against the far wall of the cellar. Doors buckled, and every window was blown out.

The family was fortunate to have survived the blasts from the high-explosive bombs, which were designed not only to blow up buildings but to create shock waves of such power that all the internal organs that were filled with air—the lungs, the stomach, and the intestines—exploded. Thus many corpses had no external wounds or damage.

One witness reported seeing a tram filled with passengers, all of them dead, killed instantly by the concussion wave from a high-explosive bomb, which had destroyed their hearts and lungs. Not one had an external wound. The windows had exploded outward, so that none of the glass had pierced their bodies. There they sat, he recalled, appearing as if they had just fallen asleep.

The Sommer family stayed in their shelter until daylight, when Gerhart and a friend named Peter, a child of the same age who lived next door, went out to investigate. Even small children had been taught how to deal with unexploded ordnance, in particular the small incendiary bombs, and the two little boys set off several that they found in the street by poking them with a piece of lumber.

Just before noon, Gerhart's brother arrived home. His ambulance, which had been transporting wounded to the Elbe Meadows, had been hit and destroyed by machine-gun fire from an American fighter plane. The mother then loaded up a four-wheeled cart with household goods and with her three children began the trek to relatives in the countryside, where they would live until the end of April.

In May, the entire family was reunited when the father returned home from the east. He and a group of comrades had commandeered a locomotive and had managed to get as far as Pirna, just a few miles from Dresden, before the engine gave out. They had walked the rest of the way home.

· · ·

All the stories told by survivors heartbreakingly underscore the true cost of air war against civilians, but that of Mrs. S., who lived at 19 Webergasse, just a block from the Altmarkt and thus at the epicenter of the firestorm, is particularly wrenching.

"Then came the second raid and we went down into the basement again," she recalled. "I carried my son and placed a wet cloth over his face because of the smoke. . . . I do not know at what time my child was dead, or my mother. I fainted. When I came to, the corpses were lying on top of me.

"I pulled myself out from under to see if there was a way out. But my legs would not support me because of a torn ligament and so I could only crawl on my knees. But I could not see an exit."

Mrs S lay there until Thursday with the bodies of her son and her mother. When they were finally dug out, she was told she was one of six survivors out of ninety-five people who had sought refuge in the cellar. "You cannot imagine how they were stacked on top of each other," she said. "Eighty-nine corpses."

More than thirty years later she still carried the photographs and the death certificates of her son and mother. "This was the little one," she said, showing her interviewer the picture of her dead son. "He was seventeen months old."

• • •

As these tragedies and dramas were playing out in the streets of Dresden, the aerial bombardment continued. The American air force, which had completed the triple blow on 14 February, was back the next day. On 15 February 1945, another 211 B-17s from the Eighth Air Force dropped another 464 tons of bombs on the crippled city. The primary targets that day were the oil refineries at Böhlen and Ruhland, but when the weather closed in over those targets, the pilots had to opt for the secondary target, Dresden.

Bombing was done by H2X, and though it was scattered and by no means as effective as during the three previous raids, it was devastating to the stunned survivors below, who were struggling desperately, searching for victims while trying to extinguish the hundreds of fires that were still burning.

And on this day, perhaps the most crushing psychological blow of all was delivered to the Dresdeners. The Frauenkirche, the Church of Our Lady, the dominant feature of the townscape, miraculously still stood after three devastating waves of Allied bombers had destroyed everything around it.

But the sandstone foundation and supports were fatally weakened by the flames that had roared around the great church since the first British planes had appeared two nights before. At 1015 on 15 February, the dome of the church, more than a hundred meters high, began to buckle. In just a few seconds the proud symbol of the Florence on the Elbe since 1734 was a pile of smoking rubble. The last vestige of old Dresden was gone.

• • •

Later that same day, at 1530, another plane appeared over Dresden, but this one was hardly noticed by the dazed survivors, if they even bothered to register its presence. This plane from 542 Squadron of the RAF had a benign mission: to photograph the carnage below. The quality of the prints is poor because of the smoke from the fires, but it is clear that the raids had their intended effect.

The areas most affected were south of the Elbe—the city center, or Altstadt, and the adjoining areas of Johannstadt and Süduorstadt— which were effectively 100 percent destroyed. Houses were destroyed or damaged as far as the suburb of Loschwitz. The Neustadt, north of the river, was less severely damaged, but the sectors near the river were essentially flattened and burned out. The Carola Bridge was judged out of service, and while the Augustus Bridge was heavily damaged it was probably usable. The railway bridge was seriously damaged as well.

Put simply, the destroyed area contained all the important cultural, religious, and civic buildings of Dresden. These included the Zwinger, the Albertinum, the Academy of Art, the Japanese Palace, the state archives; the museums of antiquities, of the army, of folklore, of history, and of prehistory; the Hofkirche, the Kreuzkirche, the Sophienkirche, and the Frauenkirche; the Semper Oper and the Schauspielhaus; the Royal Palace and the adjoining Taschenbergpalais; the Rathaus; the Zoological Garden; the Grosser Garten; the train stations; and the majority of the hospitals.

But as vast as the destruction of the cultural treasures was, the destruction of thousands of private homes and apartments, the electrical-generating system, the food-distribution system, and the sewage and water systems were the more immediate calamity. And everywhere there were the bodies of the dead, whose decomposing corpses portended a health crisis of terrible proportions.

What was to be done with the thousands of corpses being carried out of the basements or still lying in the streets? Day after day, bodies were loaded onto the only available transport, horse-drawn wagons, and taken away to be buried in vast mass graves at the Heidefriedhof, on the Dresdner Heide, the heath northeast of the city.

By the end of February, it was realized that this system could not cope with the rising health emergency. The city center was sealed off and giant grills made of girders and metal shutters from a nearby department store were erected in the Altmarkt. The horse-drawn carts with their cargoes of corpses were then diverted to the ancient square. There the bodies were stacked on the grills like cordwood, five hundred at a time, doused with gasoline, and set ablaze. Almost ten thousand of the dead were disposed of in this way, and the stench of burning flesh hung in the air for weeks.

For some of the survivors it was the smell in the streets—a sickening mixture of high explosives, phosphorous, ash, smoke, and, above all, burning flesh—that they would never forget. A woman who survived the firestorm and later immigrated to America recounted that on a visit to Dresden fifty years later she could still smell the burning corpses and was nearly overcome when she stepped out of a car at the Altmarkt.

• • •

In 1975, a gravedigger at the Heidefriedhof unearthed an urn while opening a new grave. The urn contained a report written by a young soldier identified only as Gottfried, and dated 12 March 1945.

"On 13 February we heard the early warning. Mother got ready and kept her good humor, while father was seriously concerned as he always is when danger threatens from the air. Christa [the soldier's wife] wrapped up her little Mike and we went to the air raid shelter under the house in front of ours. Everything was as usual and we hoped to be able to return soon upstairs. This was Shrove Tuesday (Mardi Gras)! But it was not long before [a neighbor] brought us the report: 'Fighter units en route to city.' A few minutes later we no longer needed an air situation report to know that this time we were it.

"The enemy planes dropped flares and the well-known 'Christmas trees' over the whole area of the city. The first detonator bombs fell. Outside the wild dance of the man-made elements of destruction. The raid lasted an eternity, finally, 'All Clear.'

"My father and I immediately went upstairs to see what had become of the house. . . . All doors and windows were torn to pieces. Both houses, front and back plus those on both sides looked awful. On the top floor of the building in back I extinguished two incendiary bombs. . . . The building along the side was already burning and a blast of wind threatened our building in the back. The wind soon turned into a storm and tore up everything inside, because there were no more doors. The house across the street was also in flames. I stood on the roof garden surrounded by a firestorm that kept getting worse. Before long, all buildings in this area were on fire. Timed explosives kept going off."

When the second raid came, the soldier, his wife, and their infant son took refuge in the basement of an already burning house, where they remained, surrounded by fire, until 0930 on the morning of 14 February. When they emerged, on the Grosse Plauensche Strasse, they could see that his parents' house had taken a direct hit and was just a smoking ruin. The entire area around the Central Station, he said, "was nothing but debris and ashes as far as the eye could see."

"Total destruction. Lunacy. . . . Only a few survivors came crawling out of their basements, no air raid wardens, no help, just nothing. We had to get the child out of this hellish smoke. I carried the boy over mountains of debris, between burning and collapsing buildings, past the dead and dying.

"Six days later I went to the wrecked house. The debris was still so hot that one could not step on it without burning the soles of one's shoes. Then I heard that the recovered bodies were being taken to the Altmarkt to be burned with flame throwers. I wanted to spare our relatives this fate."

With the help of a corporal from his unit and six prisoners of war, the young man started digging into the shelter beneath his parents' house. Even then, a week after the raid, the heat was still so intense in the cellar that they could remain there for only a few minutes. But despite the poor light, he said, "I saw the most painful scene ever. . . . Several persons were near the entrance, others at the flight of steps and many others further back in the cellar. The shapes suggested human corpses. The body structure was recognizable and the shape of the skulls, but they had no clothes. Eyes and hair carbonized but not shrunk. When touched, they disintegrated into ashes, totally, no skeleton or separate bones.

"I recognized a male corpse as that of my father. His arm had been jammed between two stones, where shreds of his grey suit remained. What sat not far from him was no doubt mother. The slim build and shape of the head left no doubt. I found a tin and put their ashes in it. Never had I been so sad, so alone and full of despair. Carrying my treasure and crying I left the gruesome scene. I was trembling all over and my heart threatened to burst. My helpers stood there, mute under the impact.

"What else is there to write? There are three copies, one I put in the urn."

• • •

Variations on this melancholy theme were played out for decades after the war. For years the skeletons of victims were discovered in the ruins of Dresden as rubble was removed or foundations for new buildings were erected.

One particularly poignant discovery was made when the ruins adjacent to the Altmarkt were being excavated in the 1990s. The workmen found the skeletons of a dozen young women who had been recruited from the countryside to come into Dresden and help run the trams during the war. They had taken shelter from the rain of bombs in an ancient vaulted subbasement, where their remains lay undisturbed for almost fifty years.

CHAPTER TWELVE

"MR. PRIME MINISTER?"

Questions in
Parliament and
World Opinion

At the Allied Air Commanders Conference two weeks after the Dresden firestorm, there seemed to be no particular concern with public opinion. And the outcry over Dresden had caused no change in Bomber Command's policies. On the night of 23–24 February, ten days after the triple blow on Dresden, some areas of which were still smoldering, Pforzheim had been subjected to one of the most devastating raids of the war. The area of destruction comprised 83 percent of the town, and 17,600 people died.

The Pforzheim attack, according to the minutes of the meeting, "had been what was popularly known as a terror attack." Harris knew that in certain quarters the value of these area attacks was disputed, but the town contained innumerable small workshops for the manufacture of precision instruments, and he said that the attack must have destroyed the "home-work" of the population and their equipment, since 25 percent of the population was now dead. Given the percentage of the population killed, the Pforzheim raid was probably the most deadly raid of the war. Bomber Command had now destroyed sixty-three German towns in this fashion.

While Spaatz and Doolittle kept silent at this meeting, they made clear elsewhere and with some frequency their opposition to morale bombing. But they had also called for widespread attacks across Germany, which, combined with heavy attacks against places like Berlin, would have had "a more decisive effect upon morale." Spaatz had, five days earlier, been singled out in a broadcast by the turncoat commentator Donald Day on the Nazi English-language radio station, who'd declared,

The Wehrmacht has decided to confer a special decoration upon Gen. Spaatz, the commander of the US bombing forces in England. This special decoration is the Order of the White Feather. The Wehrmacht thinks that Gen. Spaatz earned this decoration when he sent over a fleet of nearly 1,000 US bombers to lay a carpet of bombs across Berlin. Gen. Spaatz and the Americans commanded by him knew that Berlin was crowded with hundreds of thousands of refugees, principally women and children, who had fled before the organized savagery and terrorism of the Bolshevik Communist Red Army.

Day was referring to the thousand-bomber raid of 3 February. Berlin, he said, was already taxed to the limit housing and feeding refugees, and the planes that should have protected the city were in the east, helping the German army fend off the common foe of Bolshevism, which threatened not just Germany but all of Europe.

On the day of this broadcast, 17 February, while Day was warning of the horrors of Bolshevism, thousands of Jews were being herded along roads and highways like so many cattle, forced to make their way westward on foot in the bitter cold of an eastern European winter. These were the pitiful remnants, the last few survivors of the concentration camps in the east, which lay in the path of the Soviet advance.

While Day was ranting about American atrocities and the dangers of Bolshevism, the forced march of a thousand Jewish women from the camp at Neusalz on the Oder had reached the Neisse River—at least for those who were still alive. The survivors—there would be only two hundred at the end of the ordeal—would not reach the camp at Flossenburg for another three weeks.

The day after Day's broadcast, 18 February, the last of the few hundred protected Jews in the German homeland were ordered to collection points for deportation to Theresienstadt. There were to be no exceptions. Marriage to an Aryan no longer could save them.

Day, of course, did not mention that the American bombs also dispensed a rough justice at the court building in Berlin where the trials of the conspirators in the 20 July bomb plot against the Führer were going on. Thousands of accused conspirators had already been tried in show trials and executed.

The president of the People's Court was the rabid Nazi Roland Freisler, who did not so much preside as perform. His hysterical diatribes were cunningly devised to humiliate the defendants, cow the onlookers, and, not so incidentally, curry favor with Hitler, who viewed the newsreels of the trials.

Freisler was crushed to death as the court building collapsed around him during the raid. The trials were suspended and several of the defendants were saved by the raid and survived the war. Other plotters, such as Admiral Wilhelm Canaris, chief of the Abwehr, military intelligence, were not so fortunate. He was executed by the Gestapo on 9 April, just a month before the German surrender.

· · ·

Bomber Harris somewhat peevishly complained to his colleagues at the Allied Air Commanders Conference that although Bomber Command had been fighting Germany for five years, their role in the destruction of Germany was not being properly appreciated by the ground forces, which were just entering Germany. In response, it was suggested that perhaps air crews should visit the infantry and tank divisions and that ground forces could profit from visits to airfields.

Doolittle, mindful of the criticism of the friendly-fire disasters caused by bad navigation during close air support of ground troops, was not optimistic about such a public relations campaign. "Eighth Air Force

Crews would have to be careful not to visit an outfit that they had bombed," he wryly remarked.

Interestingly, Harris had been with Churchill at Chequers the evening of the Pforzheim attack. Churchill had returned just four days before from the Yalta Conference. When Bomber Command had finished with its task, the prime minister mused aloud over dinner, "What will lie between the white snows of Russia and the White Cliffs of Dover?" Churchill's remark to Harris can be read in several ways, but it is clear that he recognized the awful power of aerial bombardment.

He added that if he lived he would concentrate on one thing: the building and maintenance of a powerful air force. No doubt Britain, in the postwar world, would have to carve out a new niche for itself, caught as it was between the "huge Russian bear and a great American elephant."

Harris, surprisingly, demurred. He saw more promise in the German V-2 rockets. Although they were no match at that stage for the devastating power of his bomber fleets, they were clearly a portent of the future. "The bomber is a passing phase and, like the battleship, it has nearly passed," he said to the prime minister.

Earlier, as the guests had gathered in the great hall of Chequers, waiting to go into dinner, John Colville, Churchill's secretary, had asked Harris what the effect of the raid on Dresden had been. "Dresden? There is no such place as Dresden," Harris had replied.

Colville also records that during this same evening Churchill remarked that Carl Spaatz was "a man of limited intelligence," to which Harris replied, "You pay him too high a compliment."

If his book *Bomber Offensive* is any guide, Harris seemingly never changed his opinion of his American counterpart. He mentions Spaatz only once, in passing. As for Eaker, Anderson, and Doolittle, Harris wrote, "We could have no better brothers in arms . . . and the Americans could have had no better commanders than these three. I was, and am, privileged to count all three of them as the closest of friends." Harris wrote these words in 1947, when Spaatz had not only succeeded Hap Arnold but had been made head of the new and separate United States Air Force.

Churchill, when he made his disparaging remark about Spaatz, no doubt knew of the American's upcoming promotion to four-star general, which came on 11 March. Spaatz himself was informed of the promotion during a poker game. His response was in character. He ordered champagne for everyone and then returned to the business at hand. "Come on and deal," he said.

Carl Spaatz was now one of the highest-ranking men in the American military, but the European operations that he oversaw were already being relegated to second place by Washington. By late March, Spaatz let his anger at the new policies, particularly the diversion of matériel to the Far East, spew forth.

"It seems," he said, "unjustified that so great and expensive a Military Organization as the Air Force should have its potentialities limited to such serious extent by failure to set up adequate bomb production facilities."

Spaatz's cable raised hackles at the Pentagon, but no increases were forthcoming. Lieutenant General Barney M. Giles wrote to his friend that "it is most improbable that your ultimate desired requirements can ever be met."

Attention was shifting to the Pacific theater, where in a short time Spaatz himself would be running the air war. Such are the fortunes of war.

· · ·

Goebbels, when he heard the news of Dresden, wept openly and called on Hitler—who, according to his personal physician was thrown into a black depression—to repudiate the Geneva Convention and start shooting captured pilots and parachutists.

The propaganda minister issued Gerhart Hauptmann's elegy to the dead city to the press and radio. Hauptmann's work, which Goebbels extolled as exemplifying the work of Germany's most famous poet, was soon broadcast and printed around the world via the neutral countries.

As for Hitler, he quickly rallied and threatened to heed Goebbels's advice. "This constant sniveling about humanity will cost us the war," he said. A few days later, when he deigned to look at photographs of the thousands of dead Dresdeners, the Führer lapsed again into a despairing mood, but it was brief and had no effect on his resolve to fight on.

Hitler's quick recovery from his brief and uncharacteristic shock at the destruction of Dresden mirrored his attitude toward the destroyed cities of the Reich. Cities can be rebuilt, he had said more than once in response to the Allied raids. Besides, it had always been his plan to rebuild the cities according to National Socialist ideals, and he had often remarked to Albert Speer that the raids would make the rebuilding easier.

Speer was an unknown architect in 1933 when he was brought into Hitler's circle to help the Führer realize his grandiose schemes, in particular his dream of transforming Berlin into Germania, the new capital of the Thousand-Year Reich. And even though he was raised to the position of armaments minister in 1941, he continued working up plans for this vast transformation. Even as Soviet troops were on the outskirts of Berlin he and Hitler would study the architectural models.

Other high-ranking Nazis were just as zealous as Hitler in their desire to forge a Germany completely based on National Socialist ideals. If the cities and monuments of Germany were destroyed, so be it.

When Robert Ley, the German Labor Front leader, heard of the destruction of Dresden, he was exultant. Germany, he said, could "almost draw a sigh of relief. It is over now. In focusing on our struggle and victory we are now no longer distracted by concerns for the monuments of German culture." For Ley these monuments were "superfluous ballast," just so much "heavy spiritual and material bourgeois baggage."

Early on the evening of 14 February, Goebbels met again with Hitler in the *Führerbunker*. Dresden was still aflame. Goebbels denounced Göring to the Führer and called for his trial and certain execution by hanging or a firing squad for dereliction of duty, citing in particular the miserable showing of the Luftwaffe during the three-part Dresden raid. Hitler put him off.

Three days later, Goebbels resurrected his scheme to execute one Allied prisoner of war for each air-raid victim. Hitler approved, and Goebbels produced a plan justifying this abrogation of the Geneva Convention. This vengeful barbarism came to nothing when Hitler again changed his mind. Several of his henchmen took credit for the plan's demise, particularly those later arrested and tried at Nuremberg.

Dwight Eisenhower might have had something to do with the reversal as well. The supreme allied commander warned the Nazis and the German people themselves, in a widely disseminated announcement, that they would be held fully accountable for such actions.

■ ■ ■

The Dresden raids and firestorm immediately became the symbol to many of the horror of a war waged against civilian populations, and for a while in the spring of 1945 there was something of a firestorm as well in the press, the Parliament, the highest reaches of government, and military headquarters. Everyone, it seemed, now had questions about Allied bombing policy in general and the raid on Dresden in particular.

The brouhaha began just a day or two after the raid when Air Commodore A. M. Grierson briefed reporters at the Supreme Headquarters Allied Expeditionary Force (SHAEF) on the continuing air campaign. Grierson then offered to take questions from the reporters, and the very first had to do with the attacks on Dresden and other points just ahead of the advancing Red Army. As Grierson explained it, the attacks were the result of recommendations made by the combined strategic targets committee and had three purposes.

Dresden and other eastern targets were evacuation centers, and bombing such crowded places would materially disrupt the German war effort. The Wehrmacht had to reassign entire divisions to help out after the raids, and vast amounts of food, fuel, and other matériel had to be diverted to aid the refugees.

Dresden and other such cities in the east were also important communications centers, through which passed reinforcements to the Russian front, in particular troops and armaments being withdrawn from the Western Front and transferred to the east.

Finally, by heavily bombing targets so close to the Eastern Front, the Anglo-American air forces were substantially aiding the Soviet advance into the Reich. Russian troops had already crossed the Oder and were threatening Berlin.

Grierson also revealed that there were no Russians on the targets committee; it was purely an Anglo-American body. In answer to a reporter's question, he said that there had been no Russian pressure to bomb Dresden and other eastern cities, that there was no prior consultation, and that thus far the Russians had not commented on the RAF-USAAF offensive.

Indeed, according to Grierson, there was "no definite arrangement made with [the Russians] for planning beforehand or discussion afterwards at the moment." And in response to a question as to what other cities might be on the list of targets, he responded that he couldn't answer offhand but any city that lay on the east-west or north-south communications lines, any city that was a center for evacuation, and any city that had stores of emergency food supplies might be a likely target.

As for Dresden itself, while the primary goal was to blast communications carrying military supplies, there was another goal, said Grierson: "to stop movement in all directions if possible—movement of everything."

Grierson's frank and, to many of those present, disturbing comments were meant as background, but among the reporters was Howard Cowan of the Associated Press. It is little wonder that Cowan drew the obvious conclusion that bombing policy had, indeed, changed—not so much that of Bomber Command, which had called for bombing German population centers for years, but that of the American Eighth Air Force.

Cowan used the briefing as the basis for a story that ran on page one in the *Washington Star* on 18 February 1945. The article, which inexplicably passed the SHAEF censors without comment, created its own firestorm. At the Pentagon, an outraged and angry Hap Arnold fired off a cable to Spaatz, in which he quoted Cowan's piece in its entirety.

The Allied Air Commanders have made the long awaited decision to adopt deliberate terror bombing of the great German population centers as a ruthless expedient to hasten Hitler's doom.

More raids such as the British and American heavy bombers

carried out recently on the residential sections of Berlin, Dresden, Chemnitz, and Cottbus are in store for the Reich, and their avowed purpose will be creating more confusion in the German traffic tangle and sapping German morale.

The all out air war in Germany became obvious with the unprecedented daylight assault on the refugee-crowded capital two weeks ago and subsequent attacks on other cities jammed with civilians fleeing from the Russian advance in the East.

The Allied view is that bombardment of large German cities creates immediate need for relief. This is moved into the bombed areas both by rail and road and not only creates a traffic problem but draws transport away from the battlefront. Evacuation of the homeless has the same result.

Reconnaissance has shown that the best way to create road bottlenecks through key cities is to topple buildings into the streets. One spot on the Western Front recently was made impassable for nine days by such tactics. The effect on morale both at home and at the front is quite obvious.

The decision may revive protests from some Allied quarters against "uncivilized warfare," but they are likely to be balanced by satisfaction in those sections of Europe where the German Air Force and the Nazi V-weapons have been responsible for the indiscriminate slaughter of tens of thousands.

The reaction of the Germans, who still are bombing England blindly with long-range rockets, is expected to be a new outburst of violent words, but there is little more the Nazi propagandists can say—all the previous Allied air raids on the Reich have been described by Berlin as "Terror Attacks."

Arnold complained that he was already getting calls from influential radio and newspaper commentators asking who had ordered the change in bombing policy from the often-stated goal of precision bombing to area bombing. "What do we say?" he asked Spaatz plaintively.

Spaatz, who was in the Mediterranean, ordered his staff back in England to put out the fires, or at least bring them under control. On 19 February, Major General F. L. Anderson, deputy commander for operations, cabled Arnold an explanation of the public relations fiasco. Anderson quoted the "pertinent portions" of Grierson's press conference—which, he somewhat surprisingly enjoined Arnold, who knew a thing or two about security, "are not repeat not for publication."

To start with the Heavies, the overall communications plan is going ahead and in communications I include oil. I understand you have already heard something about the oil plan and the oil war generally, but the situation now is such that we might expect very big results from the bombing of the oil refineries and pro-duction plants. The bombing of communications centers and rail-ways is having an increasingly serious effect on the German economy generally and with the loss of Silesia the importance of the communications out of the Ruhr has become emphasized more than ever. I think if you will notice from now on, the sort of targets being chosen for attack by the Heavies, and for that mat-ter the Mediums as well, you will see the sort of general results of the planning which has been going on in the last fortnight.

Another matter, which has been given a lot of thought and which required a lot of careful consideration, is the employment of the Heavies against the centres of population. The effect of the Heavy raids on population centres has always been first of all to cause the Germans to bring in train loads of supplies of extra comforts and to take away the population which have been ren-dered homeless. Now that form of relief relies very, very much to a pretty great extent on rapid and sound communications be-tween the big cities and the whole of the interior of Germany it-self, so that the destruction not only of communications centres, but also of the towns where the relief comes from and where the refugees go to, are very definitely operations which contribute greatly towards the break up of the German economic system.

Although Anderson maintained that Cowan had exaggerated Grier-son's views, he admitted in the cable that "Grierson did imply that attacks were to be directed against civilian populations." However, he emphasized, "We have not, or do not, intend to change the basic policy which has governed the direction of effort of the United States Strategic Air Force in Europe from the first time they started operations in this Theater. Our attacks have been directed in all cases against military objectives."

While Arnold was no doubt relieved to hear that the chief targets of American bombers were and remained oil and communications, he cannot have failed to understand what all military commanders understand. No operation in wartime, let alone bombers operating at 30,000 feet, can guarantee that there will be no collateral damage. Oil refineries and marshaling yards are inevitably near or adjoin major civilian population centers. But Anderson (and Spaatz) insisted there was no change in policy. "There has been," the cable said, "only a change of emphasis in locale."

As promised to Arnold, Anderson met that same day with Eisenhower to draft an official and public response to the changes of terror bombing. Eisenhower's headquarters issued a denial that terror bombing was official policy and explained that Dresden was a viable military target.

Secretary of War Henry L. Stimson echoed Eisenhower's denial of a change in U.S. policy, and the *Washington Star*, which had set off the furor in the first place with Cowan's article, accepted his explanation. Cowan had simply been guilty of "an excusable but incorrect interpretation" of Grierson's remarks. This was, says historian Tami Davis Biddle, a "1940s version of spin control."

Stimson, however, began to have second thoughts about the matter and reopened the question of the Dresden raid. Arnold was having none of it. "We must not get soft," he fumed. "War must be destructive and to a certain extent inhuman and ruthless."

The New York Times was hardly less forthright. The day after the American raid, on 15 February, the paper had editorialized that if a great German city and its cultural treasures were obliterated, the Germans had only themselves and their Führer to blame.

Others were not so accommodating. On 26 February 1945, *Newsweek*, in an article headlined "Now Terror, Truly," reported the Dresden inferno and a new military policy. "Allied air chiefs have decided to adopt deliberate terror bombing of German population centers as a military means of hastening the Reich's surrender by snarling up communications and sapping morale," said the magazine.

Journalists resident in Germany from such neutral countries as Switzerland and Sweden had more or less parroted the Goebbels line that the raid had been an atrocity, and their dispatches had also begun to find their way into the Allied press. The notorious press conference at SHAEF headquarters had only added further fuel.

In Great Britain two of the most influential prewar advocates of aerial bombardment had already recanted and had written scathing denunciations of the Bomber Command policy of systematic destruction of German cities and the killing of noncombatants.

In 1943, J. F. C. Fuller said that next to Bomber Command's actions "the worst devastations of the Goths, Vandals, Huns, Seljuks, and Mongols pale into insignificance." B. H. Liddell Hart was hardly less censorious. In 1942, he wrote that the Luftwaffe and Bomber Command were now engaged in a "mad competition in mutual devastation."

Finally, the controversy spread to the House of Commons. On 6 March, a firebrand Labour MP from Ipswich, Richard Stokes, took to the floor to question the entire bombing policy of Bomber Command, in particular the Dresden raid and in general the laying waste of the cities of Germany.

Stokes's speech was brief, but it ignited a controversy—particularly his charge that history would record the raids as "a blot on our escutcheon." As the story continued to unfold, the blot threatened to tarnish the escutcheon of the prime minister himself. On 28 March he began to distance himself from his earlier policies.

Ever mindful of public opinion, of his place in history, and that his government was a coalition, the prime minister ordered a reassessment of the policies that he had set in motion. In a letter to General H. L. Ismay, his chief of staff, Churchill said, "It seems to me that the moment has come when the question of bombing of German cities simply for the sake of increasing the terror, though under other pretexts, should be reviewed."

The prime minister's reasons were not altruistic. He went on to complain that if Germany were "utterly ruined," German resources that could be used to rebuild Great Britain would instead have to be used in Germany to provide housing for the defeated enemy. But he quickly returned to questioning the policies of Bomber Command and the Eighth Air Force.

"The destruction of Dresden remains a serious query against the conduct of Allied bombing," said Churchill. "I am of the opinion that military objectives must henceforward be more strictly studied in our own interests rather than that of the enemy. . . . The Foreign Secretary has spoken to me on this subject, and I feel the need for more precise concentration upon military objectives, such as oil and communications behind the immediate battle-zone, rather than on mere acts of terror and wanton destruction, however impressive."

The record is clear on Churchill's role in developing the bombing policies of Bomber Command, so it must have been with some dismay that Ismay, Portal, Bottomley, and Harris himself were now hearing that the prime minister was not only disavowing a program that had his fingerprints all over it but also saying that it might have been a mistake.

Had not the prime minister, at the summit meeting with Joseph Stalin in August 1942, drawn a picture of a crocodile to represent Europe and then delighted Stalin by ripping at its belly and hitting it on the snout at the same time? The dictator saw at once the strategic value of attacking the "soft underbelly of Europe" and gaining a beachhead on the Continent from that direction.

And the Soviet leader was also delighted, according to both the British and the American ambassadors, Archibald Clark Kerr and Averell Harriman, who were present, when Churchill explained the RAF bombing policy put into effect the previous February: the morale bombing of the German cities. Stalin at once began to list the most important urban targets, urging Churchill to spare no one, to bomb homes as well as factories. Churchill, responding to his host's enthusiasm, promised the Soviet leader that the RAF would be "ruthless." Between them, said Harriman, "they soon had destroyed most of the important industrial cities of Germany."

The list of actual cities is not given in the accounts of the meeting, but it seems unlikely that Germany's seventh-largest city and the one closest to the Eastern Front would not have been included.

So as early as August 1942, the British prime minister had pledged to the Russians that the RAF would wage total aerial war against the cities of Germany. Civilians were not to be spared.

. . .

Ismay was not the only recipient of the Churchill memorandum. Portal received a copy, and he passed it on to Bottomley, who was instructed to get Bomber Harris's response to Churchill's allegations. But Harris was not to be shown the full text. He was to be apprised of only the prime minister's main points.

Harris realized soon enough what was afoot, and in just one day he had his reply ready. "To suggest that we have bombed German cities 'simply for the sake of increasing the terror though under other pretexts' and to speak of our offensive as including 'mere acts of terror and wanton destruction' is an insult both to the bombing policy of the Air Ministry and to the manner in which that policy has been executed by Bomber Command," he fumed. "This sort of thing if it deserves an answer will certainly receive none from me, after three years of implementing official policy."

Harris, of course, went on for several pages, explaining and justifying in increasingly outraged tones Bomber Command policy, which had been official policy since before he had assumed command, but made no apologies for carrying out his duties. "I have always held and still maintain," said Harris, "that my Directive, which you quote, the progressive destruction and dislocation of the German military, industrial and economic systems, could be carried out only by the elimination of German industrial cities and not merely by attacks on individual factories however important these might be in themselves."

Harris forcefully argued that the policies that he had pursued for three years had fatally weakened the German war effort and at that very time were enabling Allied troops to advance into Germany with "negligible casualties." Harris was, of course, referring to the more recent weeks. January and February 1945 were two of the bloodiest months of the war in Europe. Casualties on the Western Front totaled over 136,000, with a third of them occurring in the week immediately preceding and the week following the Dresden raid.

Bomber Harris was in no mood to either defend or apologize for his actions. Instead he warmed to his task of explaining to the air minister and even the prime minister what the campaign had been about and what they could expect from him for the duration of the war—and while he was at it, he gave them some advice.

"I therefore assume that the view under consideration is something like this: no doubt in the past we were justified in attacking German cities. But to do so was always repugnant and now that the Germans are beaten anyway we can properly abstain from proceeding with these attacks. This is a doctrine to which I could never subscribe. Attacks on cities like any other act of war are intolerable unless they are strategically justified. But they are strategically justified in so far as they tend to shorten the war and so preserve the lives of Allied soldiers. To my mind we have absolutely no right to give them up unless it is certain they will not have this effect. I do not personally regard the whole of the remaining cities of Germany as worth the bones of one British Grenadier," said Bomber Harris.

If one is looking for a succinct justification or rationale for Harris's actions in World II, there it is. He went on to argue that the only choice was to continue as before or "very largely stand down altogether." That would be fine with him, he said. "I take little delight in the work and none whatever in risking my crews avoidably." And what of the future? he asked.

"Japan remains," said the flinty air chief. "Are we going to bomb their cities flat—as in Germany—and give the Armies a walk over—as in France and Germany—or are we going to bomb only the outlying factories, largely underground by the time we get going, and subsequently invade at the cost of 3 to 6 million casualties? We should be careful of precedents."

This was not only an apologia. It was also a gauntlet thrown down in front of Churchill, Portal, and Bottomley, and their opposite numbers at American headquarters and in Washington. And it had its effect.

Churchill's original memorandum was immediately revised, with the offensive wording removed—Harris had called it an insult—and in a directive issued on 4 April 1945, it was announced that Bomber Command would continue as before.

But in the event there was little left to destroy. To be sure, during April there were massive raids on Hamburg, Kiel, Potsdam, Heligoland, and Wangerooge, as well as one abortive raid on Bremen. There were smaller raids as well, and the Mosquitoes kept up the pressure on Berlin, but the great campaign was winding down.

. . .

The angry exchange among Churchill, Portal, Bottomley, and Harris in March 1945 was not the first time they had crossed swords in their battle of wills. In a particularly spirited exchange of letters with Portal, from early November 1944 through mid-January 1945, the head of Bomber Command had defended his position that although the oil plan was a chimera, Bomber Command was doing its part to seek out and destroy the refineries. Portal was not convinced and even went so far as to suggest that perhaps Harris's views were filtering down through Bomber Command and creating opposition to the oil plan.

Harris was quick to respond. "I do not give my staff views," he said. "I give them orders."

The exchange between the two airmen degenerated further and became so heated that Portal finally aroused Harris to very real anger, a not too difficult task. The chief of Bomber Command, referring to what he called "an intolerable situation," by which, of course, he meant anyone presuming to meddle in how he ran his command, wrote to Portal, "I therefore ask you to consider whether it is best for the prosecution of the war and the success of our arms, which alone matters, that I should remain in this situation. . . ."

Harris's resignation would have caused another kind of firestorm, this one from the British public, and Portal damped the fires immediately. Harris responded in kind. He would follow orders and implement the oil plan, although he remained convinced to the end that it was not the most effective use of men and machines. In any event, simultaneously with the promised implementation of the oil plan, Bomber Command continued to level German cities and towns.

Unknown to Harris, Portal was in possession of information from the codebreakers at Bletchley Park that the oil plan was having a devastating effect on the Reich. This was information that one would have thought would have been disseminated as a matter of course to someone of Harris's stature and rank; but it was not, at least not sufficiently enough to convince the head of Bomber Command that his superiors in the military and the political spheres were pursuing the best policies.

. . .

The principals settled their problems and their infighting with letters and memorandums and directives, in the interest of successfully bringing to an end the war against the Nazis in 1945. However, in the postwar period both Churchill and Harris seemed to have had bouts of selective forgetting. They were more than disingenuous in their recollections of the Dresden raid and its aftermath and their own roles in the controversy.

Sir Arthur Harris, "Bomber Harris," the erstwhile hero, had become something of an embarrassment in peacetime England, and he disposed of the issue of Dresden in less than a page in his 1947 memoirs. The former head of Bomber Command said only that "the attack on Dresden was at the time considered a military necessity by much more important people than myself."

As we have seen, one of these "much more important people" was Winston Churchill, who in his multivolume history of World War II was even more succinct, disposing of the issue in one sentence. "Throughout

January and February our bombers continued to attack, and we made a heavy raid in the latter month on Dresden, then a centre of communications of Germany's Eastern Front," said the former prime minister. And once, when asked about it directly, he allegedly replied to his questioner that he would have to ask the Americans about that, since it was their show.

All efforts to ignore or paper over the Dresden raid would of course fail. It continued to fester among the victors as well as the vanquished, and in the early 1950s, the first books on the Dresden firestorm began appearing in Germany.

Sensationalist in tone and often lurid in detail, some of them became best sellers, either in spite of or because of their historical inaccuracies. First off the mark, in 1952, was Axel Rodenberger with *Der Tod von Dresden* (The Death of Dresden).

Rodenberger's book was notable for lending a false legitimacy to a clearly erroneous casualty figure and for perpetuating one of those legends that with repetition becomes a truism. He put the number of dead at between 350,000 and 400,000, a figure whose wide acceptance was in direct proportion to its inaccuracy.

Rodenberger also helped perpetuate the myth, almost certainly invented by the Goebbels propaganda machine immediately after the raid, that American fighter pilots had indiscriminately strafed crowds of fleeing refugees on the streets and in the parks of Dresden, most particularly the thousands who had sought refuge from the firestorm in the Elbe Meadows and the Grosser Garten.

However, the mythology surrounding the destruction of Dresden reached full flower in 1963, and became firmly implanted in the world's consciousness, with the publication of David Irving's *The Destruction of Dresden*.

Irving's documentation seemed exemplary, the book was well written, and it was well received. Almost at once the author became a celebrity historian, and in the next three decades he produced a series of books that were praised by such estimable figures as Hugh Trevor-Roper, A. J. P. Taylor, and John Keegan. The latter called Irving's *Hitler's War* "one of the half dozen most important books about the war," and the *Times* of London said, "Irving is in the first rank of Britain's historical chroniclers."

In 1993, however, a dissenting voice was raised by an American historian, Deborah Lipstadt. In her book *Denying the Holocaust,* Lipstadt charged that Irving had not only twisted historical data to conform to his preconceived ideas about Hitler and the Third Reich but had also in many instances distorted data to prove his points. David Irving had, she said, not only falsified the historical record but also provided ammunition for those who denied that there had been any such thing as the Holocaust. In fact, she charged, David Irving was himself a Holocaust denier.

In what would turn out to be not only an ill-advised action but a disastrous one, Irving brought suit for libel against Lipstadt and her publisher, Penguin Books. Penguin engaged Richard J. Evans, professor of modern history at Cambridge University, to help prepare the case for the defense. Evans and a team of researchers began at once to comb through Irving's entire body of work.

During the course of the trial, which began in London on 11 January 2000, Evans presented example after example of precisely what Lipstadt had accused Irving of doing, citing in particular his most famous work, *The Destruction of Dresden.* Irving had alleged that the city was of no military importance and that 135,000 people, mostly women, children, and old men, had died during the air raids and firestorm of 13–14 February 1945.

Irving's casualty figures proved to be wildly off the mark. According to evidence introduced at the trial, even though he was aware that the figure compiled by the Dresden authorities was probably closer to 35,000, Irving had knowingly published the higher figure. His reason for doing so, he argued in the book, was that the East German authorities had probably struck out the first digit in the number, changing 135,000 to 35,000, to satisfy their Soviet postwar masters. At the time of publication of the book, no one had bothered to point out the obvious flaw in Irving's argument: the Soviets had not bombed Dresden, and therefore none of the onus of the raid was attached to them.

At the trial it was revealed that Irving's original publisher, William Kember, had accused the author of "falsifications of the historical facts" and warned him that the book "could be interpreted as the work of a propagandist for Nazism who had not scrupled to distort many facts and omit numerous others in order to vilify the British War Government and in particular Winston Churchill."

Kember and his staff then set about to modify, edit, and in many cases simply omit what they saw as the more egregious examples. But the casualty figures and the overall conclusion of the book stood, and in at least two subsequent editions of *The Destruction of Dresden* Irving raised the number of casualties to 250,000.

He based the new figures on a German document, *Tagesbefehl* 47 (Order of the Day, No. 47), which had purportedly been drawn up in March 1945 by the head of the Dresden police. Irving had first been made aware of TB 47 in 1963, but he had dismissed it then as a forgery. In the interim, he had purportedly seen what he said were convincing copies of the original and he was now prepared to vouch for TB 47's authenticity.

In reality, he had seen no such thing. Irving had seen what Evans described as a "typed-up transcript at least several removes from the original." TB 47, it turned out, was indeed a forgery, concocted by Goebbels's Propaganda Ministry and first published in the Nazi weekly *Das Reich.*

Irving himself had long known of the doubtful provenance of TB 47 and had admitted as much, but the spurious data had nevertheless continued to appear in editions of the book, as did the story of the omitted digit in the casualty figure.

Even when a 1995 revision of the work appeared, retitled *Apocalypse 1945: The Destruction of Dresden,* Irving was still unwilling or unable to accept what by then had become the accepted death toll, around 35,000. Instead, he wrote, the number of dead was "sixty thousand or more; perhaps a hundred thousand—certainly the largest single air raid massacre of the War in Europe." And in his 1996 biography of Joseph Goebbels, Irving repeated his death toll of 65,000–100,000.

The minds of millions of people have remained unchanged as well, bearing out the view of L. A. Jackman, a chief historian of the Air Ministry, who wrote, "It is practically impossible to kill a myth of this kind once it has become widespread and perhaps reprinted in other books all over the world."

To a large extent this is the view of the larger public as well. In spite of the trial and the damaging revelations, Irving's 1963 descriptions—and his numbers—have remained firmly fixed in the popular imagination. A city of no appreciable importance to the Nazi war effort, filled with innocent people, mostly women and children and hundreds of thousands of refugees, was obliterated for no discernible reason with the end of the war just weeks away.

If further proof is needed of Jackman's sad assessment of the power of historical revisionism, one need look no further than a speech that David Irving gave in South Africa in 1986. "Of course now everybody talks about Dresden in the same breath as they talk about Auschwitz and Hiroshima," said Irving. "That's my achievement, ladies and gentlemen. I'm a little bit proud when I look at the newspapers every 13th and 14th of February, when the anniversary comes and they mention Dresden, because until my book was published on that subject the outside world had never heard of what happened in Dresden when 100,000 people were killed in one night by an RAF and American air force raid on one undefended German town at the end of the war."

When the libel trial ended in April 2000, David Irving's reputation as a historian was in tatters. In addition to having been exposed as a manipulator of historical data, he was also labeled by the court as a racist, an anti-Semite, and a neo-Fascist.

Deborah Lipstadt was vindicated, but the issue did not die. What she referred to in a 2005 interview as David Irving's "immoral equivalency"—the Dresden raid was as bad as the war crimes that the Nazis had committed—has been embraced and is fervently believed by many thousands of people.

Irving, meanwhile, soldiered on. In a 12 March 2002 posting on his Web site, he wrote the following comparison of the attack on the New York World Trade Center and the Dresden firestorm: "Thousands of victims were cremated in the Altmarkt square on makeshift funeral pyres of five hundred civilians at a time. (Rather more than the WTC's three thousand died in that inferno: about thirty times that number, I still aver.)"

In November 2005, Irving was arrested by Austrian authorities when he made a clandestine trip to Vienna to address a student group. He had been barred from Austria since 1989 for his views, which allegedly violated the Austrian law forbidding denial of the crimes of the Nazi years or historical revisionism that seeks to cast a favorable light on the Third Reich. He was jailed and denied bail. In February 2006, Irving was sentenced to three years in prison.

Author Kurt Vonnegut shares with David Irving the distinction of being one of the two best-known sources of information about the destruction of Dresden. Indeed, Vonnegut pays homage to Irving, of a sort, by quoting from *The Destruction of Dresden* in his satirical novel *Slaughterhouse-Five*, in which the Dresden raid is the defining event.

The principal character, Billy Pilgrim, is an American prisoner of war who is caught in the city when the bombers come. Vonnegut, who was a prisoner of war in Dresden in February 1945, was interned in the eponymous slaughterhouse of the title and witnessed the raid firsthand.

Although the novel is heavily science fiction, Vonnegut's view of the raid is never in doubt. He maintains that it was unnecessary, another slaughter of the innocents—a view that has been absorbed by countless undergraduates for whom the book has been received wisdom since its publication in 1969.

Both books appeared in the tumultuous 1960s, during the debate over the war in Southeast Asia in which thousands of civilians were dying in air attacks. It was, the historian Charles C. Gillispie remarked, a time of "romantic resentment," when it seemed appropriate to reexamine all wartime policies, both past and present.

In Great Britain, the Royal Air Force was especially sensitive to what it saw as revisionism and even the repudiation of its own noble role in the victory over Fascism in World War II. Much was made in magazine articles and reviews of Irving's book about the misgivings of the aircrews before this raid. Efforts immediately began to shore up the Bomber Command position and refute the critics. The task fell to the Air Historical Branch.

The AHB began by examining the operational record books of Bomber Command, the bomber groups, and the fifty-five squadrons that took part in the raid. There was no justification, said the reporting officer, for any of the statements that the Bomber Command crews were uneasy about the operation because of moral scruples.

One's overall impression from scrutiny of these contemporary accounts is that to the aircrew involved it was very little different from other raids, except for the distance, the fact that Dresden had not been attacked before by Bomber Command and the raid's spectacular success.

Their reaction on their return was one of jubilation the raid had been so successful, tempered by the fatigue consequent on a round trip that had lasted for some ten hours, after which many had to be prepared at short notice for another flight to Chemnitz in the same area.

There were well over 5,000 aircrew involved in the Dresden raid and it was the prerogative of all airmen, aircrew or not, to indulge in "binding." Among these men it is possible that there were individuals who may have had doubts about this raid, bearing in mind the fact that by February, 1945 there was a certain war weariness and the raid was certainly a test of endurance, but none of this is reflected in the O.R.B.s. Certainly, there is nothing to justify a general statement of this nature, as though there was a widespread mood of criticism of the raid on moral grounds. There is a possibility that after 18 years and with knowledge of the destruction and casualties inflicted some of these aircrew may have rationalized their feelings at the time and expressed doubts, but none of this is expressed in these contemporary accounts. Indeed, the comments reveal that they returned remarkably well pleased with the success of the operation.

The report includes excerpts from a cross-section of the squadron operational record books, which, critics naturally enough point out, support the conclusions already laid out as the official RAF view. But these are statements from debriefings that were made just hours after the two raids were completed, not reassessments ten, fifteen, or twenty years later. They thus carry considerable historical weight.

12 SQUADRON Bomber Command made the inevitable assault on Dresden. Thousands of incendiaries rained down on Germany's 7th. largest city. This is considered a really first-class attack. The route was satisfactory but too long.

431 (R.C.A.F) Really pranged the target. Head wind on return kept aircraft airborne for over 10 hours, so it was a very weary group that piled into bed for only, as it turned out, a few hours' sleep at the most. Only the long time in the air marred a pleasant ride.

467 (R.A.A.F) Everyone had been hoping for a "support of the army" target for some time. to-day was the day but it was the wrong way. Another full petrol load and the target is Dresden if Joe Stalin isn't there beforehand. Trip well planned and a big success for the Command.

90 SQUADRON Best attack seen so far.

434 (R.C.A.F.) Briefing lasted longer than usual for this long trip. A very good concentrated attack.

3 GROUP Attack carried out in direct support of the Russian offensive. Crews were enthusiastic. The first night on which Dresden has been attacked in force by Bomber Command.

166 SQUADRON For the first time the Squadron was ordered to take part in an attack on Dresden, a flight involved one of the deepest penetrations into enemy territory yet made. Altogether a highly satisfactory night's work.

514 SQUADRON Whole area reported as one mass of smoke and flames. Crews highly delighted.

433 (R.A.A.F.) It is understood that this raid was one of the first fruits of combined planning from the Yalta Conference thus beginning the ensuing 7,000 aircraft support to the Eastern front.

Ten years earlier an American report classified as "Top Secret Security Information" had been circulated to a small number of people. Entitled "Historical Analysis of the 14–15 February 1945 Bombing of Dresden," the report was prepared by the USAF Historical Division. Its subsequent declassification and availability has changed few minds on either side of the bombing question, particularly those whose natural propensity it is to distrust all government documents, but in spite of its provenance the report is a valuable contribution to the debate and its arguments are sound.

The impetus for the study was the increasing use of the Dresden raid by the Soviet Union and its client state East Germany to demonize the Western democracies. This is clear from the introduction, which states, "From time to time there appears in letters of inquiry to the United States Air Force evidence that American nationals are themselves being taken in by the Communist propaganda line concerning the February 1945 bombings of Dresden."

The United States at the time was involved in the Korean War, and the nation was also transfixed by the revelation of so-called security threats and the fulminations and denunciations of fervent anti-Communist politicians, most notably Senator Joseph McCarthy. Perhaps that is why the language of the report is remarkably free of the overheated rhetoric of the period.

After laying out a series of questions, beginning with "Was Dresden a legitimate military target?," the air force historians addressed the conventional belief that the 13–14 February bombing of Dresden, the famous triple blow, was a one-time, isolated event. Not so, said the drafters of the report.

Before 13–14 February 1945, Dresden had already been bombed twice, and while these first two raids were, admittedly, minor operations they served notice that the city was not off-limits to Bomber Command or the Eighth Air Force. After 13–14 February, Dresden was bombed four more times, with raids on 15 February and 2 March and two raids on 17 April. Also, as we have seen, Dresden was the alternate target for the thousand-bomber American raid against Berlin that was scheduled for 2 February 1945 but was canceled because of bad weather.

During the seven months that Dresden was a target of Allied air operations (October 1944–April 1945), some 2,448 bombers dropped a total of 7,100.5 tons of bombs—5,278 tons of high explosives and 1,822.5 tons of incendiaries.

The 2 March raid was particularly heavy. Of the 450 B-17s of the American Third Air Division, which had been dispatched to bomb oil targets at Ruhland, 406 were unable to find the primary target and dropped 1,080.8 tons of bombs on the ruins of Dresden, including 140.5 tons of incendiaries. In this raid, the last of the major Dresden landmarks was destroyed—the Japanese Palace, which housed the Dresden State Library.

The two final raids, both on 17 April, by 580 bombers from the Eighth Air Force, saw more heavy explosives dropped on the city—1,554.4 tons—than any previous raid, plus an additional 164.5 tons of incendiaries. Thus the outcry over the firebombing of 13–14 February did nothing to halt the continued bombing, at least by the Americans—Bomber Command did not return to Dresden—of what was still considered to be an important military target.

But was Dresden a legitimate target? This question has persisted for the sixty years since the firebombing and has been kept alive by both democratic and totalitarian regimes, advocates from the far left and the far right, militarists and pacifists.

Comparison with other military targets is thus not only useful but imperative. When World War II began, Dresden was the seventh-largest city in Germany, with a population of 642,143. Only Berlin, Hamburg, Munich, Cologne, Leipzig, and Essen were larger. While the size of a city does not necessarily make it a prime military target, the activities out of which large cities evolve and around which they revolve often do. Dresden was a major commercial and transportation center and the capital of the state of Saxony.

The city had since medieval times lain athwart two primary military routes: the east-west route of the valley and gorge of the Elbe River between Germany and Czechoslovakia and the east-west land route along the central European uplands.

Three great trunk routes of the German railway system converged at Dresden: Berlin–Prague–Vienna; Munich–Breslau; and Hamburg–Leipzig–Prague. Two main lines connected Dresden with Leipzig and

Berlin. In fact, the first railroad line in Germany ran between Dresden and Leipzig.

It is rail traffic that is the best indicator, however, and by any measure Dresden was an important rail hub, destination, and transfer point. The Dresden-Saxony railway system ranked seventh in the country in mileage, but it was third in total tonnage carried.

The final issue—were the factories, machine shops, and industrial sites important enough to justify the wholesale destruction of the city in order to guarantee their incapacitation?—has been more problematical for historians since the raids of 13–14 February 1945. It need not have been. According to the American air force, there were 110 such sites—all legitimate military targets—employing 50,000 workers.

These installations included dispersed aircraft factories; a poison-gas factory (Chemische Fabric Goye); an antiaircraft and field gun factory (Lehman); and Germany's most famous optical instruments firm (Zeiss-Ikon). There were also manufacturers of electrical products and X-ray apparatus (Kock and Starzel); small arms (Seidel and Naumann); molds and metal packings (Anton Reich); gears and differentials (Saxonizwerke); and electric gauges (Gebruder Bessler).

Typical was the J. C. Müller Universelle-Werke, which had been founded to make machinery for the manufacture of cigarettes. In the First World War, the company had gone into armaments, but afterward, with such activity forbidden by treaty, it went back to making cigarette machinery. Under Adolf Hitler the company grew exponentially, and by the time of the raid 4,000 workers, which included slave laborers and Jews from concentration camps, were turning out a plethora of military equipment—including machine guns and aircraft parts.

Early in the war, the Nazis had begun to transport Jews to Dresden to work in the factories. For most of them, it was only a brief stopover before they were sent on to the death camps. Later, as labor shortages became more critical, some of them avoided the further deportation to the east and even survived until the end of the war.

Not mentioned by the air force was another vital service that was centered in Dresden. The city had become a key link in the German postal and telegraph system. The central offices, in which hundreds of

German civilians and British prisoners of war worked, were located on the Postplatz, in the very center of the Altstadt. Berlin had moved other important services to Dresden as well, including the Berlin Grossbank.

Dresden was also a favored haven for refugees from the capital and other bombed-out cities of the Reich, and it still was a favorite retreat of the Nazis. Frau Goebbels herself spent much time at one of the Dresden sanatoriums, and Hitler's half sister, Angela, was married to Martin Hammitzsch, the director of the State School of Building Construction in Dresden.

As for military installations, the report did err in its estimation of the air defenses in the city. While there was a fighter squadron based nearby, the other air defenses were minimal. As we have seen, the antiaircraft guns had been moved to the east to be used as antitank weapons in the attempt to hold back the Russian advance.

There were also an ammunition storage depot and a new SS headquarters, but they were unlikely to be destroyed in any raid on the city. They were miles from the central area and far belowground.

Another continuing point of controversy has been the argument that the Russians requested specifically that Dresden be bombed. The 1953 air force report also errs in stating that it was not until early 1943 that the Allies and Russians began high-level consultations to coordinate their military efforts against Germany. Such plans began to be laid soon after America entered the war in 1941 and were discussed in earnest at the highest levels in August 1942, more than a year before the Tehran Conference of the Big Three. Stalin, up to and during the Yalta Conference in February 1945, had been repeatedly reassured by visiting emissaries and by both Churchill and Roosevelt personally that Allied bombers could be counted on to support the Russian offensive in the east when the time came.

The air force report, which dutifully laid out the facts of the Dresden raid of 13–14 February 1945, could have gone a long way to lay the controversy to rest if it had been released in 1953. But it was not declassified for public dissemination for another twenty-five years. Thus the questions were resolved only to the satisfaction of the limited number of military and Defense Department officials who were allowed to read it.

Therefore, the books and articles that condemned the raid as unnecessary—even a war crime—ensured that the Dresden controversy would not only take on a new life and interest but would grow in the intervening years. The failed U.S. intervention in Vietnam, various other American adventures abroad, and the worldwide peace movement guaranteed a continuing interest. Dresden's place on the lists of bombing atrocities, alongside Coventry, Rotterdam, Guernica, and, of course, Hiroshima and Nagasaki, was assured.

· · ·

Every book, article, and documentary concerning the Dresden firestorm rightly has extolled the city of the Augustuses as an architectural and cultural marvel, which it certainly was; but also, with a few notable exceptions, all have decried the raid as unnecessary and an act of unparalleled barbarity.

In addition, was not the war at an end? After all, the Eastern and Western Fronts were rapidly contracting, with the last vestiges of Nazi Germany being squeezed tight in the vise created by the Allied forces. Indeed, with the Soviet forces just a few miles from Dresden in mid-February 1945, was not the final collapse only days or, at most, a few weeks away?

Harry Truman's memoirs cast a revealing light on this argument. On 13 April 1945—his first full day as president and exactly two months after the Dresden raid and just three weeks before the unconditional surrender of Nazi Germany—Truman was told in a meeting with his top military advisers and the secretary of war that the assessment by intelligence sources presented to Roosevelt and Churchill at the Octagon Conference in Quebec in September 1944 still held. Germany would not be defeated for at least six months and Japan for a year and a half.

In other words, Secretary of War Henry L. Stimson, Secretary of the Navy James V. Forrestal, Army Chief of Staff George C. Marshall, Chief of Naval Operations Ernest J. King, Lieutenant General Barney M. Giles, representing the air force, and White House Chief of Staff Admiral William D. Leahy all assured Truman that Germany would not fall before October 1945, at the earliest, and Japan not before October 1946.

When Truman assumed the presidency on 12 April 1945, he was completely in the dark about the development of the atomic bomb. After a hastily convened cabinet meeting immediately after he was sworn in, Stimson stayed behind to tell the new president of "the development of a new explosive of almost unbelievable destructive power." Amazingly, that was all the secretary of war felt free to confide to his boss, the president of the United States.

The next day, James F. Byrnes, who had been director of war mobilization, came to see Truman. While he allowed that the new weapon was "great enough to destroy the whole world," he provided no further details.

The commander in chief, who, as he admitted in his memoirs, was "puzzled," did not press his subordinates for more information. Perhaps he was being deferential. While the new president was being briefed, his predecessor's funeral train was still en route from Warm Springs, Georgia, to Washington.

It was not until the next day that Truman was told of the atomic bomb by Vannevar Bush, the head of the Office of Scientific Research and Development. He also learned from Bush the startling news that the new weapon was almost ready to be tested.

Admiral William Leahy, Roosevelt's, and now Truman's, chief of staff, sat in on the scientific briefing. The admiral, who just hours earlier had concurred with his colleagues on the end dates for the war in Europe and the Pacific, now volunteered an even less prescient prediction. "That is the biggest fool thing we have ever done," he said. "The bomb will never go off, and I speak as an expert in explosives."

• • •

Dresden, the seventh-largest city in Germany, with its prewar light industries retooled and revamped to provide vital military goods and services, and with its vast network of railroads, highways, and river traffic, was clearly a viable military target. No responsible military planner could ignore it. The city was an important component of the Nazi war machine.

When the bombers had departed, much of this manufacturing capability had been destroyed or seriously crippled—though more of it would have been devastated if the massive British raids had concentrated on the industrial areas just outside the city instead of the Altstadt. Dresden would not regain the major role as a producer of armaments that it had enjoyed prior to 13 February. Too many workers were dead. Too much of the infrastructure had been destroyed. And the ensuing American follow-up raids were designed to ensure that this would remain the case.

Bomber Harris summed it up in his acerbic response to Churchill's questioning of the necessity of the destruction of Dresden. "The feeling, such as there is, over Dresden could be easily explained by any psychiatrist," said Harris. "It is connected with German bands and Dresden shepherdesses. Actually Dresden was a mass of munitions works, an intact government centre, and a key transportation point to the East. It is now none of these things."

Harris might also have pointed out that the week of the Dresden raid the Germans launched the greatest number of rockets against England of any week since the beginning of the vengeance-weapons campaign.

CHAPTER THIRTEEN

FROM THE ASHES

Dresden Is Reborn

Few cities in the world had such a concentration of cultural treasures as Dresden in 1945. All of the city's major architectural sites and art collections were in walking distance of one another and all were located within the area of total devastation—some sixteen hundred acres, two and a half square miles. Comparisons with other cities whose cultural riches lie in similar proximity provide some perspective on the loss.

Parisians would be devastated by the loss of the Louvre, the Palais-Royal, the Jeu de Paume, the Invalides, the Tuileries, the Champs-Élysées, the Arc de Triomphe, Sainte-Chapelle, the Eiffel Tower, Notre-Dame and the Île de la Cité, the Opéra, Saint-Sulpice, and the Sorbonne. In a firestorm like the Dresden raid, all of these monuments of French culture and their surrounding neighborhoods would be gutted by fire and reduced to mounds of rubble.

Londoners—whose city, of course, did suffer; many landmarks were wrecked or seriously damaged, in particular the Houses of Parliament and dozens of historic churches—might think differently about the bombing of other cities if Covent Garden, Westminster Abbey, St. Paul's, the National Gallery, the Victoria and Albert Museum, Buckingham Palace, the West End, the Strand, and all of Mayfair and Belgravia and their environs were leveled.

Americans, as well, might benefit from the cautionary tale presented by the destruction of Dresden. Imagine if, in Washington, D.C., all of the public buildings, national monuments, and museums, from the Capitol to the Lincoln Memorial and beyond, were destroyed in one great cataclysm.

The National Gallery, the White House, the Capitol, the Washington Monument, the Lincoln and Jefferson Memorials, the Kennedy Center, the Smithsonian Institution, and much of Capitol Hill and Georgetown lie well within the parameters of a raid the size of the Dresden firestorm. All would have been obliterated or reduced to smoking ruins.

In New York, a similar series of raids would lay waste a great swath of Manhattan if the central aiming point were Fourteenth Street. Everything between the East River and the Hudson River and well into Central Park would be razed. The Metropolitan Museum of Art, the American Museum of Natural History, St. Patrick's Cathedral, the Museum of Modern Art, Central Park, Times Square and the Theater District, and thousands of office and apartment buildings would be gone.

Perhaps another comparison is in order as well. The area destroyed by the 2001 attack on the World Trade Center in New York, which caused such devastation and grief, was some twenty-five acres, about 1.5 percent of the area of the firestorm in Dresden.

· · ·

February in Saxony is rainy and chilly, but there are sunny days with blue, cloudless skies. Like everywhere in midwinter, when the trees are bare and the vines leafless, the skeleton of Dresden can be seen, the underlying landscape visible. But in this old city other outlines are visible as well. When one masters the clues, one can find the scars from the firestorm more than sixty years ago.

The great open spaces, some of them still punctuated by the foundations of the buildings that once occupied the sites, are the products of explosions and fires, not the wrecker's ball. From time to time one comes upon fenced-in enclosures containing bits and pieces of statuary, broken masonry and marble, plinths and columns, architraves and garlands, and assorted other architectural elements. The shards and pieces were carefully numbered and cataloged long ago and now wait to be attached to, or perhaps reintegrated into, reconstructed buildings.

Without the softening effects of summer greenery, the ugliness of the Communist-era buildings are magnified many times. What the *Great Soviet Encyclopedia* called the "socialist reconstruction of Dresden" is epitomized on the northern side of the Altmarkt, the ancient square at the heart of Dresden. There stands the Stalinist Kulturpalast, the perfect example—or nadir—of Socialist building in Saxony. One guidebook extols this uneasy alliance as a marriage of modern urbanism with an ancient heritage. It's a shotgun marriage at best.

The new buildings combine the worst aspects of Socialist cookie-cutter architecture and the dehumanizing elements of modernism gone awry or misunderstood. And nowhere else in the world is the contrast between the beauty and the exuberance of the baroque, the rococo, and the neoclassical and the blandness of the modern more apparent than in Dresden.

In much of old Dresden, however, the eye is still beguiled and the mind stimulated by the beauty of the surviving or reconstructed buildings ordered up by the Augustuses and their successors. For while the Communist rulers of the former East Germany can be faulted for erecting buildings of a transcendent ugliness, they must also be credited with saving and rebuilding many of the major monuments.

This strange dichotomy of preserving the cultural heritage while destroying the aristocracy and the class system that created it prevailed in all the satellite states. It followed the example of the Soviet Union, which after 1917 ruthlessly liquidated the nobility but kept their palaces.

Historical preservation was not universal. Many monuments that survived the destruction of the World War II were toppled by the tribunes of the people. Statues of kings and statesmen of the ancien régime were often dismantled or melted down. In the Altmarkt, the statue of Germania was considered too representative of a militant and Fascist Germany, so it was taken away after the war. The statue of the Iron Chancellor, Bismarck, at the upper end of the Pragerstrasse; Augustus the Strong at the entrance to the Neustadt; and Martin Luther in the Neumarkt by the Frauenkirche also survived, although Luther and Augustus were severely damaged. All three were put in storage, but in a stunning example of political inconsistency, Luther and Augustus were repaired and restored to their pedestals in the 1950s. Bismarck and Germania remain exiles.

Restoration has been slow and even after six decades is not complete. The first task of the new postwar regime in East Germany was not historical preservation. The overriding priority, after clearing the hundreds of thousands of tons of rubble, was to build housing for millions of homeless and displaced people. So one is forced to understand, if not forgive, the blocks of utilitarian apartment buildings that today coexist uneasily with their exuberant baroque distant cousins.

While the aesthetics of the Communist-era public housing blocks might have been the subject of debate, their monetary value to the city after German reunification was clear. In a stunning example of the triumph of capitalism, the mayor of Dresden agreed in March 2006 to sell all of the city-owned apartments, a total of 48,000 units, to an American investment firm for $1.2 billion. The move completely retired the massive municipal debt.

The Communist regime of the GDR, like many governments in the eastern bloc, was not oblivious to the past. Employing the same arguments that were made in the Soviet Union for restoring the palaces and resorts of the czars—that princely art and architecture were the patrimony of all the people—the leaders of the GDR began to rebuild Dresden in the 1950s. What the postwar buildings lacked in architectural interest was more than offset by the German craftsmen and artisans who set to work to re-create their lost heritage with great fidelity and not a little love.

First and foremost was, of course, the Zwinger, the world-famous museum and crown jewel of the city. The Soviets, who had taken the collections away for "safekeeping" at the end of the war, heeded their fellow Communists' call to return the looted art in 1955, and the great collection of the electors was reinstalled in the meticulously restored museum.

The reconstruction efforts were by no means characterized by system or logic. Opposite the Zwinger lay another ruin, the Sophienkirche, which could easily have been reconstructed—much of the original building survived the raid—but, over much protest, the site was leveled. And across the Theaterplatz, near the Semper Opera House, the site of another famous Dresden landmark, the Hotel Bellevue—that bastion of privilege—was also completely cleared. Eventually a new Bellevue was built, by an international hotel chain, but on the other side of the river.

The oldest church in Dresden, the Kreuzkirche, which was built in the Gothic style in the thirteenth century, was destroyed by Prussian artillery in 1760. The rebuilt baroque church was destroyed by fire in 1897 but was restored. The tower and the facade survived the firestorm more or less intact, although the interior was completely gutted.

No attempt was made during the restoration of the church to replicate the fanciful baroque decorative features. Instead the church walls and vaulting were covered with a rough, concrete-like plaster, with the occasional fragment of a cherubim or angel, recovered from the ruins of the old church, embedded in the surface. The effect is restrained, reverential, and ultimately very moving, especially during musical performances of the Dresden Kreuzchor, the boys' choir that has performed in the church for almost eight centuries.

The residential neighborhood that the desperate Red Cross worker was trying to reach was totally destroyed in the raid; the ruins were leveled, and the debris carted away. Much of the neighborhood is again residential, but the prewar villas and small apartment buildings had to give way to large apartment buildings for the masses during the postwar housing crisis.

The Hauptbahnhof is the only recognizable prewar building in the immediate area, but as in the old days the Central Station, which faces onto the Pragerstrasse, functions as the major entrance to the city.

The Pragerstrasse was not rebuilt until the late 1960s, and it in no way today physically resembles the fashionable prewar avenue that connected the Altstadt and the Hauptbahnhof. The street is now a rather ordinary pedestrians-only mall, lined with shops and midpriced hotels, but whatever its architectural shortcomings, it has been reborn as a vibrant center of Dresden commercial life.

After the war, other buildings in various stages of ruin and disrepair remained boarded up, and their rebuilding and restoration proceeded at a glacial pace for the next decades. The Hofkirche was rebuilt fairly early on, but the Semper Opera House did not reopen until 13 February 1985, exactly forty years after it had been destroyed by bombs, with a performance of Weber's *Der Freischütz.*

Although the Dresden Staatskapelle had to wait forty years for the restoration of its permanent home at the Semper, the world-renowned orchestra continued to perform regularly in other venues in Dresden and to make regular concert appearances abroad.

After the reunification of East and West Germany in 1990, reconstruction and preservation became issues of national, not just Saxon, pride. East Berlin, Leipzig, and Dresden, even under the Communists, had never lost their image as powerful symbols of the great contributions to Western civilization made by German writers, philosophers, and musicians. Indeed, these cities had for centuries been the cultural patrimony of all Germans. Billions of deutschmarks became available for historic reconstruction, and of course the newly introduced capitalism spurred many projects.

The long-delayed rebuilding of the Royal Palace could now finally be undertaken. However, progress was slow, and it was not until 2005 that the work had advanced to the point that the extraordinary collection of jewels and decorative objects known as the Grünes Gewölbe could be moved from the temporary home in the Albertinum back into the building. The completely restored building was opened to the public in 2006.

Next to the Royal Palace is the restored Taschenberg Palace. The original was built by Augustus the Strong for one of his many favorites, Constantia, the Countess Cosel. Augustus had an enclosed bridge built between the Royal Palace and the Taschenberg, much like the bridge that connected the palace with the Hofkirche. But the bridge to the Taschenberg had a more secular purpose than the one to the cathedral. It ensured the king's privacy when he visited his mistress. The "Saxon Pompadour" reigned supreme in Augustus's affections for nine years until palace intrigues, some of them her own, led to her banishment to Burg Stolpen, where she spent the last twenty-one years of her life under house arrest. Her palace has a new life as the Grand Hotel Taschenberg Palais Kempinski.

Foreign largesse has been important as well in the reconstruction of what is arguably Dresden's most famous building. An international campaign was launched in 1992 to raise money for the rebuilding of the Frauenkirche. The reconstruction project attracted donations from nearly every country in the world, and the restoration of the symbol of Dresden began the following year.

During the forty-five years of Communist rule, the sad pile of rubble of the once-great church lay at the very heart of the city, in the Neumarkt. It not only served as a reminder of the horrors of warfare; it was, not so incidentally, a rebuke to the West. On 13 February each year, thousands of Dresdeners, carrying candles, gathered at the ruins and sang old songs and hymns, falling silent as every bell in the city began to toll at 1010, the precise time that the first bombs began to fall on the city on that terrible night in February 1945.

Workers began sifting through the vast pile of fire-blackened stones of the original Frauenkirche in 1993, carefully marking each stone that was still usable and could be incorporated into the fabric of the new church. In June, the badly damaged but intact pinnacle cross and its boss were uncovered, a happy omen.

In May 1994, the first of the new foundation stones was laid. The original foundation stone, which was laid on 26 August 1726, was still in place in the choir. The reborn Frauenkirche now began to rise from the blackened eighteenth-century foundation. In ten years, the outer construction was complete, and once again the great stone bell that defined Dresden soared over the skyline. A new gold pinnacle cross, an exact replica of the original, financed by British donations and made by British artisans, was set in place and crowned the church.

Within, master plasterers, painters, and artists, working from old photographs and using the latest computer technology, painstakingly restored the grand rococo interior. To the dismay of many purists, reproducing a facsimile of the original organ of Gottfried Silbermann was deemed not feasible, and a modern organ, with a baroque outer covering, was installed in the church.

Another building that has played a central role in the Dresden drama lies just behind the Frauenkirche, and every regime for the past hundred years has made use of the massive structure. In this brooding pile of a building, "enemies of the state"—common criminals, political dissidents, Jews, and homosexuals—were questioned, detained, and tortured by the Gestapo or shipped on to concentration camps. In 1938, the Gestapo and the Dresden police had an unobstructed view of the burning synagogue, situated only a block away, during the outrage called Kristallnacht.

The police building was one of the first to be restored and operating again after the war, and here the notorious Stasi, the East German secret police, intimidated and terrorized the populace, from the same offices used earlier by Himmler's henchmen. In the mid-1980s a young Soviet agent named Vladimir Putin, who would go on to greater fame as president of Russia, was a KGB operative in Dresden, where he worked hand in hand with the Stasi.

"We started the fire, and it came back and consumed us," said the mayor of Dresden on the fiftieth anniversary of the firestorm, 14 February 1995. A group of leftists disrupted the memorial service in the Hofkirche. They charged that it was unseemly to commemorate the Dresden dead when so many innocents, in particular the Jews, suffered at the hands of the Germans. "Germans were the criminals, not the victims," they shouted at the startled audience, which included Chancellor Helmut Kohl. In their view the Dresden dead were victims of the evil Nazis, not of the Allied bombers.

These young people were viewed by many as representative of a healthy German democracy that tolerated dissent. Others were not so forbearing. The German political scene is both fractured and fractious. There are leftists, rightists, centrists, old-line Communists, and a small but increasingly vocal ultra-right-wing element, neo-Nazis in all but name.

An incident on a research trip to Dresden is informative. In a café near my hotel on the Pragerstrasse, I watched as the barman became more and more agitated over the presence of three men sitting at a table. There was nothing remarkable about either their looks or their behavior, but he identified them as Turks. Finally, after much muttering, he stormed over to their table and ordered them out of the café. When they protested, he threatened to call the police. They left.

As it turned out, he would not have had to go very far for the police. After further conversation with the gentleman on my right, I found out that he was a high-ranking police official whose job it was to ferret out former Stasi agents in the new Saxon police force. He had watched the expulsion of the foreign "guest workers" with studied detachment.

On the sixtieth anniversary of the bombing, five thousand of that barman's fellow travelers from the far-right, anti-immigrant National Democratic Party marched through the streets of Dresden. In a more hopeful sign, an opposition group of nearly equal strength also took to the streets to protest against the rightists.

Perhaps more representative was a group of German students I encountered on a Danube steamer. They were outraged that the captain who was pointing out the attractions along each side of the river had neglected to tell the passengers that we were passing near the site of one of the most infamous of the Nazi concentration camps, Mauthausen. A petition was circulated, most of the passengers signed it, and the matter was put right on the public address system, which was an encouraging sign indeed.

• • •

Even if rare, any antipathy toward outsiders or lack of tolerance for liberal views is a source of worry in a country with such a violent past as Germany. So the small but active Jewish congregation in Dresden is a hopeful portent. Like all religions, Judaism was discouraged under the Communist regime, but within five years of the end of World War II a small group of Jews was worshipping again in Dresden.

In the Neustadt, the resurgent Jewish community founded the Center for Jewish History and Culture in Saxony, in a building facing the eighteenth-century Jewish Cemetery, which miraculously survived the

Nazi era. The old cemetery draws throngs of the faithful, the merely curious, and sometimes the obtuse or unreconstructed.

In order to enter the site, men are obliged to don one of the yarmulkes provided by the guides, but on the day I was there, a German tourist refused to do so. He was quietly asked to wait outside while his embarrassed wife stayed on for the tour. It is devoutly to be wished that she, and not the recalcitrant husband, is the true face of the new Germany.

Our guide stressed that the unofficial name for the Jewish Center in the Neustadt is Hatikva, "hope" in Hebrew, and hope is certainly the proper word to describe the Jewish community in Dresden, which by 2005 had grown to about 250, helped along by emigration from Russia.

More important than the size of the congregation is that the Jews of Dresden now have a synagogue, the first to be built in eastern Germany since the 1920s. Their new building sits on the site of the original synagogue built by Gottfried Semper in the nineteenth century. The dedication took place on 9 November 2001, the sixty-third anniversary of Kristallnacht, the night that the old building was burned to the ground by the Nazis.

A relic of Semper's original synagogue, a Star of David, has been incorporated into the ultramodern twenty-first-century building. A local firefighter, Alfred Neugebauer, salvaged the Jewish symbol from the wreckage on the night of the Nazi rampage and, at the risk of imprisonment or death, hid it in his home. The star is now enshrined above the entrance of the new synagogue.

Winston Churchill, celebrated by many as the greatest wartime civilian leader in history, was not so fortunate in peacetime. The great threat to England's very existence had brought Churchill to power, but now domestic issues, which had been relegated to the wings during the effort to win the war, were suddenly front and center. The quotidian, the mundane, were of little interest to the prime minister, and he made plain his annoyance with having to deal with them.

Instead of planning grand strategy involving thousands of warplanes, hundreds of ships, and hundreds of thousands of men, he was now badgered by politicians concerned by such issues as the postwar use of the soon-to-be-abandoned airfields scattered across England. Would they be available as sites for commercial aviation?

As Lord Moran recorded in his diaries, even though Churchill spent many hours with the reform-minded American president, he did not share Roosevelt's "preoccupation with social problems and the rights of the common man." The presidential concerns "struck no sparks in Winston's mind," he observed. The war was their only common interest.

Within just a little over two weeks after the German surrender, it was clear that the national government that Churchill had put together in 1940, with members of the Labour, Conservative, and Liberal Parties in prominent posts, was finished. The Labourites sensed that they were now in the ascendant and would finally be able to enact many of their long-delayed populist ideas and reforms into law. They withdrew from the coalition. Churchill had no choice but to tender his resignation, but the king immediately asked him to form a "caretaker" government until elections could be held to settle the matter as to who would govern postwar Britain.

British public opinion was not congruent with that of the larger world, which viewed Churchill as a towering figure, an indispensable man. On 25 July 1945, in a stunning reversal of fortune, Labour was triumphant, and Winston Churchill became a private citizen. Clement Attlee was now prime minister.

Arthur Harris, like his old boss, also found himself, at the end of World War II, not a nationally celebrated hero. Instead he became almost a forgotten man. Churchill had raised him from the rank of knight commander to knight grand cross of the Order of the Bath and had also offered him the post of governor general of Bermuda.

The new prime minister agreed to the appointment, and he invited Harris and his wife to Chequers by way of further congratulations. Attlee's colleagues in the new Labour government turned out to be more chary. He rescinded the offer of the Bermuda post within days.

Harris was also left out of the Victory Honours List, which was bad enough in itself, but the insult was compounded by the elevation to the peerage or a baronetcy of the other wartime military leaders. The calculated slight caused a furor in England. Many theories were put forward for the affront: the newly rediscovered pacifism of the Labourites; the settling of old scores by the many enemies Harris had made; even the embarrassment, in the postwar atmosphere, of what had been done to Germany by "Bomber" Harris.

Harris and his many supporters, for good reason, placed the blame on the machinations of John Strachey, an old adversary who had become undersecretary for air in the Attlee government. During the war, Harris had never hidden his disdain for and distrust of Strachey, whose politics had careered from the extreme right to the extreme left.

But Harris's ire had extended to everyone. Whether the supposed malefactor was an undersecretary, a member of the Cabinet, or even the prime minister, he'd cared not at all. In one particularly abusive memo to Strachey's predecessor, he had excoriated the defense establishment for not producing a workable cluster of incendiary bombs. The letter is studded with such expressions as "gross incompetence," "hopeless," "poor," "misplaced energy . . . being put into petty and useless improvements," and "deplorable." Amazingly, this letter was written ten days *after* incendiaries had devastated Dresden.

In January 1946, preparatory to his retirement from the RAF, Harris was promoted from air chief marshal to marshal of the Royal Air Force, the highest rank attainable in the RAF. And there the matter rested. There were no further official honors for the man who had taken the war to the enemy for five years.

Foreign governments were not so stingy with accolades for the leader of Bomber Command, in particular the United States. At a special service at the Pentagon in September 1946, Eisenhower himself presented Harris with the Distinguished Service Medal on behalf of President Truman and the American people.

By this time, Harris's connections, in particular his acquaintance with Averell Harriman, had led to his becoming managing director of the South African Marine Corporation, Ltd., a shipping line with offices in New York and Cape Town. He and Lady Harris maintained homes in both cities.

One of the advantages of a society with free elections is that wrongs are sometimes righted when the outs become the ins. Such was the case when Churchill was returned to power as prime minister of Great Britain on 26 October 1951, a month shy of his seventy-seventh birthday. The following April, he offered Harris the long-overdue peerage.

Harris's departure from England six years earlier had come amid much speculation that he had abandoned his homeland because of the shoddy treatment he had received at the hands of an ungrateful Labour government. He felt that once he accepted this honor from the new Tory government, perhaps these rumors, which were not completely unjustified, might at least be put to rest.

But he refused the highest honor. To be called "Lord Harris" just would not do in South Africa. As he put it, it would be "as out of place [there] as a hippopotamus in Trafalgar Square."

Opposition to honoring Harris was still strong, and according to

Churchill's private secretary John Colville, there was "consternation" at the meeting of the Honours Committee when Churchill proposed Harris's name.

The tenacious Churchill would not be denied, however, and the following New Year's Day, 1953, Harris's name appeared on the Honours List. He was to become a baronet, a title he'd chosen since he would not have to change the way he was addressed. But the overriding reason he allowed such an honor was that it would also recognize the thousands of men who had served and died under him in the war against the Axis— his "bomber boys." Not so incidentally, it would also be "a thistle for Strachey."

Sir Arthur Harris, Bt, GCB, OBE, AFC, LLD, eventually resettled in England in the Oxfordshire village of Goring-on-Thames, the name of which no doubt amused him greatly. There he lived quietly, receiving old friends and maintaining his contacts with former comrades in arms.

On 5 June 1964, the day before the twentieth anniversary of D-day, Harris received a particularly welcome message. "Dear Bert," wrote his old comrade in arms, "To you, one of my close associates in OVERLORD, I am impelled to send, once more, a special word of thanks. . . . no historian could possibly be aware of the depth of my obligation to you." The cable was signed simply "Ike."

On Arthur Harris's ninetieth birthday, in 1982, part of the celebration included a flyover by a Lancaster bomber. At noon, the old man was asked to come outside. As he stood in his garden the great plane roared in low over the town. The air marshal looked at his watch. "Late, as always," he said.

The controversy that swirled around Arthur Harris and Bomber Command continues to crop up as new revelations come to light and World War II strategy is rethought, reinterpreted, and in many cases condemned anew. The announcement that at long last a memorial to the men of Bomber Command, with a statue of the air marshal, was to be erected in front of St. Clement Danes, the RAF church, in the Strand, elicited protests from around the world, including the *Times* of London and the mayor of Dresden.

Opposition was effectively damped down, or at least muted, when one of the RAF's staunchest wartime sponsors announced that not only would she attend the ceremony but would unveil the statue to Bomber Harris herself. On 31 May 1992, Elizabeth, the ninety-two-year-old Queen Mother, proudly took her place beside the old airmen at the dedication, many of whom she had met when she'd tirelessly toured the RAF bases a half century earlier.

· · ·

With the Russian soldiers only a few streets away, Adolf Hitler killed himself in the *Führerbunker.* Joseph Goebbels and his wife, Magda— after dispatching their six sleeping children by forcing cyanide capsules into their mouths—chose to die upstairs, outside the chancellery. Heinrich Himmler was captured by the British, but he too chose death, by biting down on a cyanide capsule while being examined by a doctor. Hermann Göring, therefore, was the only one of the four highest-ranking Nazis to stand trial.

Soon after his arrest by American troops, Göring held a press conference, where he drank champagne while holding forth for reporters and photographers. The subsequent picture spread in *Life* magazine created the predictable storm, and the Reichsmarschall disappeared from sight until he testified in his own defense at his trial before the War Crimes Tribunal at Nuremberg. Rudolf Hess, Jaochim von Ribbentrop, Speer, Karl Dönitz, and other Nazi leaders shared the dock with him, but, as always, attention was squarely on Göring, who was unrepentant to the end.

By most accounts, Göring gave as good as he got in dealing with his prosecutors and inquisitors. The sly Reichsmarschall was a master show-man, but his fluency of speech and brilliance in retort could not mask his crimes and his role as one of the architects of the Nazi campaign of conquest, terror, and murder. He was sentenced to die by hanging. Göring protested that he should be given a soldier's death in front of a firing squad.

Whether the promise of a more dignified exit than death at the end of a rope would have deterred him from his final act is open to question. The night before his scheduled execution, Göring bit down on a cyanide capsule in his cell at Nuremberg and died within minutes. The provenance of the poison has never been satisfactorily determined.

Göring had been searched regularly to avoid just such an occurrence and nothing had been found on his person, so the theory that it was smuggled into him by one of his last visitors, a sympathetic American guard or doctor—he had made friends with several—has never been disproved.

· · ·

Carl Spaatz was at the schoolhouse in Rheims on 7 May when Germany surrendered unconditionally. Two days later he flew to Berlin for the formal surrender of the German general staff at the headquarters of the Soviet commander, Marshal Georgi K. Zhukov.

Carl Spaatz was also the only top-ranking American officer to meet one of the Nazi chieftains. Eisenhower refused to meet or greet any of his erstwhile enemies. Spaatz and Hoyt Vandenberg met Göring face-to-face on 10 May 1945, at Augsburg. Spaatz stirred up a controversy by returning Göring's salute, which he denied was inappropriate. Indeed, he defended it as the right and proper action from one officer to another.

The fallen Reichsmarschall told his conqueror that he had not wanted to fight the Battle of Britain because he knew that the Luftwaffe was not ready. He further admitted that his only effective bomber, the Junkers 88, was slow, had limited firepower, and needed a tight fighter escort. In that he was correct, but the Ju 88 was nevertheless an effective bomber in that it carried a sizable bomb load and was operating well within its range. With properly deployed fighter escorts—which, of course, it did not have—it could have been a formidable weapon.

Göring also insisted to Spaatz that if Germany could have held out for four or five more months, enough jet planes would have been available and enough fuel produced to turn the tide. He even maintained that there were enough trained pilots to do the job. This was clearly as unrealistic an appraisal of Luftwaffe capabilities in mid-1945, as so many of his prewar predictions had been.

In the postwar years, both Carl Spaatz and Dwight Eisenhower continued in military posts of great prominence, in Eisenhower's case to the highest civil office as well, the presidency.

Spaatz, when his task in Europe ended, was appointed air force commander in the Far East, where he helped bring a quick end to the war against the Japanese. Some of the old team was reassembled when the Eighth Air Force, still under Doolittle, was transferred to the Pacific war and was based on Okinawa. Carl Spaatz thus found himself a witness to yet more of the great events of the twentieth century.

As air force commander, he was directly responsible for implementing the order to drop the atomic bombs on Hiroshima and Nagasaki. Indeed, he met the *Enola Gay* when it returned from Hiroshima and pinned the Distinguished Flying Cross on the pilot, Paul W. Tibbets.

On 1 September 1945, Spaatz watched as the Japanese delegation was brought aboard the USS *Missouri* in Tokyo Bay for the surrender ceremony. He was thus the only officer to be present at each of the three surrender ceremonies that ended World War II: Rheims, Berlin, and Tokyo.

Carl Spaatz's central role in the defeat of the Axis was honor enough for any soldier, but perhaps his enduring monument is the separate and independent United States Air Force, which, in 1947, was finally freed of its subservience to the United States Army. In 1946, Spaatz had succeeded Hap Arnold, and he therefore had the distinction of being the last head of the U.S. Army Air Forces and the first chief of staff of the new United States Air Force.

The air force could not be truly independent, he argued, without an academy, which would be the equal of West Point and Annapolis. An air force academy was authorized by Congress in 1954, and construction began not long after near Colorado Springs, Colorado, on a site that Spaatz helped select and where, fittingly, he is buried.

The man immediately responsible for the three most controversial air raids of World War II—Dresden, Hiroshima, and Nagasaki—gave little thought to them afterward. And if he ever regretted any of his actions, he certainly never said so. On the contrary.

"Well, I had no difficulty in that," he said about ordering the raid on Hiroshima. "I ordered the drop. That was purely a political decision, wasn't a military decision. The military man carries out the orders of his political bosses."

As for precision bombing, the general admitted that so much of the bombing was inaccurate that the "general effect was the same as area bombing."

And when asked about the sometimes critical *United States Strategic Bombing Survey*, the man who directed the strategic bombing of Germany replied, "I've never been interested enough to read it . . . the successful conclusion of the war was enough to justify what we had done. If we had lost, then the survey might have meant something."

· · ·

People can evolve, cities can be rebuilt, and even disgraced nations can rejoin the world community. The firestorm that destroyed the dense urban mix that was prewar Dresden on the night of 13–14 February 1945 was not unlike the purifying fire that brings to a close Wagner's epic *Ring of the Nibelung*.

Just as that great conflagration consumes Valhalla and its corrupt gods and heralds redemption for mankind, so the fires of World War II were necessary in order to destroy an evil society and portend a new beginning for Germany.

But much of the new Germany found itself trapped in yet another totalitarian state. The eastern half, christened the German Democratic Republic, in many ways resembled the old police state of the Hitler years, except that the oppression of the Nazis had been replaced by that of the Communist Party.

However, an increasingly restive population eventually joined with the political liberalization movements sweeping the Soviet satellite countries in 1989 and deposed the ruling party. Within a year East and West Germany were reunited. The Dresdeners, who had known nothing but one-party, despotic rule since 1933, were now part of a freely elected, democratic republic.

The ghosts of despots are hard to exorcise—particularly for the victims. The crimes of the Third Reich have rightly been called crimes against humanity and must never be allowed to be forgotten. Nor should the small but increasingly vocal neo-Nazi movement that has arisen in Germany be dismissed as the ravings of a small minority. German history teaches us that to ignore any movement that appears to exist only on the margins of civilized society is to do so at great peril.

The reconstruction and revival of the city of Dresden from the ruins that served for decades as the perfect symbol of the universal barbarity of war offers more than a ray of hope for Germany and the world. Nowhere is this reconciliation more manifest than in the reconsecrated Frauenkirche, the great church that has been resurrected from the broken and charred pile of rubble that for half a century lay at the very heart of Dresden.

It is cause for rejoicing, not only for Germans but for everyone, that the Frauenkirche once again resounds with the music of Johann Sebastian Bach, the exemplar of all that was and is great in the German people.

ACKNOWLEDGMENTS

Many institutions and individuals provided encouragement and support during the research and writing of this book.

In the United Kingdom I am particularly indebted to the Public Record Office, Kew; the Imperial War Museum, Lambeth; the Bomber Command Association, Hendon, in particular Douglas Radcliffe; the British Library; the Royal Air Force Museum, Hendon; and the Air Force Museum, Duxford.

In Germany, Matthias Neutzner made available his wide knowledge and extensive research on the Dresden raids. The Stadtmuseum Dresden and the Deutsches Fotothek, at the Sächsische Landesbibliothek, in particular Bettina Erlenkamp, were most accommodating. Lutz Werner, at the Neue Synagoge, provided valuable information on the Jewish community in Dresden.

In America, I am grateful for the assistance rendered by staff at the Library of Congress; the United States Air Force Historical Research Center, Maxwell Air Force Base, Ala.; the library at the United States Air Force Academy; the library at the United States Military Academy; the Daniel Library at the Citadel; the New York Public Library; the Ramsay Library at the University of North Carolina at Asheville; the Mighty Eighth Air Force Museum and Library, Pooler, Ga.; and the Pack Memorial Library, Asheville, N.C.

The Wurlitzer Foundation, Taos, N.M., provided much needed solitude at a critical time in this book's genesis, and I was able to work in other special places through the generosity of Eleanor Crook, John Ehle, Rosemary Harris, and Fredda Culbreth.

The Experimental Aircraft Association, Oshkosh, Wisc., afforded me an indelible research experience—the opportunity to be co-pilot, navigator, waist gunner, and bombardier on a B-17 Flying Fortress, the *Aluminum Overcast,* and then take the controls of the great plane and fly it for a few unforgettable minutes over my hometown.

Vivian Dillingham was a stalwart throughout the long process, and others to whom I am especially grateful are David Phillips, Phillip Earnshaw, Arthur Humphrey, Carlos Sánchez, the late Gloria Jones, Enid Hardwicke, John R. Hearst, Budd Levinson, Ruben Johnson, Adolf Kremel, Kathy Taylor, Les Doss, Patrick Read, Liz Carpenter, Malcolm Goldstein, Dr. William R. McKenna, Dr. Snehal Vyas, and Tom McLellan.

Carole Gardiner was particularly generous with her support and offered much wise counsel.

Kate Davison was my skillful translator, and Carolyn Blakemore and the late Joel Honig provided useful editorial advice at an early stage.

However, it is Robert Loomis of Random House, that nonpareil of editors, to whom I am most indebted. He kept the faith, overlooked the missed deadlines, and urged me to press on. I owe him much.

Marshall De Bruhl
Asheville, N.C.
June 2006

NOTES

PREFACE

xii *"Limited or ambitious men"*: Michael S. Sherry, *The Rise of American Air Power*, p. xi.

PROLOGUE

xvii *"Ash Wednesday and St. Valentine's Day"*: John Colville, *The Fringes of Power*, p. 559.

xvii *"Were you there, Charles?"*: Lord Moran, *Churchill*, p. 256.

CHAPTER ONE: "THE BOMBER WILL ALWAYS GET THROUGH"

8 *"less than those sometimes suffered"*: John Terraine, *A Time for Courage*, p. 10.

8 *"As long as man remained tied to the surface of the earth"*: Giulio Douhet, *Il dominio dell'aria*, pp. 7–10.

10 *"jump over the army"*: Charles Messenger, *Bomber Harris and the Strategic Bombing Offensive*, p. 18.

10 *"If a future war can be won"*: Charles Messenger, *Bomber Harris and the Strategic Bombing Offensive*, p. 18.

11 *"Air power can be used as an independent means"*: Max Hastings, *Bomber Command*, p. 38.

12 *"I think it is well also for the man in the street"*: John Terraine, *A Time for Courage*, p. 13.

14 *"the result of incompetency"*: C. V. Glines, "Air Power Visionary Billy Mitchell," *Aviation History Magazine*, Sept. 1997, vol. 8.

15 *"had no quarrel with the administration"*: U.S. Air Force Historical Division, Oral History K105.5–35.

17 *By 1937–38, almost 40 percent*: Richard Overy, *Goering*, p. 38.
     "I am absolutely convinced": Kenneth S. Davis, *FDR*, p. 504.

18 *"The decisive difference"*: A. J. P. Taylor quoted in Len Deighton, *Fighter*, p. xviii.

19 *"He was determined"*: Kenneth S. Davis, *FDR*, p. 372.

19 *When he was challenged*: Michael S. Sherry, *The Rise of American Air Power*, p. 86.

20 *"squared with the dominant prejudices and priorities"*: Michael S. Sherry, *The Rise of American Air Power*, p. 82.

20 *The final Air Corps plan*: Michael S. Sherry, *The Rise of American Air Power*, p. 86.

21 *"long range bombers must rely"*: Papers of Ira C. Eaker, Library of Congress.

22 *"undoubtedly the most important turning-point"*: Martin Middlebrook and Chris Everitt, *Bomber Command War Diaries*, p. 31.

23 *"obvious to any literate citizen"*: Wesley Frank Craven and James Lea Cate, *The Army Air Forces in World War II*, vol. 1, p. 142.

24 *In their revised list of priorities*: AWPD-42 Target Priorities Table, reproduced in James R. Cody, *AWPD-42 to Instant Thunder*, Maxwell Air Force Base, Alabama: Air University Press, 1996.

24 *"one of the tragic mistakes of the war"*: Steven A. Parker, United States Air Force Academy, "AWPD-1: Targeting for Victory," *Aerospace Power Journal*, Summer 1989.

24 *"carried with them the reassuring weight"*: Wesley Frank Craven and James Lea Cate, *The Army Air Forces in World War II*, vol. 1, p. 667.

25 *"hysterical chatter"*: Kenneth S. Davis, *FDR*, p. 549.
    it was still at 73 percent: Michael S. Sherry, *The Rise of American Air Power*, p. 82.

CHAPTER TWO: THE ARCHITECTS OF DESTRUCTION

29 *"It is on the bomber that we must rely"*: Charles Messenger, *"Bomber" Harris and the Strategic Bombing Offensive*, p. 17.

29 *"the moral effect of bombing"*: John Terraine, *A Time for Courage*, p. 9.

29 *"We must avoid the stupendous drain"*: Lord Moran, *Churchill*, p. 81.

30 *His November 1942*: Max Hastings, *Bomber Command*, p. 180.

30 *In addition, although it was not publicly stated*: Martin Gilbert, *The Second World War*, p. 393.

31 *"You have only to look"*: Dudley Saward, *"Bomber" Harris*, p. 1.

32 *"I completed the long course"*: Dudley Saward, *"Bomber" Harris*, p. 13.

32 *"I can't fly"*: Dudley Saward, *"Bomber" Harris*, p. 13.

33 *"We just flew about"*: Dudley Saward, *"Bomber" Harris*, p. 16.

33 *"Thereafter for nearly twenty years"*: Sir Arthur Harris, *Bomber Offensive*, p. 277.

33 *"bones now lie"*: Sir Arthur Harris, *Bomber Offensive*, p. 277.

34 *Harris early on saw the power*: Sir Arthur Harris, *Bomber Offensive*, p. 19.

35 *Later, Harris credited*: Dudley Saward, *"Bomber" Harris*, p. 45.

35 *A quick advance by Germany*: Dudley Saward, *"Bomber" Harris*, p. 52.

36 *British intelligence that the Luftwaffe*: Cajus Bekker, *The Luftwaffe War Diaries*, p. 377.

37 *"batches of Hudsons and Harvards"*: Sir Arthur Harris, *Bomber Offensive*, p. 27.

37 *"I am at a loss"*: Dudley Saward, *"Bomber" Harris*, p. 60.

37 *Harris acidly observed*: Dudley Saward, *"Bomber" Harris*, p. 61.

37 *"Their major obsession"*: Dudley Saward, *"Bomber" Harris*, p. 61.

39 *"I have in the course of my lifetime"*: Sir Arthur Harris, *Bomber Offensive*, p. 33.

39 *Someone at the Air Ministry*: Dudley Saward, *"Bomber" Harris*, p. 82.

39 *Harris's credo*: Dudley Saward, *"Bomber" Harris*, p. 83.

41 *"perhaps the greatest error"*: Martin Gilbert, *The Second World War*, p. 277.

42 *"because you see"*: Sir Arthur Harris, *Bomber Offensive*, p. 64.

42 *"The idea that the main object of bombing"*: Sir Arthur Harris, *Bomber Offensive*, p. 78.

43 *"I do not, of course, suggest that bombing"*: Sir Arthur Harris, *Bomber Offensive*, p. 79.

43 *"The damage surpasses all one could imagine"*: Matthias Neutzner, *Angriff: Martha Heinrich Acht*, letter of 21 February 1945, p. 106.

47 *There was no argument about the ultimate purpose*: Martin Gilbert, *The Second World War*, p. 393.

50 *"Red Plague over Berlin"*: Roger Manvell and Heinrich Fraenkel, *Goering*, p. 116.

52 *only a prototype passed off as being in full production*: David Irving, *Göring*, p. 224.

52 *"designed to intimidate"*: Michael S. Sherry, *The Rise of American Air Power*, p. 359.

53 *"An endeavor will be made"*: "Preliminary Tactical Guiding Principles for the Employment of Luftwaffe Units Against England," 10 January 1940, Maxwell Air Force Base, microfilm.

54 *"That's just what we want!"*: Cajus Bekker, *The Luftwaffe War Diaries*, p. 126.

54 *"In the face of such arguments"*: Cajus Bekker, *The Luftwaffe War Diaries*, p. 176.

CHAPTER THREE: WEAPONS FOR THE NEW AGE OF WARFARE

56 *Indeed, when Arthur Harris assumed command*: Martin Middlebrook and Chris Everitt, *The Bomber Command War Diaries*, p. 241.

58 *"According to the American habit"*: Air University Library, Maxwell Air Force Base, Microfilm K2625.

60 *As late as 25 January 1945:* Spaatz Papers, Library of Congress.

64 *"In the evening we again":* Joseph Goebbels, *Final Entries, 1945,* p. 35.

67 *Udet had pulled off something of a coup:* Air University Library, Maxwell Air Force Base, Microfilm K2625.

68 *"We [Germany] were prepared for a short war":* "The Development of Ground Attack Aviation," Air University Library, Maxwell Air Force Base, No. 4376–584.

68 *In a surprisingly frank speech:* Dudley Saward, *"Bomber" Harris,* p. 54.

68 *"tried to assume as little":* "The Development of Jet and Rocket Airplanes in Germany, 1938–1945," Air University Library, Maxwell Air Force Base, Microfilm K2625.

69 *"The war is over!":* Cajus Bekker, *The Luftwaffe War Diaries,* p. 230.

69 *Seeing enemies on every side:* Richard Overy, *Goering,* p. 155.

69 *Thousands of these* Mischlinge: Bryan Mark Riggs, *Hitler's Jewish Soldiers,* p. 29.

71 *Hitler, who was kept apprised:* Albert Speer, *Inside the Third Reich,* pp. 362–63.

72 *However, not more than 300 jets:* Cajus Bekker, *The Luftwaffe War Diaries,* p. 356.

72 *In October 1944, according to Bekker:* Cajus Bekker, *The Luftwaffe War Diaries,* p. 356.

73 *On 10 April 1945, Luftwaffe jet aircraft:* Richard G. Davis, *Carl A. Spaatz and the Air War in Europe,* p. 584.

75 *As Molly Painter-Downs reported: The New Yorker Book of War Pieces,* pp. 56–57.

75 *"We have ample evidence":* Richard G. Davis, *Carl A. Spaatz and the Air War in Europe,* p. 261.

75 *And on 24 May 1943 he wrote to Arnold:* Richard G. Davis, *Carl A. Spaatz and the Air War in Europe,* p. 200.

77 *"Today I saw air power":* "8th Air Force Miscellaneous Correspondence, 1942–1945." 6 vols. USAF HRA/ISR. Air Force Historical Research Agency, Maxwell Air Force Base, Alabama, File 520.161.

79 *"We discovered one day":* Steven A. Parker, United States Air Force Academy, "AWPD-1: Targeting for Victory." *Aerospace Power Journal,* Summer 1989.

CHAPTER FOUR: THE FATAL ESCALATION

82 *"For centuries, it has been in our blood":* Winston Churchill, *Memoirs of the Second World War,* p. 354.

82 *"The PM seems rather more apprehensive"*: John Colville, *The Fringes of Power*, p. 245.

82 *Churchill told the general*: Martin Gilbert, ed., *The Churchill War Papers*, vol. 2, p. 852.

83 *Somewhere between the translation*: Warren F. Kimball, *Forged in War*, p. 65.

83 *"Should October pass"*: Public Record Office (Kew), CAB 66/13 WP (40) 421.

85 *As one Luftwaffe fighter pilot said*: Cajus Bekker, *The Luftwaffe War Diaries*, p. 169.

86 *The British pilots, said Churchill*: Winston Churchill, *Memoirs of the Second World War*, p. 358.

87 *He reserved "to himself personal punishment"*: Cajus Bekker, *The Luftwaffe War Diaries*, p. 172.

87 *A month before, Churchill had written*: Martin Gilbert, ed., *The Churchill War Papers*, vol. 2, p. 555.

88 *"Now they are trying to starve us out"*: Martin Middlebrook and Chris Everitt, *The Bomber Command War Diaries*, p. 77.

88 *"the law of diminishing returns"*: Winston Churchill, *Memoirs of the Second World War*, p. 372.

88 *"Far more important to us"*: Winston Churchill, *Memoirs of the Second World War*, p. 361.

89 *"a breathing space of which we had the utmost need"*: Winston Churchill, *Memoirs of the Second World War*, p. 361.

89 *"Göring should certainly have persevered"*: Winston Churchill, *Memoirs of the Second World War*, p. 361.

89 *"London was like some huge prehistoric animal"*: Winston Churchill, *Memoirs of the Second World War*, p. 377.

89 *Still, Churchill wondered*: Winston Churchill, *Memoirs of the Second World War*, p. 375.

91 *Some 380 people were killed*: Public Record Office (Kew), CAB 66/13 WP (40) 457.

93 *But myths die hard*: Allan W. Kurki, *Operation Moonlight Sonata*.

94 *"While the success of [the Americans'] attacks"*: Public Record Office (Kew), AIR 20/4826.

94 *"The risk of death from incendiary attacks"*: Public Record Office (Kew). AIR 20/4826.

96 *"Priority of selection"*: Martin Middlebrook and Chris Everitt, *The Bomber Command War Diaries*, p. 132.

96 *"Both are suitable as area objectives"*: Martin Middlebrook and Chris Everitt, *The Bomber Command War Diaries*, p. 132.

97 *" 'area bombing' against German cities"*: Martin Middlebrook and Chris Everitt, *The Bomber Command War Diaries*, p. 132.

97   *Just one-third:* Denis Richards, *The Hardest Victory,* p. 96.

98   *Did not this report give the lie:* Denis Richards, *The Hardest Victory,* p. 97.

98   *"It is very debatable":* Denis Richards, *The Hardest Victory,* p. 97.

98   *"spiked Churchill's guns":* Denis Richards, *The Hardest Victory,* p. 97.

98   *As for the success of the RAF campaign:* Public Record Office (Kew), "Weekly Résumé (no. 286) of the Naval, Military and Air Situation from 0700 15th February to 0700 22nd February, 1945," War Cabinet Files, Public Record Office (Kew), W.P. (45) 106, 22 Feb. 1945.

98   *"No dog nor cat is left":* Michael S. Sherry, *The Rise of American Air Power,* p. 150.

99   *"It has been decided":* Martin Middlebrook and Chris Everitt, *The Bomber Command War Diaries,* p. 240.

100 *"Lübeck," said Harris:* Max Hastings, *Bomber Command,* pp. 147–48.

101 *"I censured this":* Joseph Goebbels, *The Goebbels Diaries, 1942–1943,* p. 200.

101 *"There is talk about scenes":* Joseph Goebbels, *The Goebbels Diaries, 1942–1943,* p. 201.

102 *On 6 April 1941:* Martin Gilbert, *The Second World War,* p. 170.

102 *In a memorandum of 2 May 1942:* Public Record Office (Kew), AIR 14/3507.

103 *He ordered the gauleiter:* Albert Speer, *Inside the Third Reich,* pp. 279–80.

104 *"The end is in sight in Africa":* Joseph Goebbels, *The Goebbels Diaries, 1942–1943,* p. 353.

104 *"the greatest example of perfidy in modern history":* Joseph Goebbels, *The Goebbels Diaries, 1942–1943,* p. 410.

104 *The bombs fell:* Martin Middlebrook and Chris Everitt, *The Bomber Command War Diaries,* p. 411.

104 *The Americans followed up:* Roger A. Freeman, Alan Crouchman, and Vic Maslen, *The Mighty Eighth War Diary,* pp. 78–79.

105 *"The Americans quickly withdrew":* Martin Middlebrook and Chris Everitt, *The Bomber Command War Diaries,* p. 410.

107 *Historian Daniel Goldhagen has estimated:* Daniel Jonah Goldhagen, *Hitler's Willing Executioners,* p. 171.

CHAPTER FIVE: *VERGELTUNGSWAFFEN*

110 *"attack by pilotless aircraft":* Public Record Office (Kew), CAB 65/42.

111 *"England is trembling":* New York Times, 18 June 1944.

111 *He ordered the escalation:* Albert Speer, *Inside the Third Reich,* p. 356.

111 *More disturbing was the report:* Public Record Office (Kew), CAB 65/43.

112 *He immediately volunteered:* Chapman obituary, *New York Times,* 20 December 1997.

113 *During an interrogation:* Kenneth Grubb, "How We Make Captured Luftwaffe Crews Talk."

113 *103 of the 140 identified sites:* Denis Richards, *The Hardest Victory,* p. 225.

114 *Just four days after the first V-1:* Martin Middlebrook and Chris Everitt, *The Bomber Command War Diaries,* 16–17 June 1944.

115 *"On that day":* Albert Speer, *Inside the Third Reich,* p. 346.

By November 1944: Albert Speer, *Inside the Third Reich,* pp. 346–50.

116 *The Polish underground:* Martin Gilbert, *The Second World War,* p. 561.

117 *"has now been intensified":* Public Record Office (Kew), CAB 65/44, p. 213.

118 *It was estimated:* Ian Kershaw, *Hitler: 1936–1945: Nemesis,* p. 736.

119 *"justification of giving up":* Public Record Office (Kew), AIR 14/3507.

120 *"have thrown our preparations":* Joseph Goebbels, *The Goebbels Diaries, 1942–1943,* p. 435.

121 *"Losses were particularly heavy":* Walter Dornberger, *V-2,* p. 105.

121 *The next week saw some drop-off:* Public Record Office (Kew), "Weekly Résumé (no. 291) of the Naval, Military and Air Situation from 0700 22nd March to 0700 29th March, 1945," W.P. (45) 201.

122 *But at last the ten-month:* Public Record Office (Kew), CAB 65/50.

122 *"It is my duty":* Public Record Office (Kew), 410 H.C. DEB. 5s, col. 985.

122 *As for who should be credited:* Public Record Office (Kew), 410 H.C. DEB. 5s, col. 985.

124 *"The decisive difference":* A. J. P. Taylor quoted in Len Deighton, *Fighter,* p. xviii.

125 *Speer later derisively pointed out:* Albert Speer, *Inside the Third Reich,* p. 365.

CHAPTER SIX: OPERATION THUNDERCLAP

127 *"I don't know about oratory":* Lord Moran, *Churchill,* p. 13.

128 *"Those filthy Germans!":* Harold Nicolson, *Diaries and Letters,* vol. 2, *The War Years,* 16 February 1944.

130 *The use of poison gas:* Martin Gilbert, *Winston S. Churchill, 1942–1945: Road to Victory,* p. 840.

131 *"Press and broadcast should be asked":* Martin Gilbert, *The Churchill War Papers,* Vol. 2, *Never Surrender,* p. 423.

131 *The odds of being killed:* Public Record Office (Kew), AIR 20/4826.

131 *"that the time might well come":* Public Record Office (Kew), AIR 20/3227; Public Record Office (Kew), AIR 20/4831.

131 *"Attack on German Civilian Morale":* Public Record Office (Kew), AIR 20/3227.

132 *"A spectacular and final object lesson":* Public Record Office (Kew), AIR 20/3227.

133 *"The main purpose of [Thunderclap]"*: Public Record Office (Kew), Air 20/4826.

133 *"The essential purpose of the attack"*: Public Record Office (Kew), Air 20/4826.

134 *"at the best may prove the last straw"*: Public Record Office (Kew), Air 20/4831.

137 *"In this situation it is unlikely"*: Public Record Office (Kew), Air 20/4826.

138 *Neither Arthur Harris nor Carl Spaatz:* Richard G. Davis, *Carl A. Spaatz and the Air War in Europe*, p. 436.

138 *As for Harris:* Sir Arthur Harris, *Bomber Offensive*, p. 245.

138 *When they told Harris:* Richard G. Davis, *Carl A. Spaatz and the Air War in Europe*, pp. 432–33.

138 *A thousand American B-17s:* Roger A. Freeman, Alan Crouchman, and Vic Maslen, *The Mighty Eighth War Diary*, p. 273.

139 *"U.S. bombing policy, as you know"*: Spaatz Papers, Library of Congress.

139 *"We will continue precision bombing"*: Richard G. Davis, *Carl A. Spaatz and the Air War in Europe*, p. 434.

139 *The plan was scrapped:* Martin Gilbert, *The Second World War*, p. 592.

140 *"Since the Mongol invasion"*: Richard Breitman, *Official Secrets*, p. 93.

141 *"And not with Jews"*: Richard Breitman, *Official Secrets*, p. 102.

141 *"The Jewish capacity for destruction"*: Harold Nicolson, *Diaries and Letters*, vol. 2, *The War Years*, 13 June 1945.

142 *"If propaganda has imbued a whole people"*: Adolf Hitler, *Mein Kampf*, p. 582.

143 *And when the American bombers entered the war:* Conrad C. Crane, *Bombs, Cities, and Civilians*, p. 64.

144 *"It is contrary to our national ideals"*: Richard G. Davis, *Carl A. Spaatz and the Air War in Europe*, p. 435.

145 *"Our entire target policy"*: Richard G. Davis, *Carl A. Spaatz and the Air War in Europe*, p. 435.

145 *"The bombing of civilian targets"*: Richard G. Davis, *Carl A. Spaatz and the Air War in Europe*, p. 435.

145 *"ancient, compact, historic"*: Richard G. Davis, *Carl A. Spaatz and the Air War in Europe*, p. 436.

146 *"In the European area"*: Winant to FDR, 23 April 1944. National Archives; photocopy on file in David Irving Archives.

148 *"There seems to be a kind of fanaticism"*: National Archives; photocopy on file in David Irving Archives.

148 *"was very anxious to operate"*: *Historical Analysis of the 14–15 February 1945 Bombing of Dresden*, p. 4.

149 *"to discuss with you the situation"*: *Historical Analysis of the 14–15 February 1945 Bombing of Dresden*, p. 4.

149 *"Tedder outlined to Stalin":* Historical Analysis of the 14–15 February 1945 Bombing of Dresden, p. 4.

150 *But he now had to give way:* Martin Middlebrook and Chris Everitt, *The Bomber Command War Diaries,* p. 661.

154 *In the evening:* Joseph Goebbels, *Final Entries, 1945,* p. 3.
On 29 April 1944: Roger A. Freeman, Alan Crouchman, and Vic Maslen, *The Mighty Eighth War Diary,* p. 232.

154 *In a series of raids:* Roger A. Freeman, Alan Crouchman, and Vic Maslen, *The Mighty Eighth War Diary,* p. 316.

154 *In raids on 7 October:* Roger A. Freeman, Alan Crouchman, and Vic Maslen, *The Mighty Eighth War Diary,* p. 360.

154 *Entitled "Strategic Bombing":* Public Record Office (Kew), AIR 8/1745.

155 *"basting the Germans":* Max Hastings, *Bomber Command,* p. 341.

155 *The Prime Minister was concerned:* Dudley Saward, *"Bomber" Harris,* p. 282.

155 *Sinclair felt:* Dudley Saward, *"Bomber" Harris,* p. 283.

155 *"I did not ask you last night":* Max Hastings, *Bomber Command,* p. 341.

156 *The chief priority:* Dudley Saward, *"Bomber" Harris,* p. 284.

156 *While oil would remain:* Dudley Saward, *"Bomber" Harris,* p. 284.

157 *Bottomley sent a cable:* Dudley Saward, *"Bomber" Harris,* p. 285.

158 *"Evacuees from German and German-Occupied":* Public Record Office (Kew), AIR 8/1745.

159 *"Attack of Berlin, Leipzig, Dresden":* Maxwell Air Force Base, Microfilm K2625, 2078.

159 *"in conjunction with our attacks on Berlin":* Maxwell Air Force Base, Microfilm K2625, 2078.

160 *"to attack [Munich]":* Maxwell Air Force Base, Microfilm K2625, 2078.

160 *For Dresden was an alternate target:* Melden E. Smith Jr., "The Bombing of Dresden Reconsidered," p. 230.

160 *"All out effort will be placed":* Maxwell Air Force Base, Microfilm K2625, 2078.

161 *"Our estimate of the situation":* Richard G. Davis, *Carl A. Spaatz and the Air War in Europe,* p. 541.

162 *Eisenhower reluctantly agreed:* Richard G. Davis, *Carl A. Spaatz and the Air War in Europe,* p. 541.

163 *Further, said the president:* Warren F. Kimball, ed., *Churchill and Roosevelt: The Complete Correspondence,* vol. 3, p. 592.

163 *"If the United States":* National Archives; photocopy on file in David Irving Archives.

164 *"This is again 'jam tomorrow' ":* National Archives; photocopy in David Irving Archives.

165 *He asked the British and Americans:* Historical Analysis of the 14–15 February 1945 Bombing of Dresden.

165 *The limit-line agreement:* "Agreement for the Establishment of Limit Line (Prohibited Zone) for Operations of Allied Strategic Air Forces on the Front of Soviet Troops," 6 February 1945, Maxwell Air Force Base, Microfilm K2625, 2078.

166 *"Without you":* Richard G. Davis, *Carl A. Spaatz and the Air War in Europe,* p. 547.

166 *Kuter quickly realized:* Maxwell Air Force Base, Microfilm K2625, 2078.

167 *Therefore, on 12 February:* Melden E. Smith Jr., "The Bombing of Dresden Reconsidered," p. 234.

CHAPTER SEVEN: THE TARGET

171 *"belonged largely to emperors":* Robert B. Asprey, *Frederick the Great,* p. xiii.

171 *"from pleasure to pleasure":* Leopold von Ranke, *Memoirs of the House of Brandenburg and History of Prussia,* vol. 1, pp 343–44.

172 *"I have not at present":* Thomas Carlyle, *History of Frederick II of Prussia.* vol. 3, p. 135.

172 *"answered yes to everything":* Robert B. Asprey, *Frederick the Great,* p. 234.

175 *"in the presence of all":* Hans T. David and Arthur Mendel, *The Bach Reader,* p. 226.

181 *"DRESDEN is the historical capital of Saxony":* Public Record Office (Kew), AIR 14/3682.

182 *"Hospitals were denoted by":* Targeting information, Dresden, 27 February 1942, Public Record Office (Kew), AIR 40/1680.

183 *"Only a few knew what the finished product":* Matthias Neutzner, *Lebenszeichen,* p. 67.

184 *"a maximum capacity":* Targeting information, Dresden, 27 February 1942, Public Record Office (Kew), AIR 40/1680.

184 *"Dresden is one of the few direct links":* Targeting information, Dresden, 27 February 1942, Public Record Office (Kew), AIR 40/1680.

CHAPTER EIGHT: SHROVE TUESDAY, 1945

189 *"Pity that I have one screw too few":* Victor Klemperer, *I Will Bear Witness: A Diary of the Nazi Years, 1933–1941,* p. 236.

189 *Nevertheless, more than 30,000 internees:* Martin Gilbert, *The First World War,* p. 539.

190 *"On this occasion":* Victor Klemperer, *I Will Bear Witness: A Diary of the Nazi Years, 1942–1945,* p. 404.

190 *"The most cruel separations":* Victor Klemperer, *I Will Bear Witness: A Diary of the Nazi Years, 1942–1945,* p. 404.

191   *"Again a shabby house"*: Victor Klemperer, *I Will Bear Witness: A Diary of the Nazi Years, 1942–1945*, p. 405.

191   *"Now we were examined"*: Matthias Neutzner, *Lebenszeichen*, pp. 21–22.

196   *"Schörner is decidedly a personality"*: Joseph Goebbels, *Final Entries, 1945*, p. 80.

196   *"the other two who were condemned"*: Joseph Goebbels, *Final Entries, 1945*, p. 317.

197   *"The flight of January 1945"*: John Keegan, *The Second World War*, p. 592.

201   *"Really, one is compelled"*: Gerhart Pohl, *Gerhart Hauptmann and Silesia*, p. 5.

CHAPTER NINE: A PILLAR OF FIRE BY NIGHT

206   *The attacking force:* Public Record Office (Kew), AIR 14/3713, "Daily Attack Book."

206   *"I never bargained to take Tetrazzini"*: Lord Moran, *Churchill*, p. 255.

207   *En route, Churchill:* Winston Churchill, *Memoirs of the Second World War*, p. 929.

208   *The attack he feared had begun:* Author's interview with family member.

208   *The master bomber now broke radio silence:* David Irving, *Apocalypse 1945*, p. 134.

209   *The stadium had been chosen:* Target map of Dresden, Public Record Office (Kew), AIR 14/3682.

209   *Shouting, "Marker Leader: Tally-ho!":* David Irving, *Apocalypse 1945*, p. 135.

210   *"a rain of incendiaries"*: Sir Arthur Harris, *Bomber Offensive*, p. 83.

211   *By the time Victor Klemperer:* Victor Klemperer, *I Will Bear Witness: A Diary of the Nazi Years, 1942–1945*, p. 404.

215   *Only six aircraft:* Royal Air Force Operations Record Book, Feb. 1945. Public Record Office (Kew), AIR 24/307, AIR 24/309.

CHAPTER TEN: A COLUMN OF SMOKE BY DAY

217   *Some 461 bombers:* Roger A. Freeman, Alan Crouchman, and Vic Maslen, *The Mighty Eighth War Diary*, p. 439.

220   *a high school senior:* Author's interview with Margaret Armstrong Campbell.

221   *Twenty-three planes were lost:* Roger A. Freeman, Alan Crouchman, and Vic Maslen, *The Mighty Eighth War Diary*, p. 432.

222   *there was a relative newcomer:* Author's interview with Raymond G. Engstrand.

225   *The long mission to Dresden:* Author's interview with Ernest Robertson.

225   *"I was the old man in the crew"*: Roger A. Freeman, Alan Crouchman, and

Vic Maslen, *The Mighty Eighth War Diary*, p. 60. Colonel Morgan, in an interview with the author, recalled that it was St. Nazaire.

228 *The B-17s had strayed into Czechoslovakia:* In Roger A. Freeman, Alan Crouchman, and Vic Maslen, *The Mighty Eighth War Diary*, p. 439, Prague is denoted as a "target of opportunity."

228 *There was light flak:* Author's interview with Raymond G. Engstrand.

231 *On 15 October, Hap Arnold:* Letter to Joseph E. Kelly, Kelly family records, Repton, Alabama.

232 *At that moment aboard:* Author's interview with Ernest Robertson.

233 *He was awarded the Purple Heart:* Kelly family records, Repton, Alabama.

CHAPTER ELEVEN: ASH WEDNESDAY, 1945

235 *"A person who has forgotten how to weep":* Gerhart Pohl, *Gerhart Hauptmann and Silesia*, p. 8.

236 *A woman identified as Nora L.:* Matthias Neutzner, *Angriff: Martha Heinrich Acht*, pp. 130–34.

239 *"In the street all hell had broken loose":* Matthias Neutzner, *Lebenszeichen*, pp. 94–95.

240 *A Dresdener who directed a Red Cross camp:* Matthias Neutzner, *Lebenszeichen*, pp. 25–29.

244 *"After the first raid":* Matthias Neutzner, *Angriff: Martha Heinrich Acht*, pp. 103–04.

244 *Hans-Joachim D.:* Matthias Neutzner, *Angriff: Martha Heinrich Acht*, pp. 194–96.

248 *Gerhart Sommer, who was eight years old:* Author's interview with Sommer, 6 June 2005.

249 *"Then came the second raid":* Matthias Neutzner, *Lebenszeichen*, pp. 19–21.

252 *"On 13 February we heard the early warning":* Matthias Neutzner, *Lebenszeichen*, pp. 16–18.

CHAPTER TWELVE: "MR. PRIME MINISTER?"

255 *The Pforzheim attack:* Allied Air Commanders Conference, 1 March 1945, Minutes.

256 *"The Wehrmacht has decided to confer":* Spaatz Papers, Library of Congress.

257–58 *"Eighth Air Force Crews":* Allied Air Commanders Conference, 1 March 1945, Minutes.

258 *"What will lie":* John Colville, *The Fringes of Power*, p. 563.

258 *"The bomber is a passing phase":* John Colville, *The Fringes of Power*, p. 564.

258 *"Dresden? There is no such place"*: John Colville, *The Fringes of Power,* p. 562.

258 *"a man of limited intelligence"*: John Colville, *The Fringes of Power,* p. 563.

258 *"We could have no better brothers"*: Sir Arthur Harris, *Bomber Offensive,* p. 246.

259 *"Come on and deal"*: Captain Harry C. Butcher, *My Three Years with Eisenhower,* p. 770.

259 *"It seems," he said:* Spaatz Papers, Library of Congress.

259 *"it is most improbable"*: Spaatz Papers, Library of Congress.

259 *"This constant sniveling"*: David Irving, *Hitler's War,* p. 739.

260 *"almost draw a sigh of relief"*: Joachim Fest, *Speer,* p. 194.

262 *"The Allied Air Commanders"*: Arnold to Spaatz, 18 February 1945, Maxwell Air Force Base, microfilm K2625, 2078.

264 *"To start with the Heavies"*: Spaatz Papers, Library of Congress.

265 *"We must not get soft"*: Tami Davis Biddle. "Sifting Dresden's Ashes," p. 75.

266 *"the worst devastations"*: Max Hastings, *Bomber Command,* p. 176.

266 *"a blot on our escutcheon"*: *Hansard,* Fifth Series, vol. 408, col. 1901.

266 *"It seems to me"*: Public Record Office (Kew), CAB 120/303.

267 *Between them, said Harriman:* Richard Overy, *Why the Allies Won,* p. 102; Lord Moran, *Churchill,* p. 61; Winston Churchill, *Memoirs of the Second World War,* p. 623.

268 *"To suggest that we have"*: Public Record Office (Kew), AIR 20/3218.

270 *The exchange between:* Max Hastings, *Bomber Command,* pp. 332–35.

271 *"the attack on Dresden was at the time"*: Sir Arthur Harris, *Bomber Offensive,* p. 242.

271–72 *"Throughout January and February"*: Winston Churchill, *The Second World War: Triumph and Tragedy,* pp. 540–41. In the single-volume abridgement of the work, there is no mention of the Dresden raid.

273 *In her book:* Deborah Lipstadt, *Denying the Holocaust,* passim.

273 *"falsifications of the historical facts"*: Richard J. Evans, *Lying About Hitler,* pp. 177–78.

274 *In reality, he had seen:* Richard J. Evans, *Lying About Hitler,* p. 156.

274 *Instead, he wrote:* David Irving, *Apocalypse 1945,* p. 245.

274 *And in his 1996 biography:* David Irving, *Goebbels,* p. 501.

274 *"It is practically impossible to kill a myth"*: Richard J. Evans, *Lying About Hitler,* p. 169.

275 *"Of course now everybody talks"*: Richard J. Evans, *Lying About Hitler,* p. 181.

275 *When the libel trial ended:* D. D. Guttenplan, *The Holocaust on Trial,* pp. 281–83.

275 *What she referred to in a 2005 interview:* Australian Radio National, "Saturday Breakfast with Geraldine Doogue," 21 May 2005.

277   *"One's overall impression":* Public Record Office (Kew), AIR 19/1028.

281   *Under Adolf Hitler:* Frederick Taylor, *Dresden: Tuesday, February 13, 1945* (New York, 2004), p. 150.

283   *Every book, article, and documentary:* A notable exception is historian Frederick Taylor, *Dresden.*

283   *Germany would not be defeated:* Harry S. Truman, *Memoirs,* vol. 1, *Year of Decisions,* p. 17.

284   *"the development of a new explosive":* Harry S. Truman, *Memoirs,* vol. 1, *Year of Decisions,* p. 10.

284   *"That is the biggest fool thing":* Harry S. Truman, *Memoirs,* vol. 1, *Year of Decisions,* p. 11.

285   *"The feeling, such as there is":* Public Record Office (Kew), AIR 20/3218.

285   *Harris might also have pointed out:* Public Record Office (Kew), "Weekly Résumé (no. 285) of the Naval, Military and Air Situation from 0700 8th February to 0700 15th February, 1945," War Cabinet Files, W.P. (45) 98, 15 February 1945.

EPILOGUE

297   *"preoccupation with social problems":* Lord Moran, *Churchill,* p. 322.

298–99   *The letter is studded:* Public Record Office (Kew), AIR 24/309, 24 February 1945.

299   *To be called "Lord Harris":* Dudley Saward, *"Bomber" Harris,* p. 331.
       Opposition to honoring Harris: John Colville, *The Fringes of Power,* p. 644.

300   *"a thistle for Strachey":* Letter from Viscount Bracken to Harris, quoted in Dudley Saward, *"Bomber" Harris,* p. 332.

300   *"To you, one of my close associates":* Dudley Saward, *"Bomber" Harris,* p. 334.

303   *"Well, I had no difficulty":* U.S. Air Force Historical Division, Oral History K105.5–35.

BIBLIOGRAPHY

Ambrose, Stephen E. *Eisenhower: Soldier, General of the Army, President-Elect,*
1890–1952. New York, 1983.

Asprey, Robert B. *Frederick the Great: The Magnificent Enigma.* New York, 1986.

Bauer, Yehuda. *A History of the Holocaust.* New York, 1982.

Bekker, Cajus. *The Luftwaffe War Diaries.* Garden City, N.Y., 1968.

Bergander, Götz. *Dresden im Luftkrieg: Vorgeschichte-Zerstorung-Folgen.* Munich,
1977.

Biddle, Tami Davis. *Rhetoric and Reality in Air Warfare: The Evolution of British*
and American Ideas About Strategic Bombing, 1914–1945. Princeton, 2002.

———. "Sifting Dresden's Ashes." *Wilson Quarterly,* Spring 2005, pp. 60–80.

Böhm, Karl. *A Life Remembered: Memoirs.* New York, 1992.

Bomber's Baedeker: Guide to the Economic Importance of German Towns and
Cities. 2nd ed. London, 1944.

Boog, Horst, ed. *The Conduct of the Air War in the Second World War: An*
International Comparison. New York, 1992.

Bowen, E. B. *Radar Days.* Bristol, 1987.

Bowman, Martin W. *8th Air Force at War: Memories and Missions—England,*
1942–45. Sparkford, 1994.

Bowyer, Chaz. *Supermarine Spitfire.* London, 1980.

Boyden, Matthew. *Richard Strauss.* Boston, 1999.

Breitman, Richard. *Official Secrets: What the Nazis Planned, What the British and*
Americans Knew. New York, 1998.

Brereton, Lewis H. *The Brereton Diaries: The War in the Pacific, Middle East and*
Europe. New York, 1946.

Butcher, Captain Harry C. *My Three Years with Eisenhower.* New York, 1946.

Carlyle, Thomas. *History of Frederick II of Prussia, Called Frederick the Great.*
6 vols. London, 1886.

"Carpet Bombing." Air Force Historical Research Agency, Maxwell Air Force
Base, Alabama. File 519.553–4.

Chesnoff, Richard Z. *Pack of Thieves: How Hitler and Europe Plundered the Jews*
and Committed the Greatest Theft in History. New York, 1999.

Childers, Thomas. *Wings of Morning.* New York, 1995.

Chissell, Joan. *Clara Schumann: A Dedicated Spirit.* New York, 1983.

Churchill, Winston. *Memoirs of the Second World War.* Boston, 1959.

———. *The Second World War: Their Finest Hour.* Boston, 1949.

———. *The Second World War: Triumph and Tragedy.* Boston, 1953.

Clarkson, James A. "Increasing Operational Efficiency in the 8th Air Force by Analysis of Bombing Accuracy." Air Force Historical Research Agency, Maxwell Air Force Base, Alabama. File 248.532–84. 9 March 1945.

Colville, John. *The Fringes of Power.* Guilford, Conn., 2002.

Conversino, Mark J. *Fighting with the Soviets: The Failure of Operation Frantic, 1944–1945.* Lawrence, Kans., 1997.

Craig, Gordon A. *Germany, 1866–1945.* New York, 1978.

Crane, Conrad C. *Bombs, Cities, and Civilians.* Lawrence, Kans., 1993.

Craven, Wesley Frank, and James Lea Cate. *The Army Air Forces in World War II.* 7 vols. Reprint, Washington, D.C., 1983.

Dänhardt, Artur. *Der Zwinger: Ein Denkmal des Dresdner Barock.* Photographs by Erich Fritzsch. Leipzig, 1965.

Daso, Dik Alan. *Hap Arnold and the Evolution of American Airpower.* Washington, D.C., 2000.

David, Hans T., and Arthur Mendel. *The Bach Reader: A Life of Johann Sebastian Bach in Letters and Documents.* New York, 1945.

Davis, Burke. *The Billy Mitchell Affair.* New York, 1967.

Davis, Kenneth S. *FDR: Into the Storm, 1937–1940.* New York, 1993.

Davis, Richard G. *Carl A. Spaatz and the Air War in Europe.* Washington, D.C., London, 1992.

Deighton, Len. *Fighter: The True Story of the Battle of Britain.* New York, 1978.

Dietrich, Otto. *Hitler.* Translated by Richard and Clara Winston. Chicago, 1955.

Dill, Marshall, Jr. *Germany: A Modern History.* Ann Arbor, 1961.

Dornberger, Walter. *V-2.* Translated by James Cleugh and Geoffrey Halliday. New York, 1954.

Douhet, Giulio. *Il dominio dell'aria* [The Command of the Air]. Translated by Dino Ferrari. Washington, D.C., 1983.

Dumont, First Lieutenant Earle J., Jr. "Operation Götterdämmerung." Lecture, Army Air Forces School of Applied Tactics, Orlando, Florida. Air Force Historical Research Agency, Maxwell Air Force Base, Alabama. File 248.532–102. 20 April 1945.

Eaker, Lieutenant General Ira C. Oral History. January 1966. Air Force Historical Research Agency, Maxwell Air Force Base, Alabama. File K239.0512–626.

Easum, Chester V. *Prince Henry of Prussia, Brother of Fredrick the Great.* Madison, 1942.

Eisenhower, David. *Eisenhower: At War, 1943–1945*. New York, 1986.

Eisenhower, Dwight D. *Crusade in Europe*. Garden City, N.Y., 1970.

————. *The Papers of Dwight David Eisenhower: The War Years*. Alfred D. Chandler, ed. Baltimore, 1970.

Elliott, J. H. *Imperial Spain: 1469–1716*. London, 1963.

Encyclopaedia Judaica. Jerusalem, 1971.

Evans, Richard J. *Lying About Hitler: History, Holocaust, and the David Irving Trial*. New York, 2001.

Ewen, David. *The Encyclopedia of Musical Masterpieces: Music for the Millions*. 6th ed. New York, 1949.

Fest, Joachim. *Speer: The Final Verdict*. New York, 1991.

Freeman, Roger A., Alan Crouchman, and Vic Maslen. *The Mighty Eighth War Diary*. Reprint, Osceola, Wisc., 1993.

Gelb, Norman. *Ike and Monty: Generals at War*. New York, 1994.

"German Methods of Intelligence Interrogation." Air Force Historical Research Agency, Maxwell Air Force Base, Alabama. File 248.532–66.

Gilbert, Martin, ed. *The Churchill War Papers*. Vol. 2, *Never Surrender: May 1940–December 1940*. New York, 1995.

————. *The First World War: A Complete History*. New York, 1994.

————. *The Holocaust: A History of the Jews of Europe During the Second World War*. New York, 1985.

————. *The Second World War: A Complete History*. New York, 1989.

————. *Winston S. Churchill, 1941–1945: Road to Victory*. London, 1986.

Gillespie, Major James W. "Navigation Planning in Europe." May 1944. Air Force Historical Research Agency, Maxwell Air Force Base, Alabama. File 248.532–95.

Goebbels, Joseph. *Final Entries, 1945: The Diaries of Joseph Goebbels*. Edited by Hugh Trevor-Roper. Translated by Richard Barry. New York, 1978.

————. *The Goebbels Diaries, 1942–1943*. Edited and translated by Louis P. Lochner. New York, 1948.

————. *The Goebbels Diaries, 1939–1941*. Edited and translated by Frederick Taylor. New York, 1983.

Goldhagen, Daniel Jonah. *Hitler's Willing Executioners: Ordinary Germans and the Holocaust*. New York, 1996.

Grant, William Newby. *P-51 Mustang*. London, 1980.

Great Soviet Encyclopedia. New York, 1970.

Grubb, Kenneth. "How We Make Captured Luftwaffe Crews Talk." Air Force Historical Research Agency, Maxwell Air Force Base, Alabama. File 248.532–68. October 1944.

Guttenplan, D. D. *The Holocaust on Trial*. New York, 2001.

Hahn, Hannelore. *On the Way to Feed the Swans*. New York, 1982.

Halecki, O. *A History of Poland.* New York, 1943.

Hamilton, Nigel. *Monty: Final Years of the Field-Marshal, 1944–1976.* New York, 1986.

Harris, Sir Arthur. *Bomber Offensive.* London, 1947.

Hastings, Max. *Bomber Command.* London, 1979.

Headington, Christopher. *Johann Sebastian Bach: An Essential Guide to His Life and Works.* London, 1997.

Hennessy, Juliette A. *Tactical Operations of the Eighth Air Force, 6 June 1944 to 8 May 1945.* Air Force Historical Research Agency, Maxwell Air Force Base, Alabama, 1952.

Hersey, John. *Hiroshima.* New York, 1946.

Herzstein, Robert Edwin. *The Nazis.* New York, 1980.

Historical Analysis of the 14–15 February 1945 Bombing of Dresden. USAF. Historical Division. Research Studies Institute. Air University. Maxwell Air Force Base, Alabama.

History: First Air Force. Air Force Historical Research Agency, Maxwell Air Force Base, Alabama. File 420.01–4. Sept. 1940–Dec. 1943. Ms. vol. 3, pt. 10.

Hitler, Adolf. *Mein Kampf.* Translated by Ralph Manheim. Boston, 1943.

————. *My New Order.* Edited by Raoul de Roussy de Sales. New York, 1941.

Hodgson, Godfrey. *The Colonel: The Life and Wars of Henry Stimson, 1867–1950.* New York, 1990.

Hoffmann, Heinrich. *Das Braune Heer: 100 Bilddokumente: Leben, Kampf und Sieg der SA und SS.* Berlin, n.d.

Horne, Alistair. *Harold Macmillan.* Vol. 1, *1894–1956.* New York, 1988.

Hoyt, Edwin T. *The Airmen: The Story of American Flyers in World War II.* New York, 1990.

Irving, David. *The Destruction of Dresden.* London, 1963. Reissued as *Apocalypse 1945: The Destruction of Dresden.* London, 1995.

————. *Goebbels: Mastermind of the Third Reich.* London, 1996.

————. *Göring. A Biography.* New York, 1989.

————. *Hitler's War.* New York, 1977, 1990.

Kaes, Anton, et al. *The Weimar Republic Sourcebook.* Berkeley, 1994.

Keegan, John. *Churchill's Generals.* New York, 1991.

————, ed. *The Second World War.* New York, 1990.

Kennett, Lee. *A History of Strategic Bombing.* New York, 1982.

Kershaw, Ian. *Hitler: 1889–1936: Hubris.* New York, 1999.

————. *Hitler: 1936–1945: Nemesis.* New York, 2000.

Kimball, Warren F. *Forged in War: Roosevelt, Churchill, and the Second World War.* New York, 1997.

————, ed. *Churchill and Roosevelt: The Complete Correspondence.* 3 vols. Princeton, N.J., 1984.

Klemperer, Victor. *I Will Bear Witness: A Diary of the Nazi Years, 1933–1941.* New York, 1999.

———. *I Will Bear Witness: A Diary of the Nazi Years, 1942–1945.* New York, 2001.

Kollektiv Dresdner Fotografen. Dresden, 1976.

Krewson, Margrit B., ed. *Dresden: Treasures from the Saxon State Library.* Washington, D.C. 1996.

Kurki, Allan W. *Operation Moonlight Sonata: The German Raid on Coventry.* Westport, Conn., 1995.

La Farge, Henry. *Lost Treasures of Europe.* New York, 1946.

Lawrence, W. J. *No. 5 Bomber Group R.A.F.* London, 1951.

Levine, Alan J. *The Strategic Bombing of Germany, 1940–1945.* Westport, Conn., 1992.

Lewin, Ronald. *Hitler's Mistakes.* New York, 1984.

Liddell Hart, B. H. *History of the Second World War.* New York, 1971.

Lipstadt, Deborah. *Denying the Holocaust: The Growing Assault on Truth and Memory.* New York, 1994.

MacIsaac, David. *Strategic Bombing in World War II.* New York, 1976.

Macmillan, Harold. *The Blast of War, 1939–1945.* New York, 1967–68.

Manvell, Roger, and Heinrich Fraenkel. *Goering.* New York, 1962.

Marcuse, Herbert. "Social and Political Conflicts in Europe After the War." Air Force Historical Research Agency, Maxwell Air Force Base, Alabama. File 248.532. 4 May 1945.

Martin, Albert. "Airborne Radar: Operational Results in the Combat Zones." Special Intelligence Report. August 1944. Air Force Historical Research Agency, Maxwell Air Force Base, Alabama. File 248.532–59.

Massie, Robert K. *Peter the Great: His Life and World.* New York, 1980.

McArthur, Charles W. *Operations Analysis in the U.S. Army Eighth Air Force in World War II.* London Mathematical Society and American Mathematical Society, N.D.

Messenger, Charles. *"Bomber" Harris and the Strategic Bombing Offensive, 1939–1945.* London, 1984.

Michie, Allan A. *The Air Offensive Against Germany.* New York, 1943.

Middlebrook, Martin, and Chris Everitt. *The Bomber Command War Diaries: An Operational Reference Book, 1939–1945.* Harmondsworth, 1985.

Mitford, Nancy. *Frederick the Great.* New York, 1970.

Montgomery, Colonel H.G., Jr. "Night Air Attack of Tactical Objectives." January 1945. Air Force Historical Research Agency, Maxwell Air Force Base, Alabama. File 248.532–76.

"Monthly Report on Operations." Air Force Historical Research Agency, Maxwell Air Force Base, Alabama. File 519.308–4. Jan.–Jun. 1945. D6795. 03 Mar. 1945.

Moran, Lord. *Churchill: Taken from the Diaries of Lord Moran.* Boston, 1966.

Mosley, Leonard. *The Reich Marshal: A Biography of Hermann Goering.* New York, 1974.

Muirhead, John. *Those Who Fall.* New York, 1986.

Musgrove, Gordon. *Pathfinder Force: A History of 8 Group.* Somerton, Eng., 1992.

Neutzner, Matthias. *Angriff: Martha Heinrich Acht-Leben in Bomberkrieg, Dresden, 1944/45.* Dresden, 1995.

———. *Lebenszeichen: Dresden im Luftkrieg, 1944/1945.* Dresden, 1994.

The New Yorker Book of War Pieces. New York, 1947, 1988.

Nicolson, Harold. *Diaries and Letters.* Vol. 2, *The War Years, 1939–1945.* London, 1967.

"Organization of the Eighth Air Force." Air Force Historical Research Agency, Maxwell Air Force Base, Alabama. File 520.201–1. 28 May 1943.

Osmont, Marie-Louise. *The Normandy Diary of Marie-Louise Osmont, 1940–1944.* Translated by George L. Newman. New York, 1994.

Overy, Richard. *Goering: The Iron Man.* London, 1984.

———. *Why the Allies Won.* New York, 1995.

Overy, Richard, and Andrew Wheatcroft. *The Road to War: The Origins of World War II.* London, 1989.

Papen, Franz von. *Memoirs.* Translated by Brian Connell. New York, 1953.

Parliamentary Debates. (Hansard) Fifth Series, vol. 408. House of Commons. 6 March 1945.

Patton, George S., Jr. *War as I Knew It.* Boston, 1947.

Peyser, Joan, ed. *The Orchestra: Origins and Transformations.* New York, 1986.

Pogue, Forrest C. *George C. Marshall: Organizer of Victory, 1943–1945.* New York, 1973.

Pohl, Gerhart. *Gerhart Hauptmann and Silesia.* Grand Forks, N.D., 1962.

Price, G. Ward. *I Know These Dictators.* New York, 1938.

Ranke, Leopold von. *Memoirs of the House of Brandenburg and History of Prussia, During the Seventeenth and Eighteenth Centuries.* 3 vols. Translated by Sir Alexander and Lady Duff-Gordon. London, 1849. Reprint, New York, 1969.

Rector, Frank. *The Nazi Extermination of Homosexuals.* New York, 1981.

Rhodes, Richard. *The Making of the Atomic Bomb.* New York, 1986.

Rigg, Bryan Mark. *Hitler's Jewish Soldiers.* Lawrence, Kans., 2000.

Richards, Denis. *The Hardest Victory: RAF Bomber Command in the Second World War.* London, 1994.

Richards, J. M., ed. *The Bombed Buildings of Britain.* London, 1942.

Richardson, John, and Eric Zafran. *Master Paintings from the Hermitage and the State Russian Museum: Leningrad.* New York, 1975.

Riefenstahl, Leni. *Leni Riefenstahl: A Memoir.* New York, 1993.

Rodenberger, Axel. *Der Tod von Dresden.* Dortmund, 1953.

Rommel, Field-Marshal Erwin. *The Rommel Papers.* Edited by B. H. Liddell Hart. Translated by Paul Findlay. New York, 1953.

Rose, Norman. *Churchill: An Unruly Life.* London, 1994.

Rothnie, Niall. *The Baedeker Blitz: Hitler's Attack on Britain's Historic Cities.* Shepperton, 1992.

Rowe, Group Captain H. C. "Recent RAF Tactics and Late Information from the European War Theater." Air Force Historical Research Agency, Maxwell Air Force Base, Alabama. File 248.532.60. 28 July 1944.

Ryan, Cornelius. *The Last Battle.* New York, 1966.

Saward, Dudley. *"Bomber" Harris: The Authorised Biography.* London, 1984.

Schaarschuch, Kurt. *Bilddokument Dresden, 1933–1945.* Dresden, n.d.

Schreiber, Hermann. *Teuton and Slav: The Struggle for Central Europe.* Translated by James Cleugh. New York, 1965.

Sereny, Gitta. *Albert Speer: His Battle with the Truth.* New York, 1995.

Sherry, Michael S. *The Rise of American Air Power: The Creation of Armageddon.* New Haven, 1987.

Shirer, William L. *The Rise and Fall of the Third Reich: A History of Nazi Germany.* New York, 1959.

Shoemaker, Major Davis W. "Recent Observations from Europe: Intelligence Observations in the European Theater." 21 Feb. 1945. Air Force Historical Research Agency, Maxwell Air Force Base, Alabama. File 248.532–82A.

Simon, Edith. *The Making of Frederick the Great.* Boston, 1963.

Sington, Derrick, and Arthur Weidenfeld. *The Goebbels Experiment: A Study of the Nazi Propaganda Machine.* New Haven, 1943.

Smith, Melden E., Jr. "The Bombing of Dresden Reconsidered: A Study in Wartime Decision-Making." Doctoral diss., Boston University, 1971.

Spaatz, Carl A. Papers of Carl A. Spaatz. Library of Congress, Manuscript Division.

———. U.S. Air Force Academy. Oral History Interview. No. 186.27. September 1968.

———. U.S. Air Force Historical Division. Oral History Interview. No. K105.5–35.

Spaatz, Ruth. U.S. Air Force Academy. Oral History Interview. 3 March 1981. No. K239.0512–1266.

Speer, Albert. *Inside the Third Reich: Memoirs.* Translated by Richard and Clara Winston. New York, 1970.

———. *Spandau: The Secret Diaries.* Translated by Richard and Clara Winston. New York, 1976.

Spencer, Andrew John. "Of Literature and Legend: German Writers and the Bombing of Dresden." Doctoral diss., Ohio State University, 1992.

Steinbeck, John. *Bombs Away.* New York, 1942.

Sterling, Charles. *Great French Paintings in the Hermitage.* New York, 1958.

Stern, Fritz. *Gold and Iron. Bismarck, Bleichröder, and the Building of the German Empire.* New York, 1977.

Stone, Norman. *Hitler.* London, 1980.

Strawson, John. *Hitler's Battles for Europe.* New York, 1971.

Summary of Operations 8th Air Force. Air Force Historical Research Agency, Maxwell Air Force Base, Alabama. File 519.308–4. Jan.–Jun. 1945.

Terraine, John. *A Time for Courage: The Royal Air Force in the European War, 1939–1945.* New York, 1985.

Thurlow, Richard. *Fascism in Britain: A History, 1918–1985.* London, 1987.

Toland, John. *Hitler.* New York, 1976.

———. *Hitler: The Pictorial Documentary of His Life.* New York, 1980.

Truman, Harry S. *Memoirs by Harry S. Truman.* Vol. 1, *Year of Decisions.* New York, 1955.

Turner, Henry Ashby, Jr. *German Big Business and the Rise of Hitler.* New York, 1985.

Valentin, Veit. *The German People: Their History and Civilization from the Holy Roman Empire to the Third Reich.* New York, 1949.

Verrier, Anthony. *The Bomber Offensive.* New York, 1969.

Vonnegut, Kurt, Jr. *Slaughterhouse-Five.* New York, 1969.

Wagner, Richard. *Selected Letters of Richard Wagner.* Translated and edited by Stewart Spencer and Barry Millington. New York, 1988.

Webster, Sir Charles, and Noble Franklin. *The Strategic Air Offensive Against Germany, 1939–1945.* 4 vols. London, 1977.

Weekly Résumé(s) of the Naval, Military and Air Situation. Nos. 288–293. PRO W.P. (45). 166, 186, 201, 217, 243.

Weidauer, Walter. *Inferno Dresden.* Berlin, 1990.

Winterbotham, F. W. *The Ultra Secret.* New York, 1974.

Wohlfarth, Hannsdieter. *Johann Sebastian Bach.* Philadelphia, 1985.

Woolner, David B., ed. *The Second Quebec Conference Revisited.* New York, 1998.

Woolnough, John H. *Eighth Air Force Album.* Hollywood, Fla., 1980.

Zweig, Stefan. *Erasmus of Rotterdam.* Translated by Eden Paul and Cedar Paul. New York, 1934, 1956.

LIBRARIES, MUSEUMS, AND RESEARCH CENTERS

UNITED KINGDOM

Imperial War Museum, Lambeth

Royal Air Force Museum, Hendon

Bomber Command Association, Hendon

Public Record Office, Kew
Imperial War Museum, Duxford
British Library

UNITED STATES

Library of Congress
United States Air Force Historical Research Center, Maxwell Air Force,
    Alabama
United States Air Force Academy, Colorado Springs
New York Public Library
United States Military Academy, West Point
Daniel Library, The Citadel, Charleston, South Carolina
Mighty Eighth Air Force Museum and Library, Pooler, Georgia
Ramsay Library, University of North Carolina at Asheville
Pack Memorial Library, Asheville, North Carolina
EAA Aviation Foundation, Oshkosh, Wisconsin

GERMANY

Deutsche Fotothek: Sächsische Landesbibliothek, Dresden
Stadtmuseum Dresden

FRANCE

Memorial Museum of the Battle of Normandy, Bayeux
Utah Beach Landing Museum, Sainte-Marie-du-Mont
The Airborne Museum, Sainte-Mère-Eglise
Memorial Museum, Caen
American Cemetery, Colleville-sur-Mer

MARSHALL DE BRUHL was for many years an executive and editor with several major American publishing houses, specializing in history and biography, most notably as editor of, and contributor to, the *Dictionary of American History* and the *Dictionary of American Biography*. He is the author of *Sword of San Jacinto: A Life of Sam Houston* and the co-compiler of *The International Thesaurus of Quotations*. He lives in Asheville, North Carolina.